CREATE AND CELEBRATE YOUR CHURCH'S UNIQUENESS

Designing a Church Philosophy of Ministry

Harold J. Westing

kregel
PUBLICATIONS

Grand Rapids, MI 49501

Create and Celebrate Your Church's Uniqueness:
Designing a Church Philosophy of Ministry

Copyright © 1993 by Harold J. Westing.

Published in 1993 by Kregel Publications, a division of Kregel, Inc., P. O. Box 2607, Grand Rapids, MI 49501. For more information about Kregel Publications, visit our web site: www.kregel.com.

Scripture quotations are from *The New International Version of the Bible*, published by the Zondervan Corporation, © 1978 by the International Bible Society.

Cover Photo: Positive Images, Patricia Sgrignoli
Cover and Book Design: Alan G. Hartman

Library of Congress Cataloging-in-Publication Data
Westing, Harold J.
   Create and Celebrate Your Church's Uniqueness: designing a church philosophy of ministry / Harold J. Westing.
     p. cm.
   Includes bibliographical references and index.
   1. Pastoral Theology. I. Title.
BV4011.W43   1993   253—dc20   93-13813
                                      CIP

ISBN 0-8254-3977-9

6 7 8 9 10 / 04 03 02 01

Printed in the United States of America

This book is dedicated to Betty, my wife of forty-two years. Her constant patience and commitment to being my loyal team player in ministry has been the greatest human factor in making this book possible.

I would also dedicate this book to hundreds of my students. Their desire to be Christ's servants in building His church has been a constant source of encouragement to my life and writing.

Contents

   Worship/Music Tension: Contemporary or Traditional
   Preaching/Teaching Tension: Evangelism or Exhortation
   Charismatic Tension: Charismatic or Noncharismatic
   Participants Tension: Inclusive or Exclusive

   Authority/Leadership Tension: Laity or Clergy Control
   Discipline Tension: By Organization or Organism
   Membership Tension: Inclusive or Exclusive
   Nurture Tension: Non-directed or Directed Growth
   Fellowship Tension: Anonymity or Directed Relationships
   Facility Tension: Modest or Stately

Foreword

I t is not uncommon to hear pastors express their criticism of the mindless "consumerism" common among churchgoers today. With such a "pick-and-choose" mentality, lay people shop for churches much like consumers looking for a car. Many pastors long to see these people make choices based on broader issues such as where they can be taught the Word and how they can make their best contributions to the Kingdom of God.

I can't help but believe that the same criticism can be leveled against many of us who are pastors. We visit church conferences that market their philosophies of ministry, programs, and materials and then choose approaches to ministry that seems to "work best" from our limited perspective. Little do we realize that we are even more guilty of consumerism. Without addressing the deeper issues of who we are as individual leaders, what our church histories are, what our available resources are, and what God is specifically calling us to accomplish, we buy into new approaches and programs considering only what will make our churches grow faster.

Quite often I meet with church planters to discuss their future ministries. When asked what their individual philosophy of ministry will be and how they will design the organizational schemes of their churches, I often hear them refer to one of several fast-growing, nationally known churches. They tell me they plan to model themselves after one or another particular church. I typically respond by asking them to describe the downside of such a ministry model. Rarely do I receive a well-researched, thorough response. In fact, I often hear that they know of no disadvantages. I'm convinced that until the pastor and the leadership of a church understand both the advantages and disadvantages of a particular style, model or approach to ministry, they are not ready to begin or redesign a church.

In an effort to avoid traditionalism, we often embrace the errors of modernity. In an attempt to reach unchurched people, we often lose sight of making holy disciples. With the goal of marketing our ministries effectively, we drift away from dependence on the work and power of the Holy Spirit.

As I read *Create and Celebrate Your Church's Uniqueness*, I rejoiced to see so many tensions of choice being addressed. How refreshing to see a book written which tells you what your choices are instead of telling you what to do! How refreshing to see a book that stresses the importance of being what God uniquely calls an individual church to be.

Harold Westing has made an invaluable contribution to God's kingdom by helping the leadership of His church more maturely design the ministries of local congregations. Reading this book will be well worth your time.

RANDY POPE

Pastor, Perimeter Church
Norcross, GA

Preface

My own spiritual journey has been closely interwoven with my pilgrimage among American evangelical churches. As a church consultant for the last 28 years, I have become deeply involved in over 300 congregations in an effort to try to help them to be more effective in the proclamation of the gospel. I have been driven by a never-ending search for the heart of God about what He wants His church to look like as an expression of His grace in society. This has taken me into some very great congregations—and some that were not so great! I keep asking two very simple but penetrating questions: Who has God called you and equipped you to reach, and how are you going about doing it? That is another way to ask simply, "What is your philosophy of ministry?" There have been some stellar answers to those questions, but far too many times there is a great deal of uncertainty not only by the lay leaders but by the clergy as well. Early on, I left them with a challenge of trying to carve out a philosophy which is distinct and unique to their personality and to their community. I found some written guides to writing ministry goals and objectives, but unfortunately, there was little written that I could put into their hands as a guideline to accomplishing that major project. I decided some years ago that I would need to give myself to the discipline of gathering the material and laying out some guidelines so that congregations in America would be able to express their own unique approach to ministry honestly and coherently.

I am so deeply concerned that congregations become *intentional* about their ministry rather than just being sensitive about evangelism, discipleship, and other mandates given to the church through Christ. I want to help them come to see that in this day and age of specialization,

11

it is very difficult for a church to be effective when it is just general in its approach. It needs to be a specialist in an age of specialization. A church never has been—nor will it ever be—able to do everything that a church could do in society. Therefore, a congregation must realize and recognize its gifts before it can make a difference in its community.

It has been an honor to be part of the teaching faculty at Denver Seminary. This role has constantly offered me challenges and insight about what the church of Jesus Christ ought to look like in today's society. During my years of ministry as the National Director of Christian Education for the Conservative Baptist Association of America and during my tenure at the Seminary, I visited hundreds of congregations of various denominations. While I was at the Seminary, we started what is known today as the Institute for Church Development. At the time of this writing, the Institute has a database of approximately 700 congregations. These represent a broad perspective of theologically evangelical churches and a very extensive and broad geographical base of evangelical churches in America. In this book I will refer to the database and all the tremendous insights we have gained about American Christians through this study.

To help me present the process of forming a philosophy of ministry, I have been interviewing pastors across America. I consider these pastors to be effective designers of philosophies of ministry. They are people who think about their churches and God's world in a godly, biblical, and philosophical way. Out of all the ministers and church leaders with whom I have dealt, I picked fifteen ministers who I feel have done an exceptionally effective piece of work in designing creative and unique philosophies of ministry that continue to make a difference in their communities. I chose ministers and churches from a variety of denominations and different geographical areas. I did not choose these pastors because they were sinless or more holy than other ministers; I chose them because they have been excellent models of leaders who have been intentional about their philosophies of ministry with their congregations. Some congregations are very large, and others are small or medium-sized. In an individual way, each pastor has been seeking the face of God as to how each could make a difference with the gospel in the church's community. In no way do these people represent all the various facets of ministry. But they are a keen representation of the various kinds of ministries that are prevalent.

I will not try to categorize them as many authors have attempted to do. That is not the intent of this book. I simply am eager to give you the challenge of becoming creative in the way you think about and carry out *your* ministry. To be creative is to allow God to express His workmanship through His servants.

In each section of the book, I will be quoting from these pastors both about how they do ministry and how they have thought philosophically about ministry. It would be wonderful if you could read in detail all of their comments, but let me express the most salient parts of these insightful interviews. I am indebted to them for their contribution to me personally and to this work. You will find their names and the names of their churches at the end of this Preface. Personally, I have not always agreed with the way they minister or their various theological frameworks, but I have a great deal of respect for their willingness to wait on the Lord for direction about how they should do their ministries.

In addition to the statements of philosophy which I have collected from pastoral interviews, I have also collected approximately 100 other philosophy statements with a wide variety of creative expressions about ministry. I will refer to some of them and mention some other churches that I feel have allowed God to speak expressively and creatively through them. A few samples are listed for your review in the appendixes.

This book is not intended to be a step-by-step workbook to help you hammer out a philosophy of ministry. There are a couple of those books available in bookstores if that is your interest. Chapters 5 through 9 could, however, serve as a guideline for some of the major theological and philosophical issues every church must face as it seeks to fulfill the mandate of Christ for the church. The list is not necessarily complete but, from this writer's perspective, will provide at least the major issues of a philosophy of ministry.

This book also is not intended to be a theological treatise which forces the reader to think through all the issues which pertain to the various philosophies. However, in most instances you will find some strong theological presuppositions which must be considered as you think about a creative philosophy of ministry. You will find that the book deals primarily with ecclesiology rather than all the other accompanying theological tenets which you will find in most major theological studies.

Since it is primarily a book about practical theology, it is not exhaustive in dealing with the area of ecclesiology. Limited space will not allow me to be that exhaustive, but certainly you will find sufficient theology to get you started and send you in the right direction, searching and praying for further insight about how God would express Himself through you and your church in the community.

I have also tried to include in these chapters some of the major findings from my study of church life which includes the research that is going on in various quarters today.

In my pilgrimage among the Lord's churches, I have come to appreciate the importance of tensions that often help to keep evangelicalism on an even keel in its search for authenticity. As a faithful servant I have listened to and read the critics of church growth movements. You will see a reflection of those tensions later on in the book. Their writings and insights have often provided the necessary balancing pole as we all walk the tightrope stretched between the authentic Word of God and our constantly changing culture.

I want to express my deep appreciation to the many pastors who have shared their visions and hearts with me. I also thank my colleagues in ministry at Denver Seminary for the needed insight they have provided for me into the theological issues facing the church of Christ. I also would express my appreciation to both graduate and postgraduate students at Denver Seminary and other institutions where I have taught church growth, leadership, church staff, and numerous other topics that have given me insight into the church of Jesus Christ, which is rapidly altering its form in a swiftly changing society.

As you now begin the study of this text, my prayer is that God will expand your horizons, challenge your intellect, and excite you with the opportunities you have for a creative ministry in a world that is about to move into the next century. I believe that most tradition-bound churches will die out as they enter the 21st century. I pray that this book may help your church become one of the churches that really makes a difference.

Ministers interviewed by Harold Westing:

Robert Acker, Community Baptist Church, Alta Loma, California.
Tommy Barnett, Phoenix First Assembly, Phoenix, Arizona.
Don Bubna, Peace Portal Alliance Church, Vancouver, British Columbia.
Stephen Crotts, Burlington Presbyterian, Burlington, North Carolina.
E. V. Hill, Mt. Zion Baptist Church, Watts, California.
Randy Kinnison, Bethany Baptist Church, Beaverton, Oregon.

Clyde McDowell, Mission Hills Baptist Church, Denver, Colorado.
Tom McKee, Sun River Church, Sacramento, California.
David Moore, Southwest Church, Palm Desert, California.
Stan Perea, Church of the Rockies, Arvada, Colorado.
Randy Pope, Perimeter Church, Atlanta, Georgia.
Russ Rosser, First Baptist Church, Flushing Long Island, New York.
Gerald Sheveland, College Ave. Church, San Diego, California.
Jeff Giles, Bear Valley Church, Denver, Colorado.
Rick Warren, Saddleback Community Church, Los Angeles, California.

There are numerous people who have made this book possible, and I owe them a public word of appreciation. Rebecca Barnes spent many long, extra hours doing some of the typing and editing. Garry Mitchelmore helped me with some of the interviews and did some of early thinking on the design of the book. My colleagues at the Institute for Church Development, Gary Bateman and Dick Bunger, interacted with me on the manuscript design. Betty, my wife, was a constant sounding board when needed and at other times knew when not to knock at the door.

How to Read This Book

Rudyard Kipling pulled together all the interrogative pronouns of the English language in a bit of poetic doggerel, and these probing pronouns will open up any subject thoroughly: "I keep six honest serving men (They taught me all I knew); Their names are What and Why and When and How and Where and Who."

This book is written on the assumption that great wisdom is not to have the right answers but to ask the right questions. In a world where change is all around us, we cannot go to the church to find a solace from change. We should find the eternal, unchanging Word of God on its pulpit and in its pews, but the message of that Word comes in numberless expressions. In this book I am trying to aid you, the leaders of today's church, in finding a fresh and creative way to express those eternal truths in your churches and to find new pleasure in a unique expression of God's grace. I want to help you blossom where you are planted. In order to do that, you need to keep asking those critical questions.

You can read this book in a number of different ways to unlock the right keys:

1. You can read it as a collateral book for the design of a philosophy of ministry that will help you see what Christ's church looks like in American neighborhoods.
2. You can read it as a textbook to find out what kind of freedoms there are for the church today. You should be able to find out how to express the eternal truths of God's Word in the context of the 21st century. You will enjoy seeing how fifteen different leadership teams have designed and expressed their uniqueness in ministry.

17

3. You can read parts or all of it as a guide for a church staff or
    church retreat guide. It should be especially helpful as you
    seek to hammer out your church's philosophy of ministry
    statement. There are model philosophies in the appendixes.
4. This book could also aid a search committee as they search
    for a new senior pastor. It will help the committee and the
    congregation to determine what kind of pastor best fits the
    church at this time in its history.
5. This book is intended to be used in seminary and Bible college
    classrooms to help students come to grips with how they will
    design their unique ministries in their present or future
    congregations. Professors may find the outlines in chapters 7,
    8, and 9 very helpful in their classroom discussions or
    assignments. You will find additional reading for more detailed
    study on the various tensions in these chapters or in the
    appendixes.
6. Church consultants should find this text most helpful in
    evaluating churches for effectiveness in their unique ministries.
    You will find questions to ask, guidelines to consider, and
    ideas to suggest for the congregations with whom you are
    working. You will find some helpful tools throughout the
    book and in the appendixes for your consulting process.
7. If your church has not thought through and written its philosophy
    of ministry, do not feel embarrassed. Most churches have not
    done so either. You will soon learn why doing so is important
    for today's church. As you learn what a philosophy statement
    is in chapter 1, you will also come to understand the difference
    between a vision statement and a philosophy statement. Since
    a philosophy statement is built on values, you will see the
    relationship of values to a philosophy in chapter 2. In chapter
    3 you will find some basic teaching about why designing a
    philosophy of ministry statement is so critical to your church's
    future strength. This information will enable you to motivate
    your people to be diligent in the design process.

Chapter 4, "The Profile of a Ministry Architect," will give you a
reflection of how fifteen unique but ordinary, godly pastors think
about ministry. While their comments from my interviews with
them are spread throughout the book, this chapter is written
specifically to help you see what process they went through to
come up with their unique philosophy statements. This should guide
you in your thinking and study process.

In chapters 5 and 6 you will find some very necessary foundational tools that should prepare you to do your philosophy design. You will not know what to do with chapters 7, 8, and 9 without studying these guidelines.

I consider the heart of the book to be in these chapters. They list the fifteen different theological tensions which are the eternal, unchanging functions that every church leader must build into ministry if he or she is going to deal with God's mandates for today's church. You could study these chapters in any order, but it seemed prudent to me to put them in this order. Chapter 7, "Upward to God," deals with how God's people must respond to Him personally and corporately. You will study four major tensions here. Chapter 8, "Inward to His Body," deals with five tensions concerning the church's infrastructure. Then in chapter 9, "Outward to the World," you will be exposed to six tensions that explore the church's ministry in society.

You should consider all fifteen tensions even though you may not choose to have all of them expressed in some way in your statement. At the beginning of each section of the tensions, you will find a definition of each extreme on the continuum. This should give you an idea of how your congregation can express itself on each respective issue. As you read these chapters, keep in mind that the list of the tensions are not exhaustive, nor is the list of things to consider about each tension exhaustive.

Once you have decided to implement your philosophy statement, you no doubt will need some help. This is not an easy task, as I quickly point out. The last two chapters, "Security Levels and Paradigm Shifts" and "Leading the Church Through Creative Change," should provide significant help in enabling you to lead the congregation into vital new stages of growth. You can quickly frustrate your congregation by not wisely leading them through the change process. You will find a good outline with some practical guidelines in the last two chapters.

My best wishes to you for enjoyable and profitable reading as you seek to design and build your church's philosophy of ministry.

Chapter 1

Charting the Course

A group of pastors was talking about the kind of great leadership retreats they had recently conducted with their church boards. One talked about how his church had just worked through a new statement of purpose; another, about a new philosophy of ministry statement; and yet another, about how a new vision statement had been hammered out. A fourth pastor showed them a long list of strategies for the next year. As they exchanged pages from their leadership retreat work, they soon came to realize they were talking in different languages.

Congress needs to pass some laws which once and for all clarify directional terms for education and leadership. There appears to be no universal standard for the use of such terms as goals, objectives, strategies, vision, mission statement, philosophy of ministry, and purpose statement. As one searches through the literature on both religious and secular leadership and administration, there tends to be much confusion about how these terms are actually applied. Everyone seems to speak a different language while using the same terms. Since this book will deal with how a congregation and its leadership tend to do ministry, it becomes very important that the terms be carefully defined before we go any further.

Every church has been given its mission mandate from the pages of the Bible. The way a church does its exegesis will impact the way it reads and then implements that mission. Christ's mission is the mission of the church. James E. Carter states it clearly, "The church is central to God's redemptive plan. This is the institution that has extended the meaning of Christ's life into the world of today."[1] A close examination of the New Testament will show you how that ministry ought to be carried out. The functions of the church must be *koinonia* (fellowship), *diakonia* (ministry), and *kerygma* (proclamation). Carter goes on to say,

Mission of Church

Vision for Community

Philosophy of Ministry

Goals
short and long term

"To remain faithful to the biblical meaning of the church, the contemporary church will have to give serious attention to these functions. To remain faithful to them, however, does not mean that some forms will never change, that some words will never be updated, or that some actions will never be different. The church always lives in its contemporary world, and it must always witness in the world. The church cannot always be tied to a horse-and-buggy, a late nineteenth or early twentieth century form and expect to speak to a late twentieth century space-age world. But, to update the form is not to forsake the function. The inherent mission of the church remains constant. The eternal challenge to the church is to carry out its mission in its day."[2]

Each church, with its own unique fingerprint, will express the church's *mission* in words that are meaningful to it; but the church need not argue long and hard about what its mission *is*. Churches differ in the priority of time and energy they give to the various aspects of their mission. In the chapter on the issues of a philosophy of ministry, more attention will be given to what your priorities will be.

In this author's view, *vision* is what follows a clear understanding of what the church's mission is. Rick Warren says that "a vision-driven church is the key to a successful church." George Barna provides a clear definition of what vision is. "Vision for ministry is a clear mental image of a preferable future imparted by God to His chosen servants and is based upon an accurate understanding of God, self, and circumstances."[3] Vision is what really drives a church to the accomplishment of Christ's mission. This book, however, is not primarily a book about vision but about *how vision is carried out*.

A vision statement is an expression of a God-given passion for ministry to a community. Aubrey Malphurs states that a vision is "a clear and challenging picture of the future of a ministry as its leadership believes it can and must be."[4] Because God tends to give this vision to the pastor, it will become extremely important that he or she be the one who "casts the vision" to the congregation. David Moore says that, "a vision is something the pastor is willing to die for."[5] If he or she cannot communicate it to the congregation so it can truly be owned, then it will be necessary for another respected leader to do so. That may be difficult because the pastor tends to be perceived as the true leader of the congregation. "Thomas Peters and Nancy Austin (1985) argue that the creation of vision does not come from group process techniques, but that it starts with a single individual."[6] Having a vision means that the pastor can see what the members cannot necessarily see. Thus, "casting a vision" means helping the congregation to see what they need to see to become common laborers in the God-given mission. The pastor should be able to see into the future far more than the congregation can. Without question, the sign of a true leader is that he or she has a clear-cut vision of where to lead the people God has entrusted into his or her care. If the pastor is not respected by the congregation, then the congregation will have a difficult time following his or her lead.

It has been delightful to hear the heartbeat of the visions from the pastors I interviewed. God gave them their visions in a specific way. Their views of what a philosophy of ministry is were often different, and God seemed to give visions to them in different ways. However, when their minds and hearts were open, God seemed to speak. They were not satisfied with a carbon copy vision that another person had; they wanted a unique one from God. Some visions were faint at first, but others came over a long period of time. Russ Rosser received his vision over a period of time while pastoring in Flushing, New York, and studying passages like Isaiah 54 and Acts 13. In Acts he saw the vision to have multinational leaders as they did at Antioch. Dr. E. V. Hill continues to get his vision clarified and reinforced as he walks the streets with and among his people. Randy Pope spent weeks in contemplation and prayer before he had the vision clearly in mind for launching Perimeter Church. Randy Kinnison spends one day per week and one week per year to sharpen and clarify his vision for his Portland mission. Each of the pastors I interviewed had a vision for what they want God do in their community, but they also clearly had in mind how they were going to accomplish that vision as fellow workers together with God.

At first, many leaders did not distinguish the difference between vision and philosophy of ministry. They tended to see it all coming from God and knew that they were doing His will at His command. When pushed in the interview, they could begin to see the difference. They knew what they were about and felt driven by the Holy Spirit to do His bidding.

Once a church and its pastor has decided what their vision is, then they will need to decide just how that vision is to be accomplished. Some people might call that the long-range and short-range goals, but this book will specifically talk about the "how" of ministry or its philosophy. This book will be more about philosophical decisions regarding ministry than vision. It will deal with the kinds of issues that the church leadership must wrestle with before they can accurately carry out the vision. George Barna's book, *The Power of Vision*, Aubrey Malphurs' book, *Developing a Vision for Ministry*, and Warren Bennis and Burt Nanus's book, *Leaders: the Strategies for Taking Charge* all can provide great help for you to think through your church's vision.

If the vision you have received for your church is a genuine vision from God, then you have a new value in your portfolio. It will be like all the other values you know. They determine your behavior. In fact, you cannot say you have a value and yet fail to live by it. At that point, it is only a belief and not a value. A value is something you cherish or prize highly. It is something to which you give high allegiance in your life. It determines your priorities and ultimately your behavior. A leader is value-driven, both in vision and in philosophy. All major decisions which he or she makes are based upon the values of his or her life. Phoenix Assembly of God is an evangelistic church. The pastor breathes that in every breath, so you can see it and hear it in every program. That church wants to reach Phoenix for Jesus Christ, and you can see it on every page of the bulletin. Chapter 2 talks about the place of values in the leading process.

Next, be ready to give attention to your philosophy of ministry. That is what this book is all about. A vision statement must be prayed over carefully and worked out by the pastor before the leadership of the congregation designs its philosophy of ministry. If your church does not know and own a strong vision, then the congregation may wander around in an organizational and ministerial maze. Likewise, if the leadership does not have a philosophy which emanates from that vision, then it may never see the vision actualized. The vision tends to drive a philosophy, and a philosophy tends to carry a vision to fruition. Something good may be accomplished if there is neither a vision nor a philosophy, but it will be more by default than by design. Seldom will a church be able to reach its potential without either.

Both a vision and a philosophy must ultimately be owned by the congregation. The people must be so familiar with it that they find themselves praying for its fulfillment on a regular basis. Often as I visit with a congregation, I interview numerous members. I have found that the thriving and exciting congregations can clearly state the vision either in terms of the church's ministry slogan or in words that are most meaningful to them. They know that they are part of God's special movement in their community.

This book will use "philosophy of ministry" as Barna employs the term "mission statement." I have already given my definition of the mission of the church in the earlier part of this chapter. Barna says that "the mission is a definition of the key ministry objectives of the church. The vision statement is a clarification of the specific direction and activities the church will pursue toward making a true ministry impact." He further states, "the mission statement is philosophic in nature, the vision statement is strategic in character."[7] Webster's dictionary defines philosophy as "a study of processes governing thought and conduct, theory or investigation of the principle or laws that regulate the universe and underlie all knowledge and reality." The root meaning of "philosophy," then, is "love of wisdom." We agree in essence but are using the terms differently. From here on I will use "philosophy of ministry" to refer to the philosophic issues that determine how a church will think about and do its ministry.

At times you may find authors and speakers referring to a "theology of ministry." For this work, that is more of a limiting idea because theology is the study of God and the relationship between God and the universe. When the phrase "philosophy of ministry" is used, it refers to looking with wisdom at the concerted operation between man and God in the work of the church. God takes the divine initiative in the operations of the church, and man acts in a yielded way in cooperation with God and His work in the world. A philosophy of ministry, then, is evaluating (with God's wisdom) the church in a theological way and, at the same time, through human eyes (or what is called sociology). A helpful but somewhat inadequate way of looking at a philosophy is to call it a "divine synergism." That is acceptable as long as you make sure that God and man are not put on totally equal terms. God, who is always the initiator toward people, is always the initiator in the work of ministry.

This book addresses the process of how a godly congregation should honestly and wisely think about doing ministry. The church should do its theology through the study of Scripture and should also study culture to understand how God wants to express Himself in each respective society. For a period of time Denver Seminary advertised its educational philosophy by showing a pair of glasses with one lens as the Bible and the other as the globe. The seminary wanted prospective students to be both biblically and culturally literate so they can truly communicate God's redemptive grace in a language that the needy world can understand.

Chapter 2

Ministry Core Values

During my many years of travel, I have stayed in a lot of wonderful Christian homes. As I became acquainted with those people, it did not take me long to recognize that they owned some very special values. I have come to learn over the years that the values of the home make up the glue which holds the home together. During the years of those families being together, they have decided where they are going to spend their time, how they will work, where they will spend their money, and how they will treat each other. All of those behaviors emerge from some extremely important values which have been established as a foundation for their home.

In the same way, values hold a nation together. Author Charles Colson has underlined that fact clearly: "The public wants to believe that its president is guardian of the nation's morals, manager of the government, and the one responsible for getting Social Security checks delivered on time. What holds our society together is not force or law, but moral suasion."[8]

Langdon Gilkey also reflects on the critical importance of having a set of values for any society.

> As a historian, I assure you that Toynbee was right in this: all human cultures grow round a central core of moral ideas and ideals that command obedience, respect, and general observance. There is right and there is wrong, both unquestioned. This is what is called the "ethos" of a people, of a culture.
>
> Early Rome had something called *pietas*. We have borrowed the word twice, as "piety" and "pity," neither of which represents the old Roman virtue and mainstay of society: a loyalty to family and state, a courageous sense of duty, trustworthiness. Try the truth of this in all societies. Some central core holds all together.[9]

27

Since the church is defined as a family in Scripture, it is only appropriate that Christians think as well about a church being held together by its value system. Often church leaders have not written out the values. However, if you were part of a congregation for very long and listened to the sermons, heard the teaching, observed the business sessions, and watched the behavior, it would become very obvious that there were corporate values established by that community. Often a church gets into difficulty because it has not clearly defined as a corporate body what it holds as high values.

As I conducted interviews with various church leaders, it became obvious to me that all the leaders operated from a very strong values base. Some did not state those values, but it was obvious as I listened to their philosophies of ministry that there were strong core values which drove those philosophies. Perhaps the most obvious was stated by Randy Kinnison who said he tended to put a lot of meaning on the purpose of life. As one of his primary values, he hoped to help people understand the meaning and purpose of life.

Webster defines values as follows: "Value is to estimate the value of, set a price for, determine the worth of, appraise, to place a certain estimate of worth on or in a scale of values: as, I value health above wealth; to think highly of, esteem, prize; I value your friendship; and values change our lives."[10] Christians would classify their morals as one of their highest values, yet values are far more extensive than morals. Their values are the beliefs on which they place a great deal of worth in their lives.

Some churches would refer to their values as another way of talking about their vision. However, it is important to see that values are the underlying principles which help people to see a vision for their church. Many organizations, like the Conservative Baptist Foreign Mission Society, call their values the "core values." This indicates that there are many values unspoken which guide them in their decisions, but there are basic core values which are essential to the major philosophy of their ministry (see Appendix 2).

> In the Jerusalem church, the apostles' priorities and practices—to which Christians intensely devoted themselves—became a way of life. True spiritual formation requires such commitment to consistency of practice. The actions of the first church confirm discipling was at its heart, and if we had nothing but this text to show us the way, it would be enough to make our churches discipling centers.

1. A commitment to Scripture (Acts 2:42)
2. A commitment to one another (Acts 2:42, 44, 46)
3. A commitment to prayer (Acts 2:42)
4. A commitment to praise and worship (Acts 2:43, 47)
5. A commitment to outreach (Acts 2:345-47)[11]

I hear Paul saying the same thing in Colossians 3:1–2 when he urges people to set their hearts, or values, on things that are above or pleasing to God, not on things or values that come from today's culture.

Rod Acker of Alto Loma, California, apparently has gotten the values for his ministry from the book of Acts. He says, "Their values are worship, church planting, love and acceptance, prayer, spiritual gift mobilization, and target compassion ministries." Basically what they are saying is that these values will ultimately drive them to develop a philosophy of ministry which accomplishes those values and, of course, emanates out of their vision.

The First Baptist Church in Modesto, California, prioritizes its values: staff comes first; programs, second; and facilities, third. The personnel, the energy, and the finances will be allocated to those in that order. Their belief is that the staff must precede programs because staff develop programs, and programs necessitate facilities. I did not need to be around their congregation and on their campus long before I began to understand the outworking of those priorities. Although they had a beautiful auditorium, the statement of those priorities or those values kept in check the tremendous drive that some people had to build a cathedral.

I saw an interesting shift of that value at Phoenix First Assembly. They have an outstanding ministry to the poor. They go into the inner city and minister to them, but they also bring them to their very attractive facilities in the suburbs of the city. Two values are tied together there. "We want these poor people to be treated with respect," Tommy Barnett said. "So we want them to be in a beautiful setting." They place a high value on having the most attractive facility possible while at the same time giving as much help to the poor as they possibly can.

A values auction for your church leadership could be a very enjoyable and extremely profitable exercise to help clarify what the leaders think are and ought to be the values of the congregation. Each participant is awarded an imaginary $10,000 and given the privilege of buying items being auctioned. The chosen auctioneer simply auctions each item off one at a time. Each member of the group has the privilege of bidding on the various items. When all the items are sold, the members sit in triads and discuss why they bid the amounts they did on various items. This will get them to think through the importance they place on such things as a nice facility, a beautiful choir chancel, a youth pastor, a discipleship pastor, a foreign missions program, numerous converts, a day nursery, a high percentage of the congregation meeting in prayer, a ministry geared toward senior citizens, a congregation that cares deeply about the poor, and other items that are pertinent to the congregation (see Appendix 1: "Values Auction").

Ephesians 1:3–14 provides one of the most extensive lists of the spiritual gifts Christians have inherited by being in Christ. By the time Paul gets to verse 18, he makes a prayer for the saints in reference to that extensive list. Verse 18, "I pray also that the eyes of your heart may be enlightened in order that you may know the hope to which He has called you, the riches of His glorious inheritance in the saints." The last three chapters of Ephesians become the outworking of that prayer. If you see yourself properly as a true child of God, then you will walk circumspectly as children of love and as children of light. Paul is simply suggesting to the church at Ephesus that its value system needed to be changed. Logic tells people that if they could see properly, their values would be in alignment with God's desire for His children. For the same reason, John states in the book of Revelation that "he who has an ear to hear, let him hear" (Rev. 13:9). If he sees and hears properly, his values will be in harmony with God's desires for His children.

Hunter Lewis breaks that down into smaller components. He says that people's values are multifaceted in origin.

> What eventually becomes clear is that there are only six ways that we believe or know anything, and these may be summarized as follows: authority, deductive logic, sense experience, emotion, intuition, and science. These six modes not only describe how we think about things in general, they also describe how we develop and choose values. . . . Christianity has often been associated with authority, although it makes a strong emotional, intuitive, and logical appeal as well.[12]

Men and women often view Jesus differently. Therefore, they value different aspects of Him. Some women see and appreciate the soft and gentle, deeply loving and sensitive Jesus. Men, on the other hand, often appreciate the virile, highly disciplined, and involved Jesus. The men respond to Christ's words "come and follow me." Often the church tends to present more of the women's views of Jesus than the men's, which may give us an insight as to why the church always has a far greater percentage of women in attendance than men. Women find their identity as they come to church, and men tend to leave their identity at the door.

Yet another interesting view of how Christians' values are developed comes from Stan Perea. He talks about the different values Anglos put on the cross in contrast to the way Hispanics and African Americans see the cross. Because Anglos tend to be more individualistic, they highly value education, freedom, privacy, and success. When they look at the cross, they value the freedom in Christ which an individual receives as he or she comes to personal salvation in Jesus Christ. On the other hand, Hispanics and blacks more highly value intimacy, love, respect, communal family, and liberation which historically has given them freedom from suffering and slavery. When they look at the cross, they tend to appreciate the suffering Savior. This may give us some clue as to why liberation theology is more appealing to them and why certain churches have a specific set of values while other churches have a different set. This often has to do with the cultural makeup of the congregation.

As the leadership of your congregation begins to work through its vision and philosophy statement, you should quickly recognize that there are many values which are underpinnings for those two significant statements. Alan Wilkins can help you understand that values and vision are directly tied together and that the stories people tell in the organization quickly clarify what those values are all about.

> My research in organizations suggests that many of the values that are adopted as shared vision, as well as the conventions people learn, are passed on through informal stories. . . . Stories of actual events inside the organization are often more credible than official claims because the person who is telling the story may not be a company official (with obvious pro-company biases) and because the story is concrete, unlike the abstract ideas of vision statements. In addition, stories give people a chance to improve their own implementation of organization-sponsored values.[13]

Furthermore, if you have not hammered out your values carefully, your philosophy of ministry may not be an accurate representation of who you are and what you want to try to accomplish. Each phase of your philosophy such as music, evangelism, and fellowship has underlying values. Consequently the congregation may make wrong decisions about their philosophy if the values are not in place and generally agreed upon by everyone. It is so critical that the congregation's values be constantly held up before the people so that corporately they will make the proper decisions about their present and future ministries.

A certain congregation faced a tension between building a new gymnasium or adding a staff person to deal with discipleship ministries. A very influential family in the congregation, who was also the leading financial supporter of the church, was strongly in favor of the gym. The father saw it as a critical means of keeping his own children in the church as well as reaching others. Many of the other leaders in the church felt that having a minister of discipleship would strengthen the congregation and that this would be a far more significant investment of their finances. The influential financier threatened to leave the church if the gymnasium was not built. If the leadership of the church had clearly articulated their values and put them in the order of a priority, then this conflict may never have arisen. This is only one example among many of how a church may be brought to the point of chaos because individual values begin to shape the future of the congregation rather than values owned by the corporate body. Time after time I have dealt with congregations who had serious difficulties in functioning together as a congregation in ministry. Invariably, the crux of the problem was that they had not clearly thought through their values, nor had they articulated a philosophy of ministry which emanated from those values.

The Process of Building a Value

It takes an individual many years to build a solid set of values. In the same fashion, it takes a great deal of time for a congregation to change or establish its values. This becomes increasingly difficult for a congregation with a rapid turnover. It is also important to keep in mind that many scientific studies have been done on value formation. This chapter is not a scientific explanation of how values are formed. It simply states some significant ways to develop a movement toward godly values in the life of a congregation.

1. Values come from our close companionship with Him

In Psalm 46:10, the psalmist instructs us to "be still and know that I am God." Christians will not know God's heart nor His vision, His passion nor His values, until they spend a great deal of time in His presence. The megaphones of this world will speak too loudly, and the culture will influence them too strongly unless they spend adequate time listening to God. Most of the pastors I interviewed gave strong testimony to the fact that they spent long hours with God in prayer. This forced them to struggle through the value issues in their own lives. Where would they place their priorities? Where would they give their time and energy? Randy Pope spent weeks in prayer seeking God's face before he started the Perimeter Church and its distinctive philosophy of ministry. Randy Kinnison states:

> I began to practice the disciplines and keep in my walk with Christ. I became committed to spending an hour a day, a day a month, and a week a year in prayer. The hour a day wasn't difficult (or the day a month) because I would go off somewhere, usually a local convent, in which I would spend a day in prayer. But the week a year—I needed approval for that. The deacon board easily accepted, and I went to Colorado to my grandparents' cabin. I spent my first week in solitude. For the first three days, I simply fasted. The only thing I would read would be Scriptures or hymn books or worship. I read Scripture, prayed, and worshiped for three days. I did not keep track of the time. I did not worry about when I got up, when I went to bed, when I took a nap. I took one and one half days just to unwind from looking at a daytimer and worrying about the clock. It was definitely a life-changing experience. The last three days of my retreat, I brought a number of research materials on discipleship for us to launch a very ambitious program of small group Bible study discipleship at the church.[14]

2. Preaching is a values platform

Even though the American church is going through some significant paradigm shifts, the preached word on Sunday mornings still tends to be the focal point of most congregations. The pastor has an unprecedented opportunity during that preaching time to build a values base into the congregation. Even though they will not necessarily do what he challenges them to do, he is changing their way of thinking.

There is no form in the American church that better provides an opportunity to put people into the mind-set of thinking about righteousness. John 14:8 suggests that when the Spirit of God has come, He will convict the world of sin, of righteousness, and of judgment. Essentially, what the Spirit promised to do is to put in people's minds a second opinion. They already have a secular opinion. Now the Spirit comes to put the opinion of righteousness into their minds. It is important to keep in focus that people cannot own two opposing positions simultaneously. Preachers can play a major role in augmenting the work of the Holy Spirit (Col. 1:29). They put people into disequilibrium who will have to make the decision either for righteousness or for carnality. The one who stands behind the sacred desk each Sunday morning ought to recognize that holy and high calling of being a values builder. The wise pastor will see this as playing a significant role in building a foundation for a philosophy of ministry. The preacher ought to be preaching values that help facilitate vision and augment the church's philosophy of ministry.

3. Doing your theology clarifies values

Doing theology certainly includes worshiping God and consequently having your minds and hearts prepared before Him so you can honestly evaluate His Word. However, doing theology is more than thinking theologically, for theology implies also *practicing* our theology. If you are going to have a God-given philosophy of ministry, then you must be extremely honest with Scripture. A true biblical hermeneutic will give you an assurance that your values and ultimately your philosophy of ministry are in accord with the purposes of God.

David Moore of Community Church in Palm Desert, California, serves as a supreme example of the significance of doing one's theology. David took a more traditional church through a paradigm shift to become a strongly seeker-sensitive church. It took him approximately two years to lead the church leadership and the congregation to make the decision to effect that significant change. He testifies to the fact that they were able to make the change without losing members of the congregation because they had asked some very significant questions of Scripture and of themselves. They continued to ask themselves about the reasons for their existence and to search the Scriptures for two years regarding God's mission for the church. Consequently, the Scriptures (not the pastor) became the authority. This made it much easier for the spiritual leaders of the church to make a significant paradigm shift. Because of doing their theology carefully, they did not cause any serious disruption in the church life.

All the pastors interviewed gave strong testimonies about the importance of going back to the Word of God and studying the functions of the church rather than thinking about the cultural or historic forms which had been passed down to them from previous generations.

As new people continue to transfer their membership from other cities and churches, they will much more readily follow the leadership of the church once they understand that the philosophy of ministry is value-driven. If they do not sense that values are in place, then they may tend to challenge the church's philosophy of ministry and ultimately seek to disrupt the harmony of the congregation.

4. Imparting values leads people into disequilibrium

Sound biblical values do not come normally to depraved human beings. Society's tendency is to sin, to go its own way (which most often means going against the ways of God). The true prophet–leader who seeks to instill godly values in his or her congregation will walk a fine line between making the congregation feel comfortable and putting them into disequilibrium.

> Ronald Heifetz, a recognized authority on leadership, contends that exercising leadership is not the same thing as being an authority figure. To illustrate, Heifetz says the auto mechanic is an authority figure. We take our problems to him, he decides how the problem will be fixed, and he fixes it. A leader, on the other hand, doesn't fix problems. Rather he or she mobilizes others to face, define and solve the problem.
>
> This leads us to the crucial point. Authority figures are comforting and their function is to maintain equilibrium. Leadership does the opposite; it disturbs, provokes, and forces people to deal with problems they would rather avoid. For example, at BVC, I'm committed to disturb, provoke and force people to face the implications of hassle-free, comfortable churchianity when our society is in serious peril. I would agree with Heifetz that the leader's role is to generate disequilibrium. Disequilibrium will create an atmosphere for authority figures to rise up, meet the challenge, to right the ship bringing things back to an even keel.
>
> Who are the authority figures at BVC? Various staff, especially the executive pastor, function as authority figures. Most of our authority figures are people involved in ministries. As a leader, my job is to create an awareness of the need. The awareness causes disequilibrium. Then God raises up people to minister,

and they become the authority figures, they provide solutions for that need and restore equilibrium. But by the time authority figures have restored equilibrium, a good leader will have created more meaningful chaos elsewhere.[15]

Old Testament prophets tended to get stoned and thrown out of town. I have seen the same thing happen to contemporary prophets. A prophet of God who is a spokesman for God will speak sensitively against the values of a culture that is turned against God. This kind of leadership should be displayed not only in the pulpit but in the kind of leadership given to the church leaders through the programs which are established and carried out by and in the congregation. Randy Kinnison worked hard to keep the values of his congregation focused on their value of seeing people come to Christ.

> As the building was being built, we continually focused on outreach. We spent many times in prayer in the building praying for people who would come to Christ as a result of using the facility. I spent much time helping people visualize the ministry that would happen, like people coming to Christ in weight rooms and under basketball hoops. We prayed for indoor park ministries, basketball ministries, volleyball ministries. We prayed for ministries we didn't even know we would have yet. I believe most of the vision was communicated during these prayer times. I would take the staff, and we would drive around to the new suburbs. We would pray for the people in those subdivisions. Each week in the bulletin, we would pray for the neighborhood around the church. I especially prayed daily that God would give us missionaries to those subdivisions.[16]

To help the congregation not only own but also hang onto the important value of ministry during a building project is extremely important yet very difficult. The gymnasium is so visual. It is so exciting. It is much easier to focus on what is temporal.

5. Biblical behavior leads to biblical values

If you analyze carefully the general message communicated to most congregations, it has to do with one's attitude. The basic assumption seems to be if you have your attitude changed, then obviously your behavior would change. If you are going to change one's attitude, it generally will be quickened by the change of one's behavior. A great deal of Christ's teaching to the disciples had to do with His sending them forth on various missions. He did not sit around with them and say, "Get your attitude changed. Then when it is changed, I hope you will go to serve." He sent them forth two by two to witness. He sent them to get the coin out of the fish's mouth. He told them to wash one another's feet. So attitude tends to follow behavior more than behavior follows attitude.

Early in my years of ministry working with young people, I learned a significant lesson. If I would take young people away from the feeding table of the Sunday school classroom and get them into active service in some sort of missionary endeavor, I found that they were much more likely to grow faster spiritually. I am not suggesting that you do not need to talk about attitude, but I believe that you need to spend as much time planning activities and endeavors for your congregation. As they are engaged in ministry and mission, they will find that their attitude and therefore their values will be more deeply ingrained in their souls.

If you were to visit First Baptist Church in Flushing, New York, you would find that one of the values of the congregation has to do with a broad acceptance of many different races, creeds, and classes of people. As the leadership under Russ Rosser designed programs to include various ethnic groups, the congregation soon learned this was a beautiful and godly value. Years before, that message of unity was preached but never practiced. It was not until unity was practiced that it could be preached and owned by the congregation.

6. *Our values tend to come from our culture*

Joe Ellis in *Church on Purpose* explains the power of culture in the formation of people's values:

> From the time an individual is born, culture filters into him or her its assumptions about the church. Even before that child is aware of what is happening, the cultural image is well-structured into his or her thinking so that he or she tends to accept and perpetuate what has been heard and observed. The cultural versions of religion resemble Christianity in many ways and use some of the same terminology and forms, but they lack the essence of biblical Christianity. If congregations are not alert, they can be directed more by cultural images of Christianity than by what the Bible reveals as the intentions of God. The condition has been described as the cultural captivity of the church.[17]

No one knows for sure how powerful the media really is in helping Americans form their value system, but if the research from many quarters is true, it is extremely frightening. Listen and watch carefully. Are biblical or secular values more prevalent in your church life?

Several years ago the members of a congregation called me to work with them because it appeared that the church was on the brink of closing its doors after many years of ministry. After three days of interviews, it was obvious to me that the major power broker in the congregation had a value that said it was better not to rock the boat and keep the business matters in order rather than becoming a missionary church. He had played his chips for a number of years and was shrewd enough to manipulate the congregation into his way of thinking. It was obvious that he had learned his values from the business world where he spent most of his adult life. Politicking with *Roberts' Rules of Order* had allowed him to use his values to direct the business of the church for years. During my time with them, I worked hard to help them own, understand, and practice the value of giving energy and ministry to a lost and dying community. *Roberts' Rules of Order* may be way out of order when the congregation's values are not clearly defined and owned.

The next chapter will help you to understand further the need for a strong biblical philosophy of ministry.

Chapter 3

Seeing Through Your Scope Clearly

*Why it is so important to have
a philosophy of ministry*

Forgetting what is behind and straining toward what is ahead, I press on toward the goal to win the prize for which God has called me, heavenward in Christ Jesus" (Philippians 3:13-14). One of the obvious reasons for Paul's great success in planting churches on his missionary journeys is perhaps best summarized in the statement that he pressed on toward the goal to win the prize for which Christ had called him. That goal might be referred to as his vision, but it would certainly also include his philosophy of ministry, which is better explained in his various writings. When a hunter goes for his game, he sets the rifle scope before his eye and eliminates everything other than the animal he hopes to shoot. The word *goal* is the word *skopos* which refers to a mark on which you fix your eye with the intent of capturing that goal. A scope can eliminate as well as focus. A philosophy of ministry is very much like a scope. There are far more things for a church to do and for its leaders to do than they will ever be able to accomplish, but setting the scope on the particular goal they want to accomplish is vital to the success of the church.

Every church, no matter how small or large or how effective or ineffective, does have a philosophy of ministry. However, our research validates the fact that those who have set their scope specifically on a target consistently tend to be more effective than those who do not.

In the research we have done at the Institute for Church Development, we have found the extreme significance of a church that sets its scope on its goal. We have studied all the churches in the data bank that have grown at least 100 percent during the last decade and have contrasted them with the churches that have declined at least 25 percent during the last decade. The Institute's survey given to the congregation identifies thirty-four phases or facets of ministry, one of them being the people's perception of the congregation's goal or clarity of purpose. Of these thirty-four facets of ministry, the clarity of the goal continues to be the first and most important facet, as understood by the congregations in those churches which have grown 100 percent or more. In contrast, the churches that have declined 25 percent or more find that the clarity of their goal is one of the least perceived effective facets of ministry for the congregation. In my consulting work with these congregations across the country, I have seen over and over again how important it is for a congregation to clearly understand its purpose. Without question, a purpose-driven congregation has set its scope on the mission and is seeking with dogged pursuit to accomplish that mission.

Gerald Sheveland of San Diego says, "There are always philosophies of ministry in existence. In any given church, there are always multiple philosophies that are jogging for priority, energies, and resources. The key is not to find just a philosophy of ministry; the key is to mold a shared philosophy of ministry toward the accomplishment of that target."

In the next chapter, you will find some guidelines toward the establishment of a special philosophy of ministry. In this chapter, you will learn some additional reasons why it is so important to have an agreed-upon, clearly defined, and owned philosophy of ministry.

1. There is diversity in unity in Christ's body

Obviously, God has gone to a great deal of effort to make every human being distinctly different. It would seem to be utterly foolish to try to create everyone alike. In the same fashion, it would be foolish to try to make all the various churches, which are an expression of Christ's body, all alike. In 1 Corinthians 12 and in Romans 12 (these passages teach about the gifts of the body given to individual members), there is a great deal of emphasis upon diversity. The purpose of diversity is ultimately that the unity of the body of Christ might be expressed. In a sense, each church has its own thumbprint just as each individual has his or her own thumbprint. Psychologists

say that a person's sense of self-esteem and self-worth has a great
deal to do with recognizing the diversity of his or her personality.
Similarly, there is strength in a congregation when the individual
members can understand and own the diversity that allows them to
accomplish their goals in the body of Christ. Kent R. Hunter expresses
that thought beautifully when he says:

> There is unity within the Christian church, but inside that
> unity, there is a freedom for the individual congregation to fulfill
> God's plan in ways that are different. The programs, the strategies,
> the expression of worship, the ministries, and the buildings—all
> will take individual and unique shapes. But each remains within
> the context of the Christian faith, and each different shape
> constitutes a philosophy of ministry.[18]

2. Culture demands it

Ever since the Tower of Babel, different language groups have
been evolving into different cultures. Because of the migration of
the human race, those language groups have spread across the face
of the earth and have established their own expression of life in
neighborhoods and communities. Bruce Larson and Ralph Osborne
express it clearly: "The point is that a church, like an individual,
must have a distinct personality and a highly specialized emphasis
that makes it different from all other churches at that moment in
history."[19]

Peter Wagner in his book *Our Kind of People* writes extensively
about the good and the evil of culture. Culture tends to perpetuate its
own sin but also expresses the beauty of God's creation. God calls
for people to worship Him, and He expects that they will respond to
His initiation toward them in reference to their uniqueness.
Consequently it should be expected that each congregation will form
a philosophy of ministry in reference to its own culture.

3. Ministry effectiveness demands it

As Jesus was training His disciples, He taught them that He was
not satisfied if there were no results. He wanted banquet tables that
were filled (Luke 14:15-23). He wanted the prodigal son returned
(Luke 15:11-31). He wanted the ripe harvest reaped (Matthew 9:36-
38). No wise businessman would like to be in business without a
sense of success. Similarly, no church leader who has a passion for
God in his or her soul would want a church that was not productive
and effective. Kent R. Hunter expresses this well:

> A philosophy of ministry helps a congregation become a good corporate steward of time, talents, and money. It will reflect intentionality of ministry and the directing of resources according to well thought-out priorities. It will help a congregation focus on its identity; it will help the people discover who they are and who they are not. It will help show outsiders why the church is different from the one down the block. While each church has a different identity, attitude, and priorities, this foundation of concern for good stewardship will be a common theological basis for all churches and establish a philosophy of ministry.[20]

It is wise to keep Ephesians 2:10 in mind. It states that people are God's workmanship. That is, they are crafted by Him in a unique way so they might be productive. The passage goes on to say that they are created in Christ Jesus to do good works which God prepared in advance for them to do. Since the church is made up of individuals, everyone in Christ's body ought to be producing good works. A philosophy of ministry focuses their energy and helps them to be the most productive as they maximize His workmanship.

Great athletic swimmers are always interested in maximizing their strokes. During practice, they strap large squares of plastic over their hands to determine how effective those strokes are. If they are going to win the race, they must propel themselves through the water with the greatest amount of effectiveness to capture the energy which is wrapped up in those strokes. They will never win the race or be effective without maximizing their energy. Likewise, a church should design its philosophy of ministry so that each one of its strokes can capitalize on the energy which God has given to them. Like the swimmer who has limited strokes, the congregation has limited resources of personnel, finance, and time. They cannot afford to lose the effectiveness of every stroke of ministry. A philosophy of ministry will help them to stay effective.

4. Every church needs a centered focus

Most of the dying or stagnant churches in America have not defined a vision or a philosophy of ministry. Winston Churchill was right when he said, "More men fail for lack of aim than for any other reason."[21] A philosophy of ministry helps you to focus your resources on the target you have wrestled with and have decided is the wisest way for you to do ministry. It is very much like preparing a sermon. After you have done all your research and gathered all the information, then you must decide exactly what the big idea ought to be. That forces you to eliminate a lot of other things that are nice to say but are not pertinent to the topic. Bill Hybels apparently agrees when he says, "When you decide about being single-focused in who you will target, then it is like preaching a sermon or writing a book. You have a single theme which means you eliminate a lot of other things."[22]

Corporations and other institutions used to spend a great deal of time thinking about five-year, ten-year, and fifteen-year goals for their corporations and institutions. Because of the rapidity of the change of culture, people have become much more focused on the immediate. This has made them often forget about the future and just think in the present mode. Since Americans are generally no longer accustomed to thinking that far in the future, it becomes extremely important to carve out a philosophy of ministry so people will be forced to think about the future and not just about the immediate. Lyle Schaller says, "The pressure of today's immediate concerns often tempts people to postpone that more difficult question about purpose, reason for being, and role. The discussion requires people to think in a much longer time frame when it is normally easier to focus on the immediate concern."[23]

When a church for some reason or other has declined in its attendance, there is a great tendency to try to conduct all of the ministries that were carried out when they were much larger. That happens because either they have not realigned their philosophy or they never had one to begin with. There is still a great tendency to think they can be everything to everyone, but as Peter Wagner suggests, that becomes a great formula for mediocrity.

> Now if you like mediocrity, say "We're going to do a little bit of everything for everybody." Personally, I would rather do a few things with excellence than many things with mediocrity. Now radio stations know this. Radio stations know that they need to focus on certain things with excellence and other radio stations focus on other things, particularly in urban areas where they have that luxury. Some of you are listening to this tape and live in rural areas. You know that your radio station has to do a little bit of everything for everybody, but they don't have excellence in anything they do. They just have to serve that diverse audience.[24]

A philosophy of ministry is built on the idea that there is no single church in America or in the world that can do everything for everyone. That church really never existed and never will. Consequently, then, we need to deal with two big questions: to whom are we going to minister, and how are we going to do that ministry? Those are the choices that need to be made, and that is why we need a philosophy of ministry.

5. The balance of ministry demands it

The weekly pressure of people, programs, and all the various ministries makes it very difficult for the average leadership team to keep everything in perspective. Even when someone on the leadership team has the big picture of ministry, it will still be essential to constantly keep that picture before the whole team and the congregation. It would be very easy to get out of focus doing the good things, but not the best. The best things on which you have decided are the best things for you. The tyranny of the urgent becomes our greatest enemy. Barna reminds leaders that if they have not identified exactly what they are all about as a congregation, many other good ideas will creep in and greatly weaken their effectiveness. He says:

> One of the vision's greatest benefits is that it serves as a filter that allows people to say no to a variety of ministry opportunities. One of Satan's greatest weapons today is to breed confusion and dissension within the church by creating more needs in the people of society than a given body of believers can possibly address.[25]

Most of the pastors whom I interviewed testified that the same pressure often moved them away from their target. Dealing with personal problems is always a problem. Leaders tend to get bogged down in the inner workings of the church and the pressing needs of counseling the people, so they easily lose perspective on what the purpose of the church is. They must get out there and serve the world. Somehow, therefore, they need to resolve the leadership issue. Good leadership says that both management and counseling must be accomplished. Good leadership, therefore, is to clarify the balance of the pressures of ministry.

Robert Dale says the same thing: "Ministry is to the redeemed, and leading the redeeming people of God to become the kingdom dream in local communities. No church can minister effectively until it identifies and focuses on its unique ministry."[26]

6. The diversity of methodology demands it

When the concept of closure is not built into a pastor's temperament, it is very easy for that pastor and consequently, then, for the entire congregation to keep experimenting with a great variety of philosophies, never settling in on one. In my research for this book I found a strong agreement with my findings about churches. There is a great deal of burnout among the pastors. Much of that probably comes because they are painfully ambivalent, even schizophrenic, about what their role is and what the congregation ought to be doing. With the extreme amount of pressure on people's lives these days, such confusion builds added stress and strain on everyone.

My broad exposure to the tremendous diversity of ministries going on in America is a great reminder to me about how many different ways there are to do ministries. With people moving from community to community (therefore from church to church), they bring with them a pool of ideas which sometimes becomes overwhelming to the leadership. This is one of the main reasons why there must be a common agreement about exactly how each congregation will go about its unique ministry.

An unfocused philosophy of ministry can quickly undermine people's commitment to a church. In a society where commitment is so difficult to find, it becomes important for people to have a clear-cut philosophy of ministry (Alan Watkins, *Developing Corporate Character,* Jossey Bass, 1989, p. 135). I agree with Alan Wilkins as he talks about developing corporate character; the same is true with congregations. "The importance of keeping some long-term commitments is an abstract idea to capture. However, it is a critical one. If everything is up for grabs and if nothing is sacred, then there could be no meaning. There could be no character, and there could be no long-term confidence in an organization."

We cannot keep changing our target and win. Can you imagine what would happen if the next time you went to McDonald's to get a hamburger, you discover to your amazement that you need to wait for a host or hostess to seat you before a table with fine linen napkins and china? He or she would then proceed to take your order for a five-course meal. Quite likely you would not return, but go looking for another fast-food restaurant. There are succinct guidelines for McDonald's just as there are for significantly effective ministries and congregations. Church leaders have learned that you cannot continue to change the menu and continue to win in the battle for the souls of humankind.

7. Facility and philosophy are integrated

Believe it or not, it was Winston Churchill who said, "We shape our buildings, therefore they shape us."[27] By the time you are reading this book, Bethany Baptist Church of Portland, Oregon, will have finished a facility that is specifically suited to its philosophy of ministry. Randy Kinnison says, "I spent much time helping people visualize the ministries that would happen. People coming to Christ in weight rooms and under basketball hoops. We prayed for indoor park ministries, basketball ministries, volleyball ministries." They are fortunate in that they can build a facility which matches their philosophy. Many congregations build a facility without a philosophy and eventually find the philosophy being dictated by the size and shape of the facility.

Some years ago, I was in a Texas church that said it was committed to ministering to people personally, but because it did not have any educational space, the Sunday school class was held in the auditorium. This basically amounted to a second worship service of over 600 people. There was no personal touch involved any place in the congregation. Once again I saw an example of how a facility dictated a congregation's philosophy. Any changes that are going to be made in the facility may be very short-lived if you have not agreed upon a philosophy. Every time you change your philosophy, you may need to change your facility. That could become rather expensive.

8. A philosophy of ministry becomes a guide for all major ministry decisions

"Conflict arises because no single cause pulls people together. Growth is stunted because everyone does what is right in his or her own eyes. Self-interest prevails in a vacuum of vision."[28] Gary Litwiller and Donald Gerig are two consultants who have learned an important lesson. When they go to a congregation and discover an apparent strong disharmony throughout the congregation, one of the first places they will look is in the files to see if there is a philosophy of ministry agreed upon and owned by the congregation. If there is none, more times than not that will be the source of the conflict. Marriage counselors will quickly tell you that parents who have not come to a common agreement about how they will discipline their children will often have strong marital conflict. Disciplining children is very much like guiding a church to its ultimate mission. There is no one way to discipline children, and there is no one way to do ministry. When the members involved are agreed, there tends to be less conflict in the church family (who all want to see God's blessing upon the congregation). Tom McKee's comment about his dialogue with a fellow pastor will give you some insight into the type of conflict that can arise when there is not a philosophy of ministry.

> One pastor was talking about a friend of his who came to church and had a handicapped child. He said, "You know, we're going to leave the church and go to a church down the street because they have a ministry for handicapped." This pastor started to cry, and he said it broke his heart. "Here was my friend, and they were leaving my church to go to a church down the street because they had a handicapped ministry. So I quickly went out and hired a new staff person, and we started a handicapped ministry." As I sat there in the group I thought, how sad. How sad that we have to have every single ministry. I believe that God raises up ministries through the people that he brings into the church and the gifts that they have. We can focus those into our ministry. That's why we developed a very strong philosophy of ministry statement that allows us to do it. You see, there are all kinds of people that will come into your church. One week he wants to have an outreach to all the Vietnamese refugees in the city. Two weeks later he wants to lead a group of young people to Haiti to help construct a hospital. He wants the church to do it all. Pretty soon we burn everybody out, and the church becomes very spastic and jerking, groping this way and that way without any real direction. I love visionary people like that, but when you don't have a focus and you don't have a mission, it's very difficult to say no to visionaries. When you do have a philosophy of ministry it directs those.[29]

9. Calling the right staff to ministry necessitates a clarity of philosophy

One of the real tragedies I run into constantly as a consultant is that when churches call people to positions, sometimes they will spell out a ministry but seldom a philosophy of ministry. If a student is coming out of seminary to his or her first church, he or she has a certain image about what that ministry will look like. He or she has been exposed to a great variety of ministry styles and philosophies and comes with certain expectations. The same is true of staff members who come from previous ministries in other churches. They, too, have certain patterns and expectations. It will be very difficult for you to call the right staff person unless you—and they—know exactly what you want them to be and do. The more specific the guidelines and the philosophy are for the staff, the less likely they will be to burn out, plus the less likely you will have conflict with them in the future. Of course, you can also expect significant teamwork since everyone is working under the same guidelines and philosophy of ministry. As you think about hiring new staff members, I would encourage you to study chapters 11 and 12 in the *Multiple Church-staff Handbook*. You will find additional guidelines on how to hire someone who will fit in with your particular philosophy of ministry.[30]

10. A philosophy calls people to your church membership

Roy Oswald and Speed Leas provide a marvelous illustration for us of how potent a philosophy is in calling people to your church.

> When finding out why people came to church—almost all of them said something like they were coming to the church looking for what they usually described as something that would help them cope better with themselves, their family, their job, their world. Each brought the hope that the church would provide answers or help them cope better with themselves, their family, their job, their world. Each brought the hope that the church would provide answers or help them search. The clearer the church can be about what it is doing, about who it is trying to serve, and what the needs of these people are, the greater the possibility that those who are coming to the church looking for answers or help in their search will be able to make a meaningful decision about participating in the congregation. . . . We believe that clarification of "who we are and who we are trying to serve" will reduce the attrition rate, though it may not do much to increase the joining rate of those exploring the church in the attracting and incorporating stages of assimilation into the church.[31]

Great churches are like great restaurants: the word gets around the community and the intercommunity network. Once the people in the community find that your congregation will meet their needs and that you treat people in a certain fashion, they are very apt to be seated as part of your congregation.

In American history there probably never has been a stronger demarcation between generations than the one which comes between the G.I. Joe generation and the baby boomer generation. Numerous studies and volumes of books have been written about the characteristics of the baby boomer generation. Doug Murren did a thorough study in his book *The Baby Boomerang*, catching baby boomers as they return to church.[32] His book would be a tremendous aid in understanding the characteristics of the baby boomer generation. The Institute for Church Development's survey provides a breakdown of the percentage of people in the congregation who represent the various decades. As a consultant looking at the congregation, I can almost always tell which group of the congregation will like a contemporary style of worship in contrast to the group who will like a traditional style of worship. Each generation has its own set of values which guide them toward the decisions they will make. The G.I. Joe generation will want volunteers to do most of the work, while the boomers are quite ready to pay various workers since that is their particular life-style. As the leadership designs a philosophy of ministry, it will need to make a significant decision about which group they will cater to. If leaders desire to minister to more than one generation, they will need to give serious thought to some of the philosophy ministry issues that appeal to each generation. Failure to do so may bring an early death to the congregation.

If churches have failed to be open to the next generation for more than one decade, they may find themselves with primarily older congregations. There are very few congregations who can, in a short period of time, open the doors to the younger generation and expect them to come when the central focus of the philosophy of ministry and its values are primarily aimed at the older generation.

The pastor who thinks philosophically, leads the congregation to do likewise, and helps the congregation to own the church's philosophy of ministry makes a significant difference in proclaiming the gospel to the community. This poem by T. E. Lawrence makes that point very succinctly:

> All men dream; but not equally
> Those who dream by night in the dusty
>   recesses of their minds
> Awake to find that it was vanity;
> But the dreamers of day are dangerous men,
> That they may act their dreams with
>   open eyes to make it possible.

(Quoted in *Leaders, the Strategies for Taking Charge*, Bennis and Nunas)

In the next chapter we will learn more about those who think philosophically and lead dynamically.

Chapter 4

The Profile of a Ministry Architect

The person of God who is called to ministry in a sense is called to be an architect of ministry. It is a most fascinating and intriguing subject to discover how these architects think. As the individuals I interviewed talked about how they designed and built their ministries, there were certain themes which continued throughout the interviews in regard to how they went about their task.

Some of them were right-brained and some left-brained; some tall and some short; articulate or not so articulate; assertive or retiring; participative or autocratic; mavericks or party players. Yet they were all architects who were in the process of building the church of Jesus Christ. They, like all people, are expressions of God's creative brush strokes as expressed in Psalm 139:13-15:

> I praise you because I am fearfully and wonderfully made; your works are wonderful, I knew that full well. My frame was not hidden from you when I was made in a secret place. When I was woven together in the depths of the earth.

Each person is woven together with an uncanny specificity, an astonishing particularity, and a remarkable wholeness and unity that transcends the muddle and diversity of his or her life with a profound uniqueness all his or her own. Everyone is gifted, and this is the very basis upon which God set about working with and through his or her humanity. He has given everyone gifts to fulfill his or her calling—whatever that may be. This is the basis for this book and especially this chapter. He has given you specific traits, temperaments, and circumstances to work with, and you need to celebrate your giftedness.

You cannot be exactly like any of these leaders, but you can be your own person. You can blossom where you are planted; you can celebrate your uniqueness. You might have some of their same traits, and if you do, you can fan them into a flame as Paul suggested to Timothy that he ought to do.

Creativity takes some divine absolutes. They become your framework, and you can build within that framework. The church architects can rearrange the walls; they just cannot change the foundation. That is what Christ suggests when He says that He is the foundation of the church, and church leaders ought to build on that foundation. In 1 Corinthians 3:10 Paul says: "I laid the foundation as a master builder and someone else is building upon it." Christians are so honored to have such a great foundation to build on, and it is such a delight to create their own superstructure. Such a great and unshakable word from God deserves a beautiful and serviceable foundation. "Jesus leaves none of us out; there is an image there for everyone of us—sometimes several. He knew one image would not suffice because every imagination works differently and therefore is captured by different images."[33]

God is obviously doing a very significant work by using so many kinds of people and so many types of churches. He is eager to see that the gospel is spread throughout the world. The only way God can effectively minister to each individual in the world is to have beautiful and unique models of ministry.

These philosophers, like all ministers, are strategists or architects who work with God's eternal functions or principles to build His church. They are creative as to how they go about strategizing for ministries. They study the thoughts and the processes that govern the blending of the human and the divine in Christ's kingdom. This chapter deals with the recurring themes in the philosophical thought patterns of our church philosophers.

Creative Philosophers Are:

1. In Pursuit of God

Each leader in an individual way was saying as Paul said in Philippians 3:10: "I want to know Christ and the power of His resurrection and the fellowship of sharing in His sufferings, becoming like Him in His death."

Randy Pope talked about setting aside blocks of three or four days to be devoted to pursuing God solely. He wanted God to give him new ideas so that he would not lose the edge of creativity. He suggested that if you do not stay home and be still before God and know Him, then He would never be able to reveal His directions to you. So Randy spent many days waiting on God for His direction, and he now tries to spend at least an hour each day during his routine ministry. Clyde McDowell spoke of having a genuine encounter with God and His Word on a regular basis in order to find God's philosophy for his ministry. He found himself studying church books that were different from his own position to see how God was working in the lives of other people. Tommy Barnett spends two hours each day on a hill behind the church waiting on God. This is where he deals with issues in life and ministry and where God lays burdens on his heart for His people.

Randy Kinnison spent three days at the beginning of his new ministry in Portland fasting and seeking direction for the church. He said, "The prayer league of my philosophy of ministry has evolved into being a prayer retreat leader, taking our own people on prayer retreats, developing ministries of prayer and seeking and decision-making processes—to bathe everything in prayer and finding something wonderful happens. Usually consensus occurs. Even in very important and controversial decisions such as building almost a million dollar gym at our current facility, hiring additional staff in positions never before addressed."

Russ Rosser talked about seeking God in the process of sermon preparation. His devotional life tended to be built around the preparation of his messages. As Don Bubna is leading his congregation in Vancouver, British Columbia, he relates how he led the entire church through an extensive prayer time as they were thinking through their philosophy of ministry. He was intensely eager for the entire congregation to know, understand, and have a part in receiving that from God.

2. Knowledgeable About Who They Are

All of the men I interviewed spoke strongly about knowing who they were. They talked about their giftedness, their depravity, their temperament, their history, and their roots. It seemed difficult for them to lead until they had come to that knowledge. It was difficult for them to carve out a ministry until they had lived life, experienced ministry, and found out in the successes and failures of life just who they were.

David Moore said, "The first step for me was to know my gifts, strengths, and the dreams God had given me for the church." Clyde McDowell said his own strengths came with him as he moved from Minneapolis to Denver. There he really started to know himself. As he was engaged in ministry, as he was around other strong leaders, and as he finished his doctor of ministry program, it seemed that he started to understand who he was and therefore could lead the church in knowing who they ought to become.

It was originally thought that most of these people would have the same temperaments or personality traits. It was somewhat surprising to find they were all different. Yet in a sense, that was most encouraging since that can give everyone hope that God might be able to use him or her in the design and the implementation of a unique philosophy of ministry. Robert Acker spoke about the fact that he was a typical leader: "On the personal profile, I am a persuader. My teaching gifts are not as high as my leadership gifts. So I see the Lord allowing me to teach because it is where my leadership to the body is."

E. V. Hill suggests that he is not a planner by his own admission, but his congregation has great confidence in him and are happy to follow his lead. Don Bubna suggested that he has a strong dominant personality yet at the same time is very sensitive to people. He sees himself as a trailblazer with a great deal of commitment, and he is not willing to be caught in the tradition of the past.

Although these leaders did not talk about writing their own mission statements, in a sense they have it written down indelibly in their minds. Stephen Arcovey talked about the extreme importance of having a mission statement:

> A personal mission statement focuses on what you want to be [character] and to do [contributions and achievements] and on the values or principles upon which being and doing are based . . . . You could call a personal mission statement a personal constitution, like the United States Constitution. It is fundamentally changeless. In over 200 years, there have been only 26 amendments, ten of which were in the original Bill of Rights.
>
> The United States Constitution is the standard by which every law in the country is evaluated. It is the document the president agrees to defend and support when he takes the oath of allegiance. It is the criterion by which people are admitted into citizenship. It is the foundation and center that enables people to ride through such major traumas as the Civil War, Vietnam, or Watergate. It

is the written standard, the key criterion by which everything else is evaluated and directed.

The Constitution has endured and served its vital function today because it is based on correct principles, on the self-evident truths contained in the Declaration of Independence. These principles empower the Constitution with a timeless strength, even in the midst of social ambiguity and change. "Our particular security," said Thomas Jefferson, "is the possession of a written constitution."

A personal mission statement based on correct principles becomes the same kind of standard for an individual. It becomes a personal constitution, the basis for making life-directing decisions, the basis for making daily decisions in the midst of circumstances, an emotion that affects our lives. It empowers individuals with the same timeless strength in the midst of change . . . .

With a mission statement, we can flow with changes. We do not need prejudgments or prejudices. We do not need to figure out everything else in life, to stereotype and categorize everything and everybody in order to accommodate reality.[34]

In listening to these men talk about who they are, it became increasingly obvious that most of them are broad-picture people, not single-focused. In the Meyers-Briggs scoring system, they would be classified as intuitive.

Randy Pope early on had a view of how he could go about capturing the city of Atlanta for Christ. At one time in the process, he was pastoring four congregations at once. The Bear Valley staff helped to establish Mile Hi Ministries in Denver, which was a much broader reflection of what Bear Valley is all about. Stan Perea leads what he calls HIS Ministries which is a way for him to extend the ministry of his church throughout the city in an outreach to Hispanics. Each one drew around himself strong, gifted people who helped him expand his giftedness in ministry. Don Bubna and his wife Delores spend a large chunk of time every year traveling to some foreign country to train pastors and missionaries. Clyde McDowell, besides pastoring his large congregation, is a significant leader in the Mile Hi Ministries in the city of Denver.

Because each one of these people seemed to understand who they were, it was easier for them to discipline themselves toward accomplishing what they wanted to see accomplished. Clyde McDowell said, "Good leadership is to clarify the balance between the personal needs of the church members and what the mission of the church is all about." He seems to be able to keep that big picture in perspective.

Randy Kinnison said, "I shuddered at the thought of being a maintenance pastor who simply pumped out sermons week after week and kept people happy enough to retain a job. I have always had a much bigger view of ministry than that."

Knowing who they were meant that they also seemed to understand their depravity. Randy Pope said, "I know about my ego. I ask God daily in prayer to keep it in check. It can be used by God, or it can get out of hand very readily. I have selfish ambitions I don't want to be part of my life. The more secure you are, the more ego you tend to have. I have some insecurities as do all people. I always have to ask myself, 'Is it to glorify God or to glorify me?' I have two guys at the church that I meet with regularly. One of the things we do regularly is to check on each other's egos."

All the men expressed their depravity and in positive ways praised God for His faithful mercy. It was easy for them to minister to others since they had been the recipients of God's mercies.

3. Communicators of a Mission

These men all had seriously thought through their vision, their values, and their philosophy of ministry. Consequently, it was relatively easy for them to communicate that mission. Bennis and Nanus would express that when they said:

> There are a lot of intoxicating visions and a lot of noble intentions. Many people have rich and deeply textured agendas, but without communication nothing will be realized. Success requires the capacity to relate a compelling image of a desired state of affairs—the kind of image that induces enthusiasm and commitment in others.[35]

Although all of them had public communication skills, it seemed increasingly obvious that their whole life communicated their mission with a certain ethos.

E. V. Hill meets every Wednesday evening with five divisional groups. During those sessions, he gives directional messages for the leaders in his congregation who will help him carry out his ministry. These five groups take turns on Sunday evenings challenging and guiding the rest of the congregation. After more than 25 years of ministry, that was something they really expected of him. They got their directions from him as if he were the general of the army.

Ninety leaders were interviewed by Bennis and Nanus in preparation for their book about leaders. They said:

> A number of lessons can be drawn from the experiences of our ninety leaders. First and perhaps most important is that all organizations depend on the existence of shared meanings and interpretations of reality, which facilitate coordinated actions. The actions and symbols of leadership frame and mobilize meaning. Leaders articulate and define what has previously remained implicit or unsaid; then they invent images, metaphors, and models that provide a focus for new attention.[36]

Gerald Sheveland wraps up the importance of communication by saying, "It is just something that is a part of who I am. I think people who lead breathe it. We live it. We talk about it. We are excited about it. It shows up in our preaching. It shows up in the presentations that we make. I do not know how many times I have gone over putting together written materials and other means of image-generating media to demonstrate and to say to people, 'Here is where the action is at for us.' " Pastor Tommy Barnett spends time in nearly every service challenging the people about how they can participate in some new ministry. I see a lot of the success in Phoenix First Assembly of God relating to those motivational talks. The whole congregation is caught up in the reality that they are all involved in the conversion of many people coming to faith in Christ.

4. Creative Innovators

Steve Johnson, in what he calls "The Chemistry Match,"[37] classifies people's motivational roles in the following construct: creative, creative developer, developer, refiner, and maximizer. The strong majority of these leaders would be classified as creative or creative developers. Early in their ministries, they found the importance of getting refiners and maximizers around them so that the ministries which they created and developed could be refined and maximized by other people. Leaders who are good creative or creative development people who fail to get others around them to maximize their ministries will often find those ministries dying for lack of energy in the not-too-distant future.

Russ Rosser talked about the fact that all the siblings in the Rosser family were strongly affirmed and had modeled for them strong, creative parents. It is no surprise that you now see Russ Rosser leading his church in Flushing to so many innovative kinds of ministries. The one they are still working on is trying to sell air space above their building so their much-needed facility could be paid for by an office and apartment developer. At the same time, David Moore spoke about how his interest and skills with music are helping him to be creative. He expressed his creativity in many different ways.

Also, it was fascinating to see that most of them did not see themselves as very creative, but they had an ability to blend what they saw in others or in other ministries. Cheryl Forbes says it best:

> The great scientists, composers, painters, and ordinary people whose lives express equilibrium and peace in the face of triumph as well as tragedy have never neglected their imagination. . . . Our third eye, the eye of imagination, needs to be open and clear to see God, to know Him, to worship Him, and to accept the world He has given us.[38]

Gerald Sheveland would testify to that same reality when he says, "Well, I am not sure how creative I am. I suspect that is probably true. I enjoy art, painting, drawing, and those kinds of things. I enjoy attempting things in my mind first in almost every area of life, thinking of different ways of doing things." Again, Cheryl Forbes would paint a meaningful picture about that reality:

> Lewis Thomas has called the brain an old-fashioned attic, where we store all sorts of once-useful stuff: memories we're attached to, junk that we can't throw away no matter what. Modern psychiatry wants to clean up the brain—remove the clutter—much as modern architecture has deleted the attic. Yet people need clutter for imagination.
>
> The computer has a file organizer. It is a means to make our computer work better, and the expression of imagination is the same.[39]

As these people talked about expanding their creative aptitude, they seemed to feel that anyone could be creative. The chapter on paradigms will speak more on this. Rick Warren said, "God as the Creator thus puts that within us, but we need to be careful about fear and rejection which can prohibit that creativity from being expressed." Rick Warren makes his creativity successful. He writes things down all the time so his mind might be kept open to making the ministry more effective.

These men, like all other creative philosophers, are independent in their thinking. Steven Crotts of Grace Church in Burlington,

North Carolina, has a bright glow on his face when he talks about his five worship teams each taking their turn to lead worship. They range from Christian rock to Christian Bach. One of the very strong things that characterizes the leaders is that they are strong, restless thinkers who are always trying to solve problems. They are reflective as they think through all the various issues which pertain to the problem at hand. They are trailblazers who will not be caught in the tradition of the past. They are not necessarily extroverts, but they have learned in their own way how to understand and deal with people.

5. Balanced Leaders

These men would tell you that as they have been in the presence of God, He wants them to be an influence for Him in society. But to them it often means influencing others who influence others. They have come to understand strongly that everyone needs to have his or her hand held and needs to be hugged, but they also have come to see they do not need to hold everyone's hand and do all the hugging. As leaders, they would see to it that in their own hugging and hand-holding, people, in turn, would pass on the true art of biblical encouragement. Russ Rosser talked about his being a mission executive who directs the ministry of other people in his church. You can hear Randy Kinnison struggling with moving in his style of leadership:

> I fully understand the dimension of moving from a pastorate to a shepherd to a rancher. A true shepherd just learns how to shepherd at a different level. Another aspect of a personality that will not let you make the transition is that if you feel you need to control everything. I believe I have moved beyond that in allowing my many staff to function on their own level, making their own decisions, allowing them to either succeed or fail.

Gerald Sheveland also spoke to the issue. He said, "I am a type A personality. I like to see things happen. I like to see things happen quickly. Nevertheless, I have been able to see some great ministry effectiveness by attracting a handful of people or a few dozen people to a cause, letting them invest (simply gaining the permission of the congregation even before gaining the broad enthusiasm of the congregation), then seeing that built and adopted over a period of time as being normative."

Because the church is simultaneously a sociological and a theological institution, it becomes extremely difficult to balance ministry and people, bodies and buildings. Those ideas need to be built in a philosophy, but the good philosophers need to lead in such a way that balance is always maintained. "Great churches are built by ordinary men who won't quit."[40]

6. *Influenced by Others*

It should be no surprise to anyone that great leaders have been the recipients of a tremendous amount of influence both from the family in the growing up years and from other significant adults in their maturing years. Although all the leaders did not testify to having strong, encouraging parents, it was easy to see the value or the lack of value regarding that kind of influence in their leadership style. Tommy Barnett attributes almost all his creative ability to his father's strong innovative leadership as a pastor in Kansas City for 40 years. Don Bubna says that being a teacher taught him to have clear objectives in ministry. Stephen Crotts was a philosophy major in college which strongly influenced him to think philosophically about ministry. In observing these men in leadership, you could also see the strong influence of their mentors. Gerald Sheveland said, "I had the opportunity of being mentored in the ministry of Mission Hills under Charles Verstratten. I watched Chuck's deep belief that prayer changes communities, changes churches, changes people. I watched his piety, his passion about prayer, his deep commitment to the shepherding. These things have affected me."

One of the major surprises was to see how many of the leaders called upon consultants to help them hammer out their churches' philosophy of ministry. On the surface this seems to be unique in light of their creativity and their strong respect from the congregation. Yet they recognize that they could not see all the issues, nor were they always able to communicate them to the congregation.

Another ongoing influence which seemed to be pervasive among all of them was the fact that they were avid readers. Rick Warren tries to read a book a day. Russ Rosser has 8,000 books in his library and is constantly reading no matter where he is. It was fascinating to recognize that even though all of them were extremely busy, they all had time to learn from others. David Moore said, "The only communication books I read were secular. I never had a course on homiletics. I study very diligently the text. I believe it is important to say what the Scripture says, not just what I think about it. I want to keep the preaching biblical, but I want to give the words a very colorful meaning when I expound on it [Scripture]."

The source of influence comes from wide and varied writers, but one thing is obviously clear. They are all greatly influenced by the books and authors they read.

7. *Students of Culture*

In his or her own way each person has his or her tape-recording mind on steady record. Each one is constantly asking, "How do people function, think, and hear in society? What can I learn from them today that will help me lead them as a congregation and to communicate to the society around us the message of Christ?" Russ Rosser learned early on in his working with African Americans that they were oral communicators and not written communicators. This changes the way of working with those people. He went on to say, "Everyone in New York is a specialist (like any other big city). I learned how to understand the Chinese mind from Moses Yang, a friend in college who helped me to see that you can understand and love those of other ethnic groups. In New York City, everyone is a specialist. We have specialists on our boards, and they do what they specialize in. New York City lives in apartments, and you cannot change light bulbs there." Stan Perea, who is an Hispanic, not only spends time with the Hispanic people whom he knows, but he has gone to the homes of the Vietnamese in his neighborhood to try to learn how they think, hear, and receive messages.

If you have met E. V. Hill, you can visualize him walking the streets of Watts almost every day with dictaphone and paper in hand. He says that is where he receives his inspiration for messages and his vision for ministry.

All the men seemed to spend time among people in their society so they could understand their hearing grid. Randy Pope has been able to start a Bible study at the tennis club where he regularly plays tennis. David Moore says, "I spend a good bit of time with non-Christians at the golf course. I see them as victims of the enemy and not the enemy. I want to be the best communicator I can be. So I began to study Jesus; He told stories and asked questions. We have pulpits all over America ignoring the greatest preaching model of all time. He was talking to crowds of people where they lived." Listen to Gerald Sheveland talk about what he has learned from his culture and how he adapts to it. He says:

> In our setting here at College Avenue, we face the issue of the
> Southern California mind-set. Basically, they are a group of people

who are independent and play hard and work hard at their play. When they do work, they work hard at their work. They see things come and go [so often] that almost anything you propose will seem immediately as a new program that will come and go like all of the rest. The positives are that the cultural setting is filled with people who have handled so many change issues in their lives that they are not opposed to change for change's sake.

You cannot ignore or overlook the fact that if you are going to communicate as Christ did, you will need to live among the people to whom you are carrying the message.

Chapter 5

Build Your Own Thumbprint

I don't know what possessed me that particular Tuesday morning of my sophomore year in high school, but for some reason I found myself getting up from my chair and walking up to the front of the class. There I wrote my name on the blackboard. As I sat down, I began to reflect on what I had done. Probably most of the 120 members of the Campbell High School band had never seen that name before, for I was a very shy, quiet sophomore. The instructor stood before the band and said, "Today we're going to have tryouts for student director," and he said we could use any piece of music from our band folder. I got excited because there in our band folder for the trumpet part was "The Stars and Stripes Forever," a John Philip Sousa march.

You see, from the time I was about ten years old I had practiced leading that march because my parents had the record. I knew every crescendo. I knew every entrance of every instrument. I knew when the piccolo part would come in and the trombones and the cymbal crashes, and I had practiced with great enthusiasm, moving my little arms all over the place, waving in every instrument. As it came time for me to stand before the band, I picked up the baton and tapped the music stand as I had seen our director do many times, and I held up my arms. With evident confidence I pulled up my arms, and every single band member whipped up their instruments, and we were off. As I began to lead, a chemistry began to develop between the band members and myself. The more they got into it, the more I got into it—and the bigger my movements and the more dramatic and exact my cues for entrances.

Now to be really honest with you, I had no idea what was happening in the music because I didn't know how to read music. I just had the sounds of that march going in my brain because I had heard the record so many times and I had practiced so well. Now I don't remember if it exactly happened that way, but it seems to me that I almost got a standing ovation when I finished the great march. As I sat down and the election was taken, I knew that I won that position by an overwhelming majority, for the band thought that I was the greatest student director ever elected. As I walked down the halls of that high school the next three weeks, to the 120 members of the band, I was well known. Ten minutes before the election nobody knew who I was. After the election, everybody knew who I was. I was the student director of the Campbell High School band.

It was an exciting time for me for three weeks. Then after three weeks it all came crashing down when my band director, Mr. Perkins, called me up one day. He said, "Harold, I want you to lead this piece of music." There he laid before me a Bach chorale. Now I hadn't heard that record. I didn't know how it went, and I didn't know how to read a conductor's score that spreads all the way across the page. I picked up the baton, and I tried to start leading. By the time we were in the third or fourth measure, the band was lost, I was terribly humiliated, the trumpet section was embarrassed, and Mr. Perkins was very angry, for he saw a student who was a total phoney standing up before the band. From that day on, I had a position in name only. I was the student director of the Campbell High School band, but I didn't know how to lead. Therefore he didn't call on me again for the rest of the year.

As I've thought of that story throughout the years, it's been analogous to what I've seen happen to the church so many times. Constantly, we in leadership positions in the church have new pieces of music thrown at us, and if we don't know how to read the score, we don't know how to interpret. We don't know how to be leaders, and we start saying, "But wait a minute. I haven't heard that record before." There are so many leaders in church who are just like me: things keep changing, the tempo keeps changing, the volume varies according to every tape, every teacher, every philosopher, every politician, and every seminar that people in our church hear. They come in with a great idea. We listen to it and try it, but we don't know how to interpret what is going on. We need to have some specific principles of how to lead. We like to call it our philosophy of ministry.[41]

With the rapid change of culture all around us, we continue to be given new scores of music that we need to learn how to direct. Consequently, it becomes extremely important for us to learn the various principles and guidelines which help us to form a creative philosophy of ministry. Failure to do so may keep us from being director of the orchestra. It appears to me that many pastors are like I was. They only know how to lead one philosophy of ministry. Thomas Carlyle observed more than a century ago, "Nothing is more terrible than activity without insight." Unless service for the Lord is guided by biblical insights, it will be frustrating and possibly even destructive. A biblical philosophy of ministry can help determine one's priorities and shape his activities. So a wise leader will be able to work with a set of principles after sorting through the values by which his ministry will be prioritized, structured, and planned. This philosophy of ministry becomes a reference point for evaluating, developing strategy, making decisions, and goal-setting.

There are approximately 375,000 churches scattered throughout the landscape in America. Each one is distinctly different. They are as different as every individual's thumbprint throughout the world. Thumbprints are clumsy and awkward, yet in every crime lab, license bureau, and in every hospital where babies are born, fingerprints or thumbprints are taken as a way of identifying the uniqueness of those individuals. Since God has put so much effort into making all of us distinctly different, it seems absolutely ridiculous to try to make each one of us the same. In the same fashion, each church is distinctly different, and it is ridiculous for us to try to make each church alike. Bruce Larson and Ralph Osborne underline the importance of that distinctiveness. "The point is that a church, like an individual, must have a distinct personality and a highly specialized emphasis that makes it different from all other churches at that moment in history."[42]

Because a congregation has a distinct personality, it—like the personality of an individual—has a sense of self-worth or self-esteem. Sociologists and psychologists write and talk a great deal about the importance of having healthy self-esteem. Unfortunately, many churches have very poor self-esteem. Often this comes from not knowing who they are or what they ought to be doing or from many failures in the past creating an ineffective ministry in the present. We are taught that our behavior is a direct result of our self-image. If we have a poor self-image, then we tend to behave accordingly. The same is true for churches since they are corporate beings. If they have poor self-esteem, then their entire behavior and often their entire ministry is very weak and ineffective. If an individual sees himself or herself as walking close to Christ and energized by the Spirit, then it will be very easy for him or her to witness. This is often true of an entire congregation that is energized by the Spirit, feels very good about itself, and is actively making a difference in society.

One of the numerous principles William Easums enunciates validates this perception. He says, "Growth is directly related to the unpaid staff's perception of the congregation's size and ability rather than the reality. Most often the unpaid staff think of their church as much smaller and weaker than it really is. As a result, such a church offers weak and ineffective ministries."[43]

Again, I would suggest that churches are like individuals who sometimes live in nostalgia, thinking about that great history in the past. Of course, there is a danger about living in a fantasy world and only thinking about what you might become in the future rather than living in the realistic present. Philosophies of ministry and clear vision statements help us to live in the present reality and to feel healthy and positive about who we are.

One of God's universal principles, expressed in numerous places in Scripture, is that among unity there is diversity. 1 Corinthians 12 and Romans 12 certainly reflect that fact. Not only are individuals unique and distinct, but churches are as well. Peter Wagner, as he was addressing a group of pastors, suggested the same. "And then there's the national scale, we've got great diversity and yet we're one body, we have one Father, the Lord Jesus Christ, one baptism, and we just all feel like we're part of the same body of Christ, even though most of us, I mean all of us, there are more Christians in our city that we don't know than we know. And we say there is a certain unity because we're all one in Christ. All I'm saying is that the diversity is something that we're used to and we know how to live with it."[44]

In the design of a philosophy of ministry, be careful not to be too specific lest you cease being all that you can be. Keep in mind that the church is a mystery, and the philosophy of ministry needs to be broad enough to reflect that reality. Be careful as well that you do not develop a philosophy to bring closure on certain issues. This can lead to serious stagnation. Philosophy, then, is more of a direction, a way of deciding—not a *destination* but a *direction*.

I need not remind you that every church already has a philosophy. The problem is that only the pastor and a few of the leaders may know what it is. Unless it is clearly defined, written out, and communicated to the people, new members who join the church may cause a great deal of conflict among the congregation before they ever find out what that philosophy is. Therefore it becomes important for you to make it preachable, teachable, transferable, and memorable.

Now it is time to go about defining and designing your own unique thumbprint. When I started this project a few years ago, I was rather confident that after I had interviewed a number of creative church philosophers, I would find a certain pattern developing among them. To my surprise, that was not the case. Again, there was another distinct reflection of God's imprint upon each leader's character. However, I did find in interviewing them and observing their ministries that there were certain factors that tended to be reflected in their designs. Kent R. Hunter spoke further of those influences. There are various influences that helped to shape the attitudes and philosophy of ministry of congregations. Hunter lists the following. "Previous church experience of the congregation, traditions, denominational affiliation, theological emphases, gift mixes and leadership styles, development of leadership styles and goal or relationship orientation, the pastor, the leaders, location and environment, transitory philosophy of current history."[45] To help you as a church leadership team think philosophically about your unique design, I have selected seven items which I believe serve as a very strong model for designing your own thumbprint of ministry.

Each leader reflected in some way that the design, and the development was an ongoing process. It sometimes seemed to be in a constant stage of flux, but each continued to work with certain basic principles that were unique to the leader and the congregation. At times, I almost had the feeling they were shooting at a broad target, after which they drew the circles on the target. Because of the clarity of their vision, the leaders knew basically what they wanted to do, but they were not able to see exactly what kind of philosophy to design until they had tried it on for size. When it worked and it became theirs, then they wrote it down and communicated it to others. Usually leaders who spend a week, a month, or a planning retreat hammering out their philosophy of ministry find that it is short-lived and quite ineffective. Everyone in the congregation must understand that it is like a jewel whose facets are developed over a great period of time.

1. Seek the face of God

As I talked with each pastor, I always came away with the feeling that they truly believed that unless the Lord builds the house, the builders labor in vain (Psalm 127:1). All of them had different prayer habits, but it was obvious that there was a great dependence upon God for building the church. Randy Pope talked about spending three or four days at a time in a cabin without any interruptions and asking God, "What is it that will make the church more effective in reaching people?" All of a sudden, ideas began to roll and produced other ideas.

Another prominent thought was that they all want to reflect the glory of God through their ministry and their congregation. In Ephesians 3:21, Paul says, "To him be glory in the church and in Christ Jesus throughout all generations." This tended to be a strong emphasis among them. They understood that glorifying God is projecting His image, which means giving a true reflection of His attributes. A third biblical idea that guides their seeking the face of God is found in Psalm 15:1-3: "Lord, who may dwell in your sanctuary, who may live in your holy hill?" The psalmist goes on to explain the specific expressions of that holiness. "He whose walk is blameless and who does what is righteous." So, true worship is responding to God's revelation of Himself to us, and practicing righteousness in our lives. John provides additional insight into that kind of worship. In John 14:21 Jesus says, "Whosoever hears my commands and obeys them, he is the one who loves me. He who loves me will be loved by my father, and I will love him and show myself to him." It is important to recognize that as you obey God and respond to His revelation, He will make Himself known to you. It is important to understand that His revelation to us will partially include how He wants us to go about doing ministry. When the Lord promises in 2 Corinthians 3:18 that He will change you from one phase of glory to the other as you look upon His face, that in a sense becomes an expression of your philosophy of ministry.

2. Define your vision

"Aristotle taught us that 'Why?' is the most important question we can ask. It may also be the most difficult. If there is no reason to exist, cosmetic changes will not solve the deeper problem. At that point, the organization either needs to choose a purpose for being closed down or be changed at random by some internal and external pressures."[46] Once the pastor has defined the vision, he has, in a sense, answered the question why. After the pastor has sought the face of God for wisdom and direction and has defined the vision, then everything else should flow from there. "The boy Samuel ministered before the Lord under Eli. In those days, the word of the

Lord was rare, there were not many visions" (1 Samuel 3:1). What was true for Samuel's day is also true for our day. For people of God who do not study the Word of God, there will not be many visions. When they do seek Him, God will reveal the direction and provide the inspiration and, consequently, the vision for ministry.

Bennis and Nanus, in the research which they conducted about effective leaders, discovered that all ninety leaders they interviewed gave clear indication that they managed through a vision. This allowed them to create a focus of work. I found the same to be true with those pastors whom I interviewed in preparation for this book. "The leader who has a vision must play the role of vision-cultivator, vision-communicator, vision-clarifier,"[47] as stated by Malphurs.

The necessity that the leader have a vision prior to a philosophy of ministry was covered in chapter 1. Here it is important to see that a vision plays a very important part in developing a philosophy of ministry because the philosophy flows out of the vision and is a means of accomplishing that vision.

3. Do your theology

An automobile without an emblem designating its designer and manufacturer would be like a church without a theological imprint upon it. Every philosophy of ministry, if it is to be valid, must be an accurate expression of the church's mission as it is being translated through the vision of its individual leader or leaders. I agree strongly with Perry and Shawchuck who suggest the importance of a theological imprint upon a philosophy. They suggest:

> Christ consistently urged His followers to take a good hard look at the needs of the world around them when determining their mission: "But I say to you open your eyes and look at the fields!" John 4:35. He sets the conditions of final judgment to include a review of the extent to which they actually respond to those needs (Matt. 25:31-46). That is what Christ expects from you and your church. Certainly, He expects you to look into Scripture for information regarding the mission of your church, but He also expects you to look at your congregation, community, and world for additional, equally important information. The church that fails to do this will someday be called upon to tell why.[48]

In my interview with E. V. Hill, I definitely felt that he works out his philosophy of ministry on a regular basis in the same way. When I asked him where his philosophy of ministry came from, he said he develops it week in and week out as he walks on the streets with the people. He receives both inspiration for his sermons and a design for his philosophy of ministry as he lives and walks among his people nearly every day. I was so impressed as I talked to David Moore about how he led his congregation from a very traditional model to a very contemporary model without losing any members. He talked about the fact that for two years they studied the Word of God on a regular basis to determine exactly why it was that God wanted them to be there. He said, "I had the big picture in my mind on what had to happen. The first step was to know my gifts, strengths, and the dream God had given me for the church. Next, the elders had to buy in and make it their dream too, 'our dream.' First thing we did was begin to talk about why we existed, our purpose. We used small group dynamics to make that kind of thinking begin. We asked 'Why are we here?' at meetings and would stumble and finally reach that state."

Gerry Sheveland also spoke with strong convictions about the importance of biblical integrity when he said, "A strong commitment to believe that a philosophy of ministry has to have biblical integrity, a belief in what the Holy Spirit modeled, for example, in the life of Acts. Jesus' model to His disciples needs to have some cultural adaptations for a normative church. So there is something common with the philosophies that I am putting together with what Scripture says."

Any bonafide denomination in America has deep roots and strong theological and biblical persuasions. In the early days of America, many denominations spread across the country because of the strong convictions of their founders. It is hard for most American Christians to realize that denominations are a form of the function of church planting. Not only were those denominations often formed out of biblical convictions, but more often than not, out of ethnic backgrounds. They have been the ones that have told us how to do church, and we have continued to follow their ways for many decades. Unfortunately, many of those churches became so busy *running churches* that they forgot to *do ministries* for society and for the people where God had planted them. Numerous authors are speaking these days about the demise of denominations. While some are still growing, many of them are struggling to make a significant impact for Christ in America. Lyle Schaller, in his talk to the Church of the 21st Century Conference in Dallas, Texas (July, 1992), said that denominations perhaps would not survive if they did not become more mission-oriented. This would necessitate their trusting the people in truly biblical, autonomous ways.

It is certainly not dangerous to pick up the theological strains of your denominational background, but it is important as you do so to make sure that your philosophy of ministry is not something handed down to you by the church fathers. Rather, your philosophy of ministry must be genuinely your own.

Rick Warren, who calls his church a life development church, reflects a strong biblical impact upon his philosophy of ministry. These four guidelines guide them in their ministry: (1) we believe that every believer is a member of Christ's body (Romans 12:5); (2) we believe that every believer needs maturing (Ephesians 4:13); (3) we believe that every believer is a minister; and (4) we believe that every believer is a missionary (Acts 1:6).

If you need some help from Scripture as you study how to design a philosophy of ministry, the following list will be of assistance to you: Matthew 28:19-20; Acts 1:8; Ephesians 2:1-9; 2 Corinthians 4:3-4; Colossians 3:12-16; 1 Peter 2:1-5; 9-12; Matthew 16:18; Acts 2:42-47; Ephesians 4:11-16; Hebrews 10:24-25; Colossians 4:5-6.

4. Assess your environment

I do not believe there is a stronger admonition in Scripture to do an assessment of your environment than the words which Christ gave us in John 4:35: "Lift up your eyes and look on the fields." There must be a strong recognition that those fields keep changing, and they are different in every society. They all need to be harvested. In Matthew 9:36 we get the strong impression that Jesus actually tailored His ministry to meet the needs of those people once He had looked upon them. Shawchuck helps us understand that when he says, "To the hungry, He gave food. To the sick, He gave healing. He could not do otherwise, for He looked so intently at the people and communities around Him that Scripture declares the sight of the people moved Him with compassion for them."[49]

I heard some interesting expressions of contemporary ways of looking at the harvest. Randy Kinnison, who by talent is a very outstanding athlete, uses his talent as he participates with other athletes in his community. It is no surprise that athletics plays a major part in his ministry in Portland, Oregon.

Rick Warren, when he started his church in Los Angeles, went door to door doing interviews. Those interviews were not just questions to people about who they were but about what they would want if they were to attend a church. It is also no surprise to see that Rick made a very significant impact in the Saddleback area as he started his church in the early 1980s.

As a consultant with a number of churches, I have used community inventory demographic surveys to determine the group of people whom each congregation feels that it could best target for outreach ministry. It is the easiest way I know of to determine a profile of each individual community. Of course, that same information would be available to you in your city library, the city hall, the long-range planning committee, school districts, or other community services.

As a consultant for the last 28 years, I have worked in numerous churches to help them analyze not only their own ministries and congregations, but also their communities. I heartily agree with Perry and Shawchuck about the importance of this process. There is no other single activity you can do in your church that has greater potential for generating energy or action than congregational assessment. The Sunday the congregation fills out the extensive questionnaire is called "Say-so Sunday." A number of churches who have gone through the process have asked the special question in the questionnaire about the significance of the congregation taking time away from their normal worship service to complete such a questionnaire and to engage in the evaluation process. In all cases, every congregation has given at least a 90 percent agreement to the process.

In Appendix 8, you will find a cover letter and a short questionnaire which I often use when I am visiting communities to determine why it is that people no longer attend church. You are free to adapt this questionnaire to your own needs. Numerous congregations are constantly involved in reviews by using different methods. Some put a short questionnaire in the weekly bulletin to get feedback on certain decisions for ministries that the church is currently undertaking. Others have done house meetings where board members meet with sections of the congregation to evaluate what is currently happening and what needs to happen in the future.

Carl George of the Fuller Institute for Church Growth has suggested that there might be a significant parallel between the evangelists of the fifties and the church consultants of the eighties and nineties. Each would go into a congregation to get a feel for the current spiritual condition of the congregation and speak as a prophet of God about what the congregation ought to do to strengthen itself. I suggested earlier that there are more than 200 references in Scripture that directly or indirectly deal with the need for and process of evaluation. It deals with every phase of the Christian life and with every part of the church and its ministry.

Not to evaluate constantly is in fact to commit the sin of disobeying Scripture. "It is a badge of honor to accept valid criticism."[50] A good consultant can either play the role of a catalyst, a process-helper, a solution-giver, or a resource-thinker. An outside consultant can help a congregation get a truly objective view of what is happening. If you want to find out what the water is like, don't ask the fish. They are too much like it. In the same way, members of a congregation often cannot understand what is happening in their church because they are so much a part of it. If you are going to design an adequate philosophy of ministry, you must have a good handle on who you are, where your ministry is, and the group of people to whom you are seeking to minister.

5. Study your history

A congregation that has been in existence for a year already has history. One of the things that gives the congregation a great sense of meaning is to build upon its history. Alan Wilkins talks about how critical this is in keeping corporate character. Every congregation has a corporate character, and if it is going to carry on a long history, it must build upon that character.

William Banowsky gives us another view about the significance of keeping history in perspective.

> When the postmortem on San Francisco State's worst riot was complete, Dr. Hayakawa says he was surprised to learn that students in the field of history had not participated in the disturbances in equal proportion to students from other social science fields. "I attribute this," he explains, "to the fact that the study of history had rendered them too realistic to fall for the easy Utopian shibboleths."
>
> Recently, I visited one of the infamous Nazi extermination camps, the one in Dachau, Germany, which is now a museum. I was shaken by the ghastly artifacts of death, the pictures, and documents. I would have joined those who urged us to forget the past. Then approaching the exit, I saw posted on the stark stone wall separating the camp from civilization a quotation from George Santayana, "Those who cannot remember the past are condemned to repeat it."[51]

God reminds the children of Israel over and over again to remember the past. He calls them to worship in reference to the past. He challenges them to walk with Him based on lessons they learned from the past, and He has given them a sense of identity in reference to their past. Every congregation has some history, good and bad. All of that history gives a sense of who they are and what they can become because of who they have been. Another important way to look at the past is to study the specific stage in the congregation's current life cycle. He says, "We must understand at the outset that the life cycle of a congregation has little, if anything, to do with chronological time. A calendar cannot be used to predict the outset of a particular stage in the life cycle. It has to do with the relationship and balance of certain 'gene structures' common to congregational life." He goes on to talk about those gene structures or factors. They are energy, program, administration, and inclusion. These can be considered the gene structures of the congregation which combine differently in each stage of its life cycle. If a congregation knows where it is in the cycle, it will better understand the kind of energy that needs to be applied in order to help it into the next stage or cycle of growth. Saarinen identifies those stages as "birth, infancy, adolescence, prime, maturity, aristocracy, bureaucracy, and death" (Martin Saarinen, *The Life Cycles of a Congregation*, Alban Institute, 1986, p. 6). A study of Saarinen's book would be extremely helpful in understanding where you are historically and the kind of leadership which needs to be applied to your congregation at this time in your history.

Yet another very important way to look at your history is to understand the size of your church. Two important works could be of assistance to you at this point: *The Middle-Size Church: Problems and Prescriptions* by Lyle Schaller (Abingdon Press, 1985) and *Breaking the 200 Barrier* by Bill Sullivan (Abingdon Press). Both authors speak strongly about the significance of being one size for too many years. A congregation which does not consistently grow through different size barriers may find it extremely difficult to do so.

Schaller talks about this middle-size congregation in a way that can help us understand the significance of the history of each congregation that can be classified as a middle-size congregation. He says, "The distinctive characteristic of these churches, however, is not the common denominator of the size. That is a convenient way to categorize them, but knowing the size of these congregations tells us little. A far more useful conceptual framework is to focus on the congregational culture, the distinctive personality in the internal dynamics. These churches, who range around the 200 mark, make up approximately 30 percent of the people who attend church in America."[52] If the church leaders do not understand the significance of the size of their congregation, then they may not be able to provide adequate leadership that the congregation needs at this current time in its history.

Sullivan has discovered that a congregation that did not move through the 200 barrier within less than three years probably will not grow beyond that point. It is important to understand that a church is not only a theological institution but a sociological institution as well. Many of the sociological factors which make up a congregation and its bondedness or lack of bondedness have a great deal to do with its ability to impact the community.

Schaller gives one insight that might help you to understand the significance of size and how a congregation goes about growing. "The difference between the organizational life of the small membership church and the middle-size congregation is a conceptual difference. The eighty-five member congregation can be described as a congregation of eighty-five individuals, and a reasonable expectation is that each of the eighty-five can call the others by name. The primary relationship of most of the members is to the congregation as a whole. It may be more useful to conceptualize a 385-member church as a congregation of groups, circles, choirs, organization, and cells. . . . One implication of this is that an enhancement of congregational life as a whole should be a high priority in the small-membership church."[53]

Alan Wilkins summarizes for us the importance of keeping in touch with the past as we forge out a significant philosophy of ministry for the future. He says, "This sensitivity to past commitments, past skills, and past purposes is what I call honoring the past. The point is not that we should cling to the past, rather we must recognize what makes up a distinctive organizational character and realize how difficult it is to develop and how easily it can be lost."[54]

6. Design your ministry

Every congregation that has ever been in existence has some strengths. If a congregation continues to ignore the commitments and the skills of the past, they tend to scramble to reach the future. Failure to recognize those strengths may destroy the faith of the congregation and their ability to use those strengths. As the consultants go into each congregation using the evaluation instrument of the Institute for Church Development, they seek to determine what the top ten strengths of the congregation are. These are selected from thirty-four identifiable facets of ministry for each church. Unfortunately, this study also pinpoints the weaknesses of the congregation. If at that point a church is to concentrate on those weaknesses and forget their strengths, they may soon lose their strengths because all of the energy of the congregation and leadership goes toward their weaknesses. This whole idea is built on the fact that we cannot be and do everything. Therefore, what God has gifted us with ought to be our focal point.

It was so obvious to me that the First Baptist Church of Flushing, New York, under the leadership of Russ Rosser, had a unique team concept among its staff. Each one of the staff members gave some leadership to one of the five ethnic congregations. The strength of the staff was seen throughout its ministry and, from my perspective, tended to be one of the facets that made the congregation so effective. Russ Rosser himself felt that he wanted a staff that was brighter and better trained than he was. It was fortunate that he was not threatened by them. That kind of compliment to the staff built a very strong congregation.

I also learned the importance of not necessarily defining a philosophy until it had been tried and found effective, not tried and found wanting. "McNeil [1987] argues that action should proceed any grand announcement of a new vision. Only after the leader has 'lived' the vision for a time does it make sense to publicize it. There may be occasions when leaders can maximize their impact by making grand announcements, but more often than not, grand announcements provide a focus for opposition. Such an announcement may also create cynicism if the leader later feels unable or unwilling to live the vision."[55] Leaders who tend to write better than lead may find themselves in serious trouble if they come up with a "cutesy" philosophy or slogan of ministry but are never able to carry it off. I believe this is important because there is no exact scientific formula for the guarantee of any philosophy of ministry. All leadership is based on some sense of risk and wisdom, but there always is a chance for failure. It is better to aim toward ministry and then draw the target. The congregation may move with the leadership much more readily.

Part of the grand design is learning to deal with the tensions which I have identified in chapters 7, 8, and 9: *upward* to God, *inward* to the church, and *outward* to the world. Once the leadership has determined its position on the various tensions, they need to proceed with a great deal of confidence and come to feel comfortable with living within those tensions. By the time you get to those chapters you will learn in more detail how to deal with those tensions.

After a number of years of being a consultant I have learned that perhaps the most significant litmus test to determine the sincerity of ministry has to do with whether or not people want to be evaluated. If they do not want to be evaluated, it seems to me that they are working often out of a sense of duty rather than genuinely wanting to be effective. If they are sincerely interested in being effective, they will generally be willing to write down what they are doing or be evaluated on paper. There seems to be a sense of finality when a philosophy of ministry is written down. It is very difficult to evaluate what is not written down. It is also extremely difficult to communicate the philosophy to the congregation if it cannot be conveyed on paper. It tends to be far too elusive if it cannot be read.

The characteristics of a philosophy that makes a difference are that it is *scriptural, simple, transferable*, and *flexible*. The Sun River Church has given us a beautiful example of the clarity, yet the great impact, of their philosophy. Their statements are succinct and understandable, and they provide a powerful direction for choices in ministry. Some are as follows: (1) we are a Bible church, not a tradition church; (2) we are a lay ministry church, not a staff-centered church; (3) we are *a* church, not *the* church; (4) we are a reproducing [a church-planting congregation] church, not a superchurch; (5) the church is people, not a building; and (6) we call ourselves a worshiping/teaching church, not a lobbying church.

7. *Evaluate constantly*

If I have benefited at all from the far too many hours of watching college and NFL football, it is that I have learned the importance of the half-time. The half-time is an opportunity for the team to stop in the midst of their pursuit to win the game and see whether or not their strategy is working. Obviously, the goal is the same: win the game. However, the way they are going about it perhaps needs adjustment. The wise team that learns how to make that adjustment is usually the champion. The same is true with churches. There must be that half-time when all the leaders involved sit down long enough and honestly enough to see whether or not the strategies of ministry are working.

Robert Acker at Alto Loma seems to have learned the importance of this exercise. "Here's another key part of our philosophy. Once a year our staff invests three days for goals and planning. That is everybody on staff and their teams. So there are ten or eleven full-time equivalents on the ministry staff and their part-time staff. So we had about twenty-four people meet earlier this month. We started with prayer, and then we evaluated some surveys that we did with the congregation. Then we came back to what our key values are, and what are the things the Lord wants to do, we think, coming out of those values. So new ministries, programming changes, things to emphasize and do— everything goes back to our values."

All the pastors I interviewed had some format for critiquing and evaluating their ministry. They were most anxious to see if they were accomplishing their philosophy of ministry or if it was only some document they had talked about or had written on paper.

Chapter 6

Working with Tensions

In my early years as a professor at Denver Seminary, I quickly learned that tensions made the Seminary go around. It took me some time before I learned that tensions are very healthy. We are fortunate that we have tensions in our society for they make our society more effective. We enjoy a great deal of beauty and an unbelievable amount of productivity out of nature because of the tensions which exist in the various forces of our universe. In the same sense that there is a tension at the Seminary between the practical and the theoretical, there are tensions at work in the church.

The tensions I will look at in this chapter are not necessarily written into the philosophy of ministry, but before you can design a philosophy of ministry, you and the congregation must thoroughly understand the reality of these tensions. They can either be a tremendous benefit to you, or they can cause so much strain that the church cannot function appropriately. Because many Christians feel that Christianity ought to be always in harmony, they are reluctant to accept any tensions. As in an engine, so in a church—without facing and recognizing those tensions, the church may not move forward with great force and energy in today's society.

In this chapter I will deal with the philosophical mind-set which precedes building your own unique philosophy of ministry. These issues may not necessarily be written into your philosophy, but without an understanding of these principles, it could be almost impossible to write a proper philosophy of ministry and, more importantly, to lead the congregation in the design and the implementation of a philosophy. In this chapter I am not intending to be completely comprehensive regarding the various principles which guide you as a philosopher, but it has been my experience in dealing with thousands of people in churches that these are the critical issues that must be dealt with as the church goes through the design process.

1. Deal with tension of cause, community, and corporation

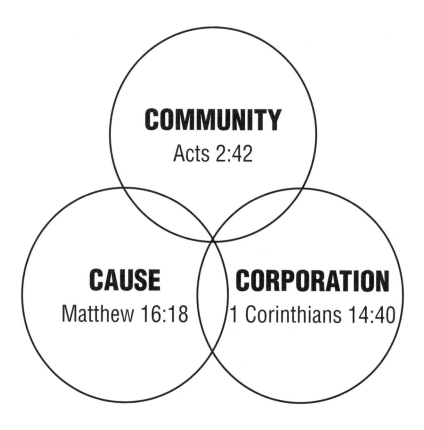

We are indebted to Jim Dethmer for a simple but profound understanding of the tension between cause, community, and corporation of a congregation.[56] There are numerous places in Scripture where these three "C's" are mentioned, but for a simple introduction to them I will refer you to three passages. The cause is expressed to us in Matthew 16:18: "I will build my church." This deals with winning a war. Community is expressed in Acts 2:42: "The church grew in fellowship." This expresses the love of the church. The corporation is expressed in 1 Corinthians 14:40, "Everything should be done in a fitting and orderly way." This deals with a church's effectiveness, efficiency, and frugality. Most good church leaders will understand that these three dynamics are at work in a congregation, but they may not be aware of the extreme importance of seeing their interrelatedness. What leaders must come to realize is that each force drives or impacts the other two. Some people have a very difficult time understanding the importance of doing everything decently and in order because in their minds, they tend to think that it hinders the work of the Spirit. To the average Christian, cause and community seem far more spiritual. The way people see these three issues may have a great deal to do with their temperament or their background. In the picture of the three circles, you must come to understand that they can stand alone and have some impact upon the congregation, but if they are to have the most significant impact upon a church, they must move in toward each other so they will be closely interwoven.

The cause of the church is very much like the vision we spoke of earlier in the book. The community has to do with its fellowship or love. So as the cause may go sour and the church may lose its vision, a congregation can similarly lose its sense of community and develop what is generally known as *koinonitis*, not *koinonia*. The corporation is the structure and the system which drives the community toward the accomplishment of its cause. A cause will soon die out if it does not have a community to carry it into action. When the organizational corporation of the church is not in force, the community may be in disarray, and therefore the cause will not be completed.

In the early days of a church, *cause* tends to be the most important of the three. Most churches never get off the ground if there is not a strong, driven cause. As the congregation increases in size and the community increases, the *corporation* aspect of the church becomes increasingly important. The larger the church, the more significant corporation is to its success and effectiveness. Small congregations are generally afraid to lose their *community*, but the genuine dynamic of the Christian community or organism really loses its effectiveness because the cause becomes sterile once it does not continue to move out centrifugally from the congregation to make a difference in society. Clyde McDowell spoke of this tension in my interview with him. He said:

> I constantly feel the tremendous tension between the machinery of the church and the problems of the people. How can I deal

with their personal problems without getting bogged down in the inner workings of the church? They are in constant need of Christian counsel. It is so easy for me to lose perspective on what the reason for the church is. We must all get out of the church building and serve the world. Somehow we need to resolve this leadership issue. My task is to see that both the machinery of the church and the needs of the people are met. Good leadership is to clarify the balance between the two. My task is always to see that the organization of the church only helps us to move toward keeping the people in order. That really facilitates the communication among the congregation.

As a consultant for churches, I can find the difficulty in their ministry by simply analyzing these three items. If one of them stands alone and is not interfacing with the other two, it could very quickly point to a slowly developing disease within the congregation.

2. Differentiate between forms and functions

During a recent conference with some pastors and an evangelist, we had a most fascinating conversation. One of the pastors was talking about his son being genuinely converted at a Christian rock concert. The evangelist spoke out vehemently by saying that obviously the boy was not genuinely saved since no one could be saved at a Christian rock concert. Of course, this is only one of hundreds of comments I hear from people in churches demonstrating their inability to receive new forms of the functions of the church of Jesus Christ. This is probably most often felt between the generations, and of the generations the most serious rift is between the G. I. Joe generation and the baby boomer generation. The acceleration of change between those two generations, no doubt, has been more rapid than in any other generation the world has ever known. Gene Getz puts it in focus for us: "One of the key problems with the evangelical churches in the twentieth century is that we have allowed nonabsolutes to become absolute."

Dealing with the form and function issue is certainly not an easy task. Many of the theological arguments going on in the church today have to do with distinguishing between forms and functions. Jim Peterson has given us a clear understanding of the difference between the two:

> Form and function have as much to do with Christian mission
> as they do art. The Bible contains a number of illustrations of the

> interplay between form and function. All teach the same lesson: function creates form. Forms are the pattern an activity assumes, but once created, they tend to become virtually indestructible. They live on and on, surviving their original functions to become part of culture's tradition. Evangelism comes to be equated with reading someone the contents of a certain booklet. Worship is defined as singing hymns accompanied by an organ. Such forms acquire an authority of their own. Then it becomes heretical even to question an established form. Function, or the purpose behind the form, is fragile and easily lost, but function is where the meaning is.[57]

At times form "relics" hold us hostage to the past and make it difficult to create new forms or paradigms that can more readily take us into the next generation. Christianity is culturally adaptive as long as such adaptation doesn't violate its message.

The following list of functions is not comprehensive. But by taking a look at these, you might have a better understanding of the scope of the functions of the church. These are the things that the organism is to become and to practice: worship (personal and corporate), fellowship, stewardship, evangelism, service, hospitality, intercession, edification, discipline, and the assembling of the believers. All of these functions are to transcend culture. Gene Getz points out the importance of these forms not transcending culture:

> Had God absolutized in the area of form and structure, He would have "locked us in" to the New Testament culture. More specifically, He would have "locked us in" to the middle-eastern society in the first century world. Christianity would have either become an ethnic religion in a particular area of the world or it would have died out. As it is, it became neither. It has spread to every culture of the world. Christianity has made its "own way," creating its own forms and structures, and will continue to do so until Jesus Christ comes again.[58]

The honest way to design the forms your church will use is to make sure you have searched the Scripture to determine what principles apply to each respective function you will use. For instance, when you are going to work with the function of evangelism, you need to make sure that the Word of God is honestly and accurately presented. If not, then no matter what the form is, the function will be wrong.

Here are a couple of important illustrations that depict the way that the functions have stayed true to the biblical instruction, but at the same time the forms have changed dramatically. You will notice how strong, biblical principles are also in order as each one of the forms change.

Leith Anderson talks about how the church has gone about evangelizing American society during past decades: from 1900 to WWII through the Sunday school; from 1970 through 1990 through the Sunday morning service; and from 1990 through weekday activities.[59]

Jim Peterson has given us another example of changes in the forms of evangelism from 1970 until 1990: [60]

Function: Evangelism

Forms—1979	Forms—1990
City-wide crusades	Home Bible studies
Door-to-door witnessing	Network of non–Christian friends
Single gospel presentation	Ongoing discussions about the gospel.

Gene Getz further reminds us that Jesus Himself used different forms to accomplish His eternal purpose. "Jesus fed the crowds. Jesus preached from the deck of a boat or on a grassy field so His listeners could better see and hear. Jesus changed the water to wine for their convenience, and convenience is merely a means to reach people and become all that God wants the church to be. What is the other choice—to be intentionally inconvenient?"[61]

May God have mercy on the church if the church is not willing to change the forms of its ministry. While on the other hand, may God have mercy on the church if it changes its functions. Neither one, however, will guarantee spirituality. Ralph Neighbor makes that clear:

> Countless renewal groups have developed within the land. They live inside and outside the church walls, with and without budgets, clergymen, programs, committees, or formal services. The disillusioning thing about practically all of them is the fact that they have the same basic people problems that the institutional churches have. People who are carnal in the old structure are going to be just as carnal in the renewed structure! What God's children need first of all is a renewing of their lives to be made conformable to His will and His direction. Unless and until that

happens, the newly devised forms are going to be as powerless as the old.[62]

Every brand of Christianity and every theological persuasion has numerous people within its folds who represent that same spiritual stagnation. Both the liberals and the extreme fundamentalists can be equally guilty. Every one of the pastors whom I interviewed has been dealing in one way or other with the tension between form and function. Gerry Sheveland talked about dealing with the seemingly eternal Sunday school movement in order to deal with the spiritual nurture process. He said, "Having found in my own ministry that I couldn't find enough capable adult Sunday school teachers or build space fast enough to keep up with multiplication growth when it begins to take place, I considered the concept of using homes and using small group leaders. They don't have to be strong teachers but can be good facilitators and pastor leaders in the life of the group. That concept of a cell group in large church ministry where growth is taking place has been a good key." Randy Kinnison also found himself dealing with one of the sacred programs of the church. His congregation apparently was willing to make the change. He says:

> I believe the church responded to the willingness to let go of Wednesday night Bible study at the church, which they have held for years, because (1) there was little interest in it, and (2) they had come to, I believe, trust me as their pastor. I had done my homework. I brought before them a well-researched program that I believed met the needs of our specific church, and I had just spent a week alone in prayer and solitude believing that the Spirit of God had directed and brought a deeper sense of purpose and unity to my life. Once again, discipleship and evangelism were reemphasized in the philosophy of ministry. Out of this change came a new component, a deep walk with Christ primarily through the ministry of prayer.

Perhaps the most sacred of all is to touch the Sunday morning worship service. I thought it extremely important to recognize that worship is our individual response to God's initiated love toward us. Because we are all individuals who respond to God in a unique way, we have learned certain forms of responding to Him. When the church tends to alter those forms, we readily feel that we are no longer genuinely worshiping Him. Of course, there is a great deal of truth to that, but if we are to reach the next generation, we may need to change the forms of worship. We may all need to make a certain shift because we are asked to respond corporately to God.

3. Maintain a spiritual life balance

Here is one illustration of the lack of balance. It is exciting to see that the American church is thirsty for revival. At times it appears many Christians want to reintroduce Pentecost to the twenty-first century. If only the Holy Spirit were to come back in full power, the church might make a more significant impact upon our society. Most of the recently- formed denominations appropriately have in their charters a keen desire for that kind of spiritual renewal. As in each and every new movement, there is a potential for error. On the heels of the form and frenzy idea, we need to deal with the spiritual life balance. Wallace Hensley points out that "structure must come before filling. The 'form' church must understand that the reason for the structure is to receive the filling. The 'frenzy' church must grasp the fact there must be structure so the wind will have something to fill. Dead form in the extreme is unyielding objectivism. Dead frenzy is mushy subjectivism."[63] Wallace Hensley goes on to emphasize the extreme importance of keeping balance between "cosmos" and "chaos." Listen to his carefully chosen words about Satan's attack on the church in this regard. He says:

> The devil's aim in throwing the church off balance is to cast her into chaos or disorder. The fundamental struggle in the universe is between cosmos and chaos. It is the tension between order and entropy. The conflict comes into the church through those restless with institutional and traditional immobility on the one hand and those who want to preserve the status quo on the other. The tendency of those wanting freedom from the chains of institutionalism is to rush to the extreme of throwing off all controls. The bent of those wanting to hold on to things as they are is to impose rigid form. . . . Cosmos is things holding together, consistency. Chaos is things coming apart, decay and disintegration. Rigid form results when man tries to impose cosmos. Yet, if he doesn't, frenzy results from chaos.[64]

The objectively imbalanced church that tends to put too much emphasis on the content of the Word of God will be immobile even when God seeks to move it forward. The subjective church, on the other hand, which is so much into feeling and often may move away from the Word of God, will be an imbalanced church that may easily be moved, "tossed to and fro" by every wind and doctrine. Here is another one of those critical tensions which keeps the church alive and well. Failure to be sensitive to it could take the congregation to its death on either side of the spectrum.

4. Coming to grips with phenomenology and theology

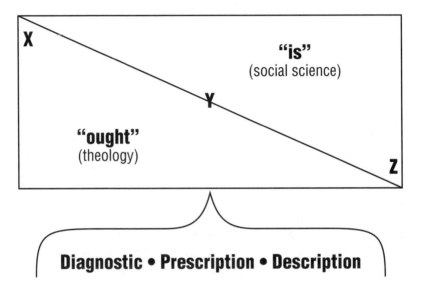

Every leader must also come face to face with the reality between what is and what ought to be. Pastoral leaders are very much like landscape architects. When they build a campus, there is a great tendency to want to put in very fancy sidewalks that lead from building to building, but a more astute architect will wait until the people have walked from building to building and have developed their traffic patterns. Then when you put sidewalks in, you will not need to build fences to keep the people in. That illustration is somewhat like coming face to face with people's life-styles. Some of it is simply cultural; the rest might be antibiblical. The long continuum drawn above illustrates the reality that every decision the board makes is some place on that continuum with a combination of both the "is" and the "ought." Therefore, when they diagnose a problem or make a prescription for that problem, the diagnosis is going to have a certain amount of the *is* and a certain amount of the *ought*. This idea relates to that wise old thought which we have been using for years: learn to live with things the way they are (being satisfied with what is), recognize that sometimes there are things you can change and others you can't, and learn to know the difference between the two.

Most of us would say it would be wonderful if all congregations were integrated, people were not divorced, and leaders did not gossip. If we truly hold to the biblical standards for leadership in 1 Timothy and Titus, we probably would not have any leaders in the church. A strong biblical leader is the one who has the ability to walk that tightrope, which is somewhat like form and function, but here we are dealing with more gray areas.

Stan Perea has found, along with his congregation, that the neighborhood is rapidly changing from an Anglo neighborhood to an Hispanic one. He is not willing to see the congregation pull its head in under the pillow. He is teaching it how to integrate the Hispanic families into their homes and into their ways of church life. Certainly, it has not happened as quickly and as completely as he had wished, but by being patient to live with the tension, the community will have a wonderful representation of what the gospel of Jesus Christ ought to look like. Congregations across America are dealing with these kinds of tensions on a weekly basis. Some give in to one side over the other in an effort to make Christ known. The important issue, however, is how mature and godly the congregation ultimately will be by the way it handles these issues.

5. Looking through four sets of contextual lenses

If you are going to understand your church sufficiently before designing a philosophy of ministry, you are going to need to look at it through four dimensional glasses or lenses: the national and local contextual lenses and the national and local institutional lenses. Each one is separate, yet in a sense, each one significantly influences the others. The intent of this section is not to expose you to all of the facets of these four lenses, but simply to suggest ideas so you can continue to be aware of these forces as you seek to understand your church and your community.

National contextual lenses

Every economic change within a region and every demographic change in America will influence your congregation, whether you are aware of it or not. Arnold Mitchell[65] talks about the fact that every region within America has a different set of values and, in a sense, has its own culture. No one in America is exempt from the paradigm shifts that have come because of the Baby Boomer

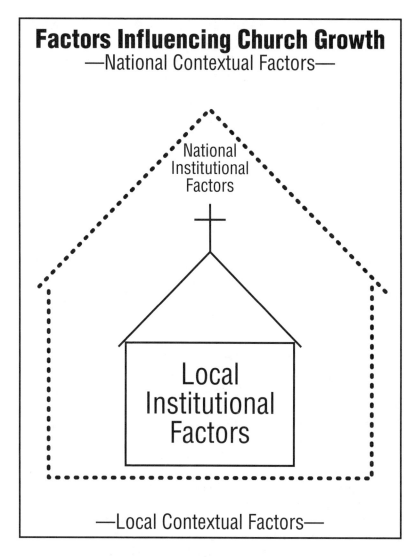

Factors Influencing Church Growth
—National Contextual Factors—

National Institutional Factors

Local Institutional Factors

—Local Contextual Factors—

generation which comprises approximately one-third of American society. Numerous books have long lists of paradigm shifts such as the one which suggests that Americans have moved from self-denial to self-fulfillment. Most of these shifts have a significant impact upon the people who attend your church.

Joel Garreau tells Americans how the shape and size of our cities have influenced the sense of community in our churches. He says our world is primarily made up of "edge cities."

"The edge city is the twenty-first century information age, middle-class place that almost never matches political boundaries on a map. Each has megaoffice space, at least one megamall, and more jobs than bedrooms. This is not a suburb. It is its own "urb." There are now two hundred edge cities and only thirty-five downtowns of comparable size. People tend to live in one, play in a second, and shop and work in a third in unlimited combinations. Edge cities are a monument to a culture that puts almost unlimited value on individualism and freedom."[66] Other factors like the gross national product, unemployment, wars, and political changes all significantly impact who comes to your church and what kind of message they hear when they attend.

Lyle Schaller talks about the trends which are coming to the church because of the national demographic factors. The percent of divorced adults quadrupled from 1950 to 1986. The number of unmarried couples living together increased ten times from 1970 to 1985. The number of blended families tripled from 1970 to 1985. The number of single-parent households doubled from 1970 to 1985. Working mothers went from one-fifth of the mother population in 1970 to one-half in 1985.[67]

The local contextual lenses

Every community in America has a different personality, just like every church has its own personality. If a church is going to make an impact on its society, it needs to culturally reflect, as reasonably as possible, the same culture as its community. Consequently, you will want to do an analysis of the work patterns in the community. A study of life-styles by Teck Sample provides a marvelous insight into the various cultures which exist within your immediate community and how they influence the makeup of your congregation. He talks about the cultural left, the cultural right, the cultural middle, and how these people tend to cluster in homogeneous units within congregations. [68]

The newness of your community also significantly impacts your effectiveness to reach those people for Christ. The receptivity access says that visitors to your church are far easier to reach than people who have no contact with your church and that new arrivals in a community are more receptive than long-term residents. Responsive new arrivals are more receptive than indifferent new arrivals. People with felt needs which you can meet are far more responsive than people with other needs. Friends of new converts are easier to reach than acquaintances of new converts. Anything that is unique or abnormal for your community will impact your church's ability to bring your community to Christ.

National institutional lenses

A good view through the national institutional lens suggests that whatever is happening in American religion will have some impact on your ability to reach the people in your community. The rise and fall of other churches and denominations in your part of the city or in your local community will either open or close people's eyes and ears to your message.

Most authors readily acknowledge that denominational influence is seriously in decline. No one is suggesting that denominations in the twenty-first century will not be in existence, but it appears at this time that they will play a much less significant role than they did in past years in America. Denominational affiliations were lined up ethnically or theologically and became the regulatory agencies for churches. Now parachurch organizations play a much more significant role in church life in America. This is certainly impacted by the fact that we are more into *networking* than we are into *belonging* as Americans.

Denominations that succeed in the next century will play a much more significant role in mission than they have played in the last few decades. Churches that seem to be extremely effective no longer emphasize their denominational affiliation. It has been my experience that many members of prosperous churches with denominational labels do not even recognize the denominational label. Churches are dropping their denominational labels from their billboards in almost epidemic proportion. This appears to be especially true with churches that are growing substantially. Nonetheless, church alignment, affiliation, support, financial, prayer, and personnel support will still continue to help new churches in their earliest stages of development. Certain denominations will continue to have more impact in certain regions of America than others. This has a lot to do with where the denomination had its earliest stages of development.

Local institutional lenses

Imagine that you are standing on the church roof and looking down through a "steeple scope" in order to understand the life and vitality of a congregation.

There are innumerable internal factors which will either open or close doors to your community. To translate the life of your church properly, you will have to understand its history. What is its spiritual vitality? Do its discipleship and evangelism programs creatively meet the needs of the community? Is there diversity in the services and vitality in its worship and prayer life? Is the congregation mobilized for ministry?

An often unmentioned and misunderstood factor concerns the congregation's authority base. The authority may come strictly through the denomination. The church's values, authority base, and life-style may be established by the congregation itself, or it may be established basically upon biblical principles, each person having his or her own prerogative as to how he or she will live out those principles. Congregations tend to cluster according to their authority base far more than the average person realizes. This becomes particularly important to people who desire to transfer membership from one congregation to another. If they are accustomed to setting their own life-style standards and find in a new church that it is established for them—contrary to their own beliefs and practices— they usually will not become members of that church.

Other factors such as the size of the congregation, the life stage the church is in, and whether or not the facility is adequate all play a significant part in whether or not the church will be effective in impacting its community.

Introduction to Theological Tensions

The next three chapters will guide you through the process of making decisions about where you are going to position yourself in the theological functions of the church. This list is by no means exhaustive, but from my perspective it covers the issues that gain the most attention in churches across America today. I do not list various choices in these chapters but simply expose you to the tensions and the factors which you should keep in mind as you move toward either the right or the left of these tensions. You may not necessarily change your paradigms by working your way through these three chapters, but they will help you to think through the issues. If you are honest, you will understand your position better than you ever have before.

Each week Denver television stations show the drawing of the lotto numbers for the week. People all across the state of Colorado are sitting on the edges of their chairs to see whether or not they are the lucky ones to have their combination of numbers drawn. It is a rather crude illustration; nonetheless, it illustrates a tremendous potential for the unique combination of positions that you will hold. There are literally thousands of combinations and options for each church, and in our individualistic society this is far more common than it has ever been before.

Even though this book is not designed as a workbook, at this point it will provide for you (if you choose) a helpful way to get group consensus. In Appendix 3 you will find a list of the fifteen tensions to be considered. After reading these chapters, the leaders of your congregation should each mark his or her choices. Then make a composite of these choices to determine approximately where your church would land on each continuum. This will give you a broad profile of who you are as a congregation and, consequently, how you could go about designing a philosophy of ministry that best reflects who you are, how you think, and how you want to go about ministry.

Chapter 7

Upward to God

Midway between two piles of hay, the animal starved to death because it spent its time just standing there evaluating the two stacks. It preferred to die rather than give up its neutral position. It preferred to die rather than make a decision, a choice. Many church leaders find themselves standing between two very good ministry options. They both look so right. They both have some eternal value, but the leaders cannot make up their minds. So they choose not to choose, which now often means to lose. Choosing between two or more different forms of ministry is what it means to develop a philosophy of ministry. God has set forth in His Word many biblical mandates for His church. These mandates are the church's functions. In the following three chapters, you will be introduced to fifteen different functions of the church which are all mandates from God. Remember that functions all have cultural forms. You will examine tensions that express the extremes of these various functions.

Some of the most critical decisions church leaders will make have to do with where they position themselves on the continuums regarding these various issues. Failure to make critical decisions on these issues will be like the church that starved for lack of effectiveness in ministry.

As a congregation you will constantly need to wait upon God for wisdom to make these critical decisions because they have so many ramifications. You should see each issue on a long continuum with opposite poles that are kept in emotional, psychological, or spiritual tension. The great danger is that some church leaders think they can encompass all the issues on each continuum and therefore meet everyone's needs. I question if this is possible—leaders must come to the conclusion that they cannot be all things to all people. Then they need to make a decision about what they specifically are going to do.

That is what a philosophy of ministry is all about: finally making a decision about what the leadership will be, not trying to be everything to everybody, which is a wise decision. How the church needs wisdom! When you are seeking wisdom, you are studying and asking both men and God how you can truly reflect Him where you are planted.

There will not be a tension about where you will put Christ and the Bible. Those absolutes are taken for granted and will become part of your mission statement. Everything in your philosophy should be biblically sound and Christ-centered. The real issues here are how you will go about ministering for Christ through your congregation.

One thing that will make this difficult is that all other tensions are influenced by each individual decision. Not one of them stands in isolation, but for the purpose of thinking through all the issues, each will be presented individually.

You will find yourself struggling with the "is" and the "ought." You will find yourself, like a parent, always trying to decide what is good for the child and always being in tension about what the child will accept. Being in ministry is like being a parent who is on a lifelong trip as a disciplinarian. What makes it so much more difficult is that you have to deal with a large and extremely diverse family. You not only need to deal with the children you now have but with those you are planning to adopt into your family as well. Are you only going to parent current family members, or are you going to ask God for a larger family?

Keep in mind as you make these decisions that you will be doing so in a multi-level, not just in a lineal fashion. It is very much like playing a 3-D tic-tac-toe game. Every move affects nine different games simultaneously, not just one. Design engineers are already talking about the next generation of computers that will function with neural networking or artificial intelligence. This process deals with many things simultaneously while keeping them in tension. Tensions are so important in the design of a philosophy of ministry because they force leaders to consider all the variables and all the possible alternatives on any given ministry mandate. It is very likely that leaders will discover a more efficient or more godly approach to ministry for the church by using something which at first may seem to contradict what they first anticipated. To some it may appear that paying an outside, highly trained and gifted teacher to come in and teach the adult Sunday school class would draw many more people to Sunday school. But they need also to take into consideration the mandate to equip and engage their congregation for ministry. If they are not training and putting their adults in places of service outside their own church family, then, in fact, they may be depriving their own people of the growth and delight which comes from a broadened ministry. A good design for ministry includes all the factors that come to bear on any decision. The mind is like a computer that deals with multi-level thinking. Both must have adequate input before they can have wise output. This kind of study should help you to make wise ministry decisions because it will provide the multi-level thinking necessary for such a process.

If your church should make a decision to be a mission outpost church, then almost all other tension decisions will be influenced in your neural network. The kind of worship service you conduct may eventually influence all other ministry decisions. The style of music you choose to use will influence those who will attend your church.

You may not want to process all fifteen of the functions listed in the following three chapters, but you should be aware of all the issues as you make your decisions. If your board and staff are engaged in a planning retreat to think through these issues, you may choose to deal with a few that currently seem to affect your congregation most significantly.

It would be good to have your congregation think through their three relational styles as reflected by the three chapters—"Upward to God," "Inward to the Church," and "Outward to the World."

"Out of one's commitment to Christ and to the church must flow a concern for the world which Christ died to redeem. This same logical sequence is seen in John: 'remain in me' deals with worship (v. 4), 'love each other' deals with the infrastructure (v. 12), and 'go and bear fruit' deals with the church going outward (v. 16)."[69]

Each of the fifteen sections will follow a somewhat similar pattern. First, the function extremes will be defined on each one of the continuums. Second, the most critical theological principles or issues and the implications of those issues will be stated to help you make an appropriate decision for your church. In some cases, you will find some guidelines about how those decisions affect other tensions. Third, there will be creative ministry models to reflect how the various leaders have thought through the issues and have made decisions appropriate for their culture.

Once you have a basic understanding of the various issues, it will be important for your leaders to rank the three most critical tensions for your church. Consider which tension drives or influences the other tensions.

Every decision you make in some way will impact all of the other functional decisions. Once you have listed the functions your leadership team is dealing with, then place alongside them all of the other functions that are going to be influenced by that decision. Here is a simple example about how you will think through the way each decision will affect your primary decision. Consider the Preaching Tension:

Evangelistic (left) 3 2 1 0 1 **2** 3 (right) Exhortation

Other tensions affected by this decision:

Inclusive worship style: Right **1**—ministering primarily to believers, but not excluding unbelievers.

Family reunion target: Left **2**—We will minimize everyone knowing each other so seekers can feel at home.

Anonymity fellowship: Left **1**—We will let people seek their own networking since we want to facilitate the seekers' relationships.

This kind of multi-level thinking will help you make certain that you have reached the right conclusion for your church about where you will land on the continuum.

UPWARD TO GOD

The four tensions in this chapter primarily deal with the four functions which most directly influence the way a church is engaged in its adoration and exaltation of God.

What a marvelous day we live in! In the midst of so much confusion in our world and so much diversity in our church life, people seem to be more interested in worship than they have been in many decades. People are seeking to put the mystery of God back into their lives. The way worship is conducted is so critical because it will determine whether or not people will worship in a meaningful way and also be faithful in their attendance.

Rick Warren suggested that the ten largest Baptist churches in America during the 1990s found worship as the most attractive thing that brought people through the front door.

Churches who ranked worship as one of the most effective things about their congregation grew at least ten percent a year through a decade. Churches which declined twenty-five percent in a decade ranked worship as one of the least effective things about their church's ministry.[70]

Seeking to define the extremes of the music worship continuum seems to be extremely difficult. Contemporary and traditional are very relative terms, yet they seem to be understood in reference to music and worship by the average worship attendee. Leith Anderson gives us some interesting insights:

> Sometimes the contemporary can be very old and traditional can be up-to-date. It is the subjective judgment combining numerous factors . . . . The difference in the meaning of tradition occurs because seldom does the tradition mean the same thing to the subsequent generation as it did to the previous generation . . . . In order to be Christian, a church must be traditional because the gospel message itself has been handed down. More practically, the popular notion of a traditional church is one where the symbols and stories were inherited rather than created. The list can be very long but includes order of service, role of clergy, leadership of laity, music, governance, style of prayer, symbols, collection and distribution of money, dress, and practice of baptism and communion . . . . Contemporary, however, is merely a contrast to traditional. It means that it originated during the present generation rather than inherited from the previous generations. It is not better or worse. It is just later.

It is very hard for people to understand that what is contemporary in today's worship and music will be strong tradition in tomorrow's church. Unfortunately, this is one of the most divisive things in congregations today.

Worship Principles

Before you can make some "heart" decisions about music and worship, there are some strong biblical principles that you must keep in mind. "Soren Kierkegaard, a 19th century Danish theologian, sensed this problem about worship. In an oft-quoted analogy, he likened Christian worship to the theater. 'Many Christians,' he wrote, 'tend to view the minister as the actor, God as the prompter, and the congregation as the audience.' But actually, according to Kierkegaard, the congregation is the actor, the minister merely the prompter, and God the audience."[71] Most congregations will need to be taught about their role in the worship drama, and all the worship prompters will need to make certain that they are leading that drama and not trying to be one of the main players in worship drama itself.

Also keep in mind that the Scriptures not only teach what a true worshiper is, but they also give a description of a false and a vain worshiper so we will be certain to keep the right one in perspective. False worshipers worship idols. Vain worshipers worship the right God but do so in the wrong way. Mark 7:6-7 says, "Isaiah was right when he prophesied about you hypocrites. As it is written, these people honor me with their lips, but their hearts are far from me. They worship me in vain. Their teachings are but rules taught by men."

Ezekiel defines a church service which you may have attended or been a participant in at one time or another: "My people come to you, as they usually do, and sit before you to listen to your words, but they do not put them into practice. With their mouths they express devotions, but their hearts are greedy for unjust gain. Indeed, to them you are nothing more than one who sings love songs with a beautiful voice who plays an instrument well, where they hear your words but do not put them into practice" (Ezek. 33:31-33).

In contrast to false and vain worshipers, John 4:24 explains what a genuine worshiper is: "God is spirit, and his worshipers must worship in spirit and in truth." He reminds us that true worship is rooted in the truth, so what we believe sends us in the direction of worshiping Him. Unfortunately, we could be in error since it could be the wrong truth done in the right spirit or, in contrast to that, the right truth done in the wrong spirit. He wants to make sure that our spirits connect with His spirit because true worship must take place internally. "Spirit" includes our minds or the intellect, and the "heart" includes our affections and feelings which are a part of genuine worship. It also has to do with your will which may be classified as your 'spiritual backbone." Worship becomes the action of the will by which you affirm your commitment to Him.

As you sit down to make a decision about what kind of worship will characterize your service, you will need to keep in mind style, goal, liturgy, and the relationships inculcated in worship. These factors will set the pattern for your normal worship service or services.

It is also critical to keep in mind that worship is to be your response to God's initiative toward mankind. If it is to be personal or subjective, then it should be a reflection of your own temperament, personality, or the way you tend to respond to God. To force a person or group of people to worship in a fashion that is contrary to their way of relating, is in a sense to ask them to be engaged in hypocritical worship. It appears that many people are changing churches because of worship styles and are doing so because they are asked to worship God in a way contrary to their nature.

The following diagram should provide a helpful tool in coming to grips with the tremendous conflict in our churches over the style of worship. [72]

Dr. Shelley's diagram will help you come to grips with what theological worship is and, at the same time, how it has been changing

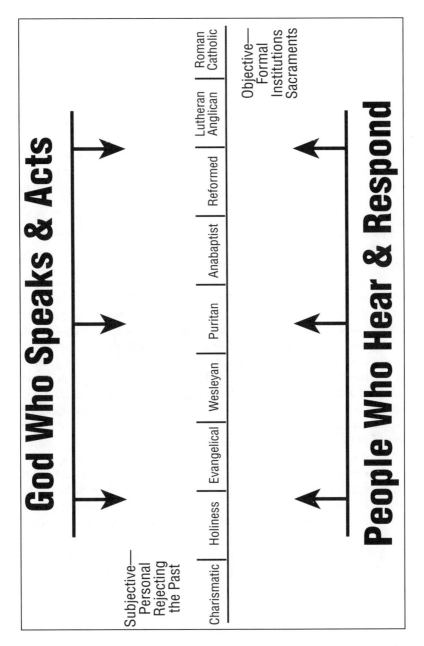

changing for generations. All of the stages on the graph currently exist in the American church. If you understand anything about the movement of church life and worship in society, you will come to understand that the prominence of the style of worship is far stronger on the left side of the graph than on the right side—there is a great movement in that direction. The right side of the graph is primarily related to the past. The sacraments were formal. Institutions deserved one's loyalty. The individual did not count as much as the individuals who are represented on the left side of the continuum.

The left side of the graph relates to the future. Here the institutions are not needed as much because God is in us and at work through us. Thus, worship relates to the individual. If this graph existed some decades ago, church leaders could have almost anticipated that worship was going to be far more subjective and personal than it was in the past. Certainly, your choice of worship will reflect your theology but at the same time you will need to take into consideration whether or not you want your worship to be more formal and objective or subjective and informal. Many people want to worship in the same manner that their ancestors worshiped.

Further consideration of the style of worship will be reflected in the following diagram which has to do with the church's goal of worship. Is it to be evangelistic, or is it to be concentrating on the adoration of God? This diagram shows three positions on a continuum (they are not absolutes). The diagram also illustrates the interaction of the four elements of growth shown in Acts 2:42-44 which were occurring in the New Testament. The diagram shows four different views about the relationship of those four elements. First, the reformed theologians suggest that if the person genuinely worshiped God, he or she would present his or her body as a living sacrifice to be engaged in service. You will see in a study of Isaiah 6 that a proper view of God does drive people to certain responses such as offering oneself to God's service. The middle of the chart is a reflection of the general evangelical churches in the last three or four decades. Worship services during this period tend to reflect an interesting mixture of fellowship, instruction, mission/evangelism, and worship. In most cases you would find instruction as being the primary or central focus of the service while the other elements at times do not generally relate to the preaching. The diagram illustrates the constant movement and at times the seeming unrelatedness of the elements of the service. It often appears that no one has sat down and asked the big questions, "How do all these things relate, and what are we trying to accomplish?" The diagram on the right shows a major shift in the role of the worship service. Because we are in a culture where church life is declining (or as some say, we are in a "post-Christian era"), then you can no longer *expect* people to come to church and worship. This position basically says you have to evangelize society before you can get them to think about showing value for God in their lives. A growing number of churches that take this position, like David Moore's church in Palm Desert, California, have worship at a different time during the week since they use their Sunday morning gathering primarily for evangelism. Helping people to see God is certainly a common element here, but there is a greater emphasis on the individual's need of the Savior. These congregations probably would identify themselves as seeker-sensitive churches.73

Drives of Ministry – Acts 2:42–47

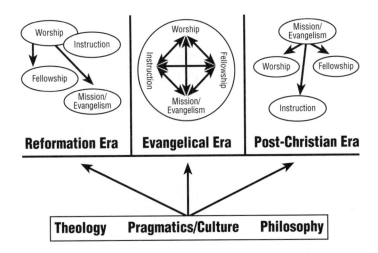

The four categories and seven issues on the graph on page 104 pinpoint what appear to be the seven issues that need to be addressed in making a decision about the form of worship that your church will follow. Most of these issues are addressed in this chapter.

A careful study of these texts and the two diagrams will provide an extremely helpful tool for you to think about what you are trying to accomplish in your worship service. It is not only important that the leadership or the prompters understand what is going on, but everyone in the congregation must come to grips with what the church is trying to accomplish. Leaders should have a meaningful discussion about how their worship experience impacts the church's evangelism program.

Worship Form Tensions

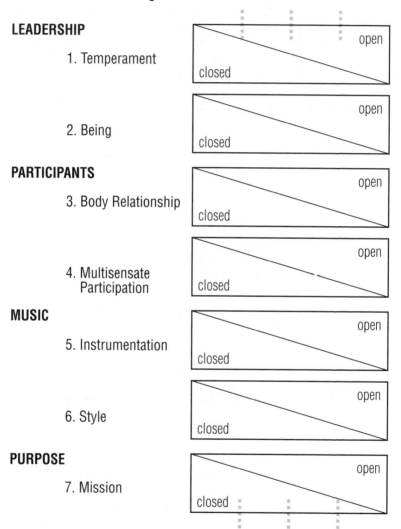

LEADERSHIP

    1. Temperament

    2. Being

PARTICIPANTS

    3. Body Relationship

    4. Multisensate Participation

MUSIC

    5. Instrumentation

    6. Style

PURPOSE

    7. Mission

The Work of the People

    The place of liturgy is the third item to consider in the design of your worship service. It is appropriate to keep in mind that all churches have some form of liturgy in their service because it means the work of the people. Therefore, the key question is not whether or not you will have liturgy; it is whether or not it will be formal or informal church liturgy. Craig Erickson suggests a moderate position which should help you understand the extremes. He says that worship ought to be "a planned spontaneity: where freedom and structure enjoy a reciprocal relationship. One cannot exist without the other. The Spirit moves through form and structure. The challenge is to keep a balance between these two shifting elements."[74]

Many people feel that they cannot worship God without dignified piety or formal words and in a formal environment. They sense that this is the best way to show awe and respect toward God. Liturgy has long, historic roots in the church, and consequently, many people want to worship as their ancestors did. Donald Hustad warns us that, "in many situations, our worship has approached a solemnity and formality that bordered on sterility."[75]

In my years of consulting with churches about contemporary and traditional worship, I found that often a congregation tends to be split in almost three directions regarding worship style, purpose, and content. Approximately one-third prefer more traditional. One-third want more contemporary. One-third would leave it as it is. [76] This often has to do with the fact that there are two or three generations in a congregation. Each would like worship packaged in the way that best suits their culture. Certainly these factors will need to be taken into consideration in the design of worship.

A fourth factor to consider is whether your worship will be corporate or individual. In a society that has moved from a corporate focus to an emphasis on the individual, there will be a tremendous pull in the latter direction. Hear the words of Craig Erickson about the biblical mandate for corporate worship: "The church is a royal priesthood (1 Peter 2:4-5). In worship, its identity is most fully revealed. Because the church is a priestly body and a royal dwelling place of the Holy Spirit, worship ought to be participatory. It is only natural that the church should demonstrate collectively its character in worship. A clergy-dominated performance of the liturgy before a passive congregation obscures the priestly character of the entire church."[77]

Recently a lady whom I was interviewing in a church said that she did not want the church to have two services because she might miss the appearance of the Spirit of God in the other service. Other individualistic expressions you may have heard may sound something like, "If this service does not meet my needs, then I will go to a place where my needs are met." If there is an extreme difficulty here, it would be the necessity of getting a corporateness of worship built into the service without losing the uncommitted individuals.

Passages of Scripture to study in preparation for this decision are Exodus 24:1–8, 1 Chronicles 15, Deuteronomy 4:9, Psalm 95, Acts 2:42–47, Hebrews 10:24–25.

Worship Music

UPWARD TO GOD				
Worship / Music	Contemporary			Traditional

Most of the major texts in Scripture that deal with worship also deal with music because music is such a vital part of our expression of praise and adoration toward God. We often hear that Americans find it very difficult to be in touch with their emotions. That is why music is such a significant part of worship; it allows us to express emotions which often we cannot do in our own words.

If there is controversy about a style of worship in a congregation, it often revolves around the selection of music. Music styles tend to attract or distract people from a church perhaps more than any one other factor. Music inspires, guides, and enriches people's worship. It is the very act of worship itself. Don Hustad defines the biblical words which talk about music listed in Ephesians 5:19 and Colossians 3:19—"Psalms, no doubt, included all the psalms and canticles common in Jewish worship. Hymns were probably new songs that expressed the Christology of the new sect. . . . They were written to express and thus teach Christian doctrine. Spiritual songs described ecstatic singing that was either wordless or had unintelligible words—singing in tongues."[78] Margaret Clarkson enriches Hustad's definitions by saying:

> Hymns are expressions of worship. They are man's glad and grateful acknowledgment of the "worth-ship" of almighty God, his confession of his own creatureliness before his Creator, his bowing before the transcendence of God. Hymns are a celebration of what God is and what he has done: songs of praise, thanksgiving, and joy in God. Christians sing hymns because God is worthy to be praised.[79]

Today's culture seems to influence music in the church perhaps more rapidly than any other one factor in our culture. One church's musician recently evaluated the congregation's musical preference by finding out what radio stations were most listened to by the members. The leaders did this to help determine what style of worship music would be most appropriate for the church. It came as a surprise to the leaders that seventy percent of the congregation listened to secular rock stations during the week. You can count on this: as often as the calendar changes, music changes. If you do not like the music, you can say as you do about the weather: just wait a short time, and it will change! Hustad again says:

> One might as well ask what will be the next cultural or philosophical or theological emphasis on the American scene. For the total value system of a generation and its art have always been closely linked.
>
> Of course, psychologists had already paved the way for this with their insistence that repression of one's deepest feelings was emotionally unhealthful. Sensitivity training and group therapy were commonly practiced to repair the psyche.[80]

As David Moore was working through the revision of the mission of his church, he saw worship not as a place to come and hide but as a place to celebrate. It fits clearly into the cultural norm of this day. Music certainly is a factor that helps us to express that celebration. Christians need to learn to celebrate and rejoice in a world where there is not much celebration. The growing Latin population in America may be influencing this shift strongly. "Hispanics are becoming the largest minority in the United States. . . . By the year 2070 the Hispanic population in the United States will have grown from the current 21 million to 57 million. Of the current 21 million, about 20 percent are Protestant. One factor leading to the phenomenal exodus of Hispanics from the Catholic Church to evangelical churches (60,000 defections per year) lies in the expression of worship. Evangelical Latinos long for a fiesta on Sunday mornings, rather than the solemn worship found in most parishes."[81]

Volumes have been written and will continue to be written about the music of our churches. Of course you need to be a student of that literature if you are going to make a proper decision about the style of music. There are four factors to consider as you think through what kind of music you will use in your congregation. First, you need to determine if music itself, distinct from the lyrics, is a moral or amoral issue.. There are few places where people's emotions will influence their decision more than this issue. Understandably so, music touches our emotions. However, do not forget that perception is reality in the average person's mind.

Close on the heels of that question will be the question about using or participating in traditional or contemporary music. See Leith Anderson's comments earlier in the chapter about those two tensions. In the ICD data base, 16 percent of the people in the data base prefer less traditional and 16 percent desire more traditional music, while 63 percent say they want the same amount of traditional music currently being used. In reference to the contemporary music style, 14 percent want less, 23 percent want more, and 58 percent want the same. Just looking at those figures, you can readily see why it is so difficult to please everyone in a congregation. Rick Warren uses very strong Christian rock music because he is targeting the boomers of southern California, and they are into that kind of music. Many congregations try to have a blend of the two in an effort to appease both age brackets in the church. It does not take long to find out where that change came from. It appeared to the youth of the '60s that their parents' Christianity was cold and cognitive. They heard it in the hymns and saw it in the worship style. The reaction of the youth caused the pendulum to swing to a subjective free style of Christianity, and music seemed to lead the way to the right. Therefore the boomers prefer more emotional music because they like to *feel* their music. The G.I. Joe generation likes to *think* their music. Therefore, they have more cognitive hymns in their repertoire.

All of this has led to what are sometimes called praise choruses, but Don Hustad calls them tiny hymns. It is utterly amazing how much controversy there is in our churches about using this kind of music, especially when it is on an overhead screen and not in a hymn book. Hustad says:

> This new form suggests "praise and worship" texts are new, and that is surely not true—our hymnals are full of worthy "praise and worship" words. These new pieces are short, often no longer than two lines. Their main characteristic is simplicity. Usually the idea is stated, and it may be repeated many times. They have their roots in a much stronger oral tradition . . . and today simplicity is in. In nineteenth century revivalism, the refrains or choruses of gospel songs were often sung without using stanzas . . . and they could be sung spontaneously from memory. These earlier forms were all products of renewal movements in the church, first in the highly emotional brush-arbor camp meetings of the early nineteenth century.[82]

The way many congregations deal with these tensions is to offer two styles of worship on Sunday morning. If you are going to appeal to a broader segment of society, that seems to be the best way to go. However, many churches still feel that they need to duplicate the second hour what they have done in the first hour. Gerald Sheveland talks about what has happened in San Diego.

If you came to College Avenue on a Sunday morning, you would be able to go to church at 8:45 in the gymnasium among young singles and young families in our Sunday celebration service. You would find a whole network of ministries built around that celebration service geared toward that target group. You would see young faces on the platform. You would see a contemporary band and drama and a number of media presentations that are geared toward that segment. You could then at 9 a.m. walk into the sanctuary and see a very traditional service (and a second very traditional service that will take place at 10:30 a.m.). You can go back into the gym at 10:15 and see a ministry that is geared straight toward university students and military personnel. The music is closer to hard rock than anything else. Skits and dramas tackle issues that never get tackled on the platform in the sanctuary, like dealing with the issues of sexual temptation, lust, relationships, and other similar kinds of issues. You would find around them teams of people who, like parachurch organizations working within a larger church, have a very focused ministry of what they are supposed to accomplish. College Avenue is really more than a church. It is a movement. It is made up of networks of ministry teams committed to reaching certain segments of people in our church.

Preaching/Teaching Tension—Evangelism or Exhortation

UPWARD TO GOD				
Preaching / Teaching	Evangelistic			Exhortational

When we think about the key role of prayer in the church, we might say it is the best of times, it is the worst of times. Thirty years ago in America, a long pastoral prayer was a significant part of the service. Church services that have a great volume of liturgy in their Sunday morning format will often engage the congregation in numerous and long prayers. Prayer does not seem to be as common in the morning service as it used to be, but the good news is that many people are praying in their homes and small groups throughout the week.

"Andrew M. Greeley, the sociologist-novelist-priest, says more than three quarters (78%) of all Americans pray at least once a week; more than half (57%) report praying at least once a day. Indeed, Greeley finds that even among the 13% of Americans who are atheists or agnostics, nearly one in five still prays daily, siding (it seems) with Pascal and wagering that there is a God who hears them."[83] We need to be theologically correct in our prayers in public worship since people tend to emulate the prayer they learn in church. The danger is that since we are a therapeutic society, we tend to skip over focusing on God for who He is and instead go to God for counsel. Larry Crabb said recently that "we are not really worshiping God when we go to Christ for counsel."[84] God expects people to seek His face for help and to be engaged in supplication for their friends, but genuine worship is focused on adoration of Him and is seated in a lack of righteousness. When people truly worship Him, He ultimately will grant them His righteousness and meet their needs. Spiritual leadership should be concerned with a balanced prayer emphasis during services.

It is important for the leadership to keep in mind that the members of the congregation learn how to pray through what they hear and participate in during the formal worship service. Poor corporate prayer practices among the body perpetuate poor private practices in prayer.

Gary McIntosh suggests that the congregation ought to be learning and expanding their disciplines of prayer. He suggests:

> Churches and individuals go through a process in their understanding and practice of prayer. We classify this prayer process on a scale using six levels: introduction, initiation, imitation, intercession, investigation, and invasion. If you believe your church is at this level you should engage people in warfare praying. Encourage prayer for entire towns, cities, and metropolitan areas. Intensify warfare praying against the power of the Evil One. Train people in the discipline of fasting. Fasting gives intensity and focus to prayer. It is a weapon in the upper levels of invasion.[85]

Good leadership should be aware of where the congregation is in their spiritual journey and the congregational prayers should be consistent with the level of maturity of the congregation in their pilgrimage.

Recently my wife and I visited a congregation with a couple who had been in Denver for a long period of time. As they stood at the exit observing the hundreds of people leaving this megachurch, they commented on how they saw people who had left their church after each one of the last three pastors had come into leadership. People had left because of dissatisfaction with the new styles of worship and music which had been introduced by each new pastor.

It appears that every congregation faces these same kinds of issues today. The choices that are made in the philosophy of ministry about worship and music significantly impact the movement of today's mobile society. There are very few Americans who can appreciate the loss of community and the sense of bonding which comes through long-term commitment to a congregation. All of those who are in leadership today understand the difficulty of building community and commitment into the local assembly.

If the church moves in the other direction and structures worship primarily toward outsiders, then they may quickly lose that sense of community. They may also tend to seek professionals rather than getting the laity involved in the worship. That, too, has its consequences. I do not imagine that these pressures will go away. They only force the church more toward doing what it feels is right in the eyes of God. Make your choices about worship and vote on God's side. For further study, read Allan and Bore, *Worship: The Missing Jewel*, Killinger, Stevenson, and Hayford, *Mastering Worship*; and Robert Webber, *Worship Is a Verb*.

Anyone who understands anything about the church would be hard pressed to prove Easum wrong when he says:

> Worship can be filled with good content, but unless that content is presented in a way that awakens the imagination and stirs the emotion of the congregation, seldom does anything lasting occur. Like any good drama, worship must have movement that ebbs and flows, without long dead spots. The service must build to a final act and clamor for a response from the congregation. If the drama is well done, the congregation will become part of the cast of characters. The people will sense that everything is designed for their response. They will feel as if the final scene in the dramas will be determined by what they do with their lives.[86]

Preaching is the essential element of worship. "Today the average visitor comes to church to hear a sermon, not to participate in corporate worship . . . . The larger the church, the more important it is for the senior pastor to be in the pulpit at least forty-four Sundays a year."[87] Furthermore, preaching is the primary means of exposing the community to Jesus Christ.

Not only is preaching essential for the preacher, but also for the people who come to church. They expect the same. Leith Anderson reminds us, "When I go to a restaurant, I expect to be served food. At a concert, I expect to hear music. In an art museum, I expect to see art. In a doctor's office, I expect there to be talk about medicine. I am never surprised or offended when these people and places present what they represent. The same goes for the church. Churches are people and places where God is expected to be present, and His book is no surprise."[88]

Because preaching is such a central point for the congregation, the community, and for the clergy, there has often been conflict about exactly what it ought to accomplish. It is extremely difficult to define evangelism as one end and exhortation as the other end of the continuum because there is a little bit of each in the other. Most preachers will tell you that they are doing some of both, but most give in to one end of the tension or the other, often without recognizing they are doing so. Some would say that they do evangelism with historical, exegetical, and philosophical thought. Others feel that their motivational narratives and strong emotional appeals are providing both exhortation (which they would classify as expositional preaching) and evangelism (which would also be accomplishing the mandate for the church).

If your church says its preaching is primarily for evangelism, then perhaps nearly every Sunday's services will be geared toward bringing the lost to Jesus Christ. These pastors will see themselves as mission pastors, not the ones who would classify themselves as guiding a household of faith. Tommy Barnett would agree with Callahan "that the day of the professional minister is over. The day of the missionary pastor has come. The professional minister movement born in the church culture in the late 1940s simply ceased to be functional on the mission field of the 1980s. That way of being a minister had worked for nearly forty years. When it became dysfunctional, it no longer worked."[89] To Barnett every Sunday is super bowl Sunday. He plans, studies and prays that it will be that kind of an evangelistic service. To communicate the gospel he often plans what he calls "illustrated sermons" (in keeping with what Jesus would call His parables). He believes that Christians will also gain greatly from the truth of the Word of God, but his prayer is that seekers will find Christ. The congregation is highly motivated to bring the lost to services. They often go into the inner city of Phoenix to bring sometimes as many as one thousand people off the streets so that he can preach Christ to them. Jim Abrahamson and his four classifications of churches would classify that church as a reaching-out congregation rather than a handing-down congregation.[90]

On the other hand, those churches and pastors who classify themselves as expositional or exhorting pastors would primarily hold the position that churches are places for Christians, and they need to be exhorted about their spiritual lives, their value systems, and their walk with God. In these churches, it may be unusual to find numbers of people being asked to make public decisions for Jesus Christ. These churches, if they are growing, tend to be built primarily by transfer growth rather than conversion growth. "It is my contention," writes John R. Stott, "that all true Christian preaching is expository preaching. The classical Reformed method is to take one or more verses of Scripture, distill the central theme, and then organize the material with several subdivisions."[91]

Because preaching is such a critical item, it should be considered as a primary issue in every church's philosophy of ministry. A strong decision here will provide a very specific direction for the pastor and will help the congregation be more sympathetic with the pastor's continuing themes on preaching. Some churches choose once a month or perhaps once a quarter to concentrate on evangelism with the idea that the congregation can bring their unsaved friends with them and pray particularly on that Sunday that many people will profess Christ as Savior.

Through the research we have done at the Institute for Church Development, we have consistently seen that the effectiveness of preaching is one of the top three items that help a church grow numerically. It is our guess that strong expository preaching is also a major factor in the spiritual growth of the congregation. Kirk Hadaway's research tends to validate the same.[92] He has identified the key issues which help churches grow off a plateau or who have been in decline. This study of a number of churches suggests that churches that are growing off a plateau have sermons that are more challenging than comforting. Those churches that are breaking off the plateau are rated, by their congregations, with a 70 percent effectiveness score in contrast to those who are on a plateau or decline as being 40 percent effective. These churches tend to see preaching as heralding the truth of Christ or storming the citadels of the soul and urging people to make a response to Christ.

Douglas Webster has given us another insight which helps us understand the extremes on the preaching continuum. He contrasts the household of faith congregation and preaching with a market-oriented congregation and preaching. He distinguishes the two in the following way:

> Household of faith preaching is concerned with teaching the whole counsel of God in a faithful and timely way. The congregation is appealed to through faithful exposition and compelling application of the Word of God to their personal

lives as well as to the body life of the church. Preaching is effective both in evangelism and disciple-making.

Market-oriented preaching is seeker sensitive, felt-need oriented, and focused on the individual. The audience is appealed to through humor, moving illustrations and personal anecdotes. A practical distinction is made between preaching and teaching—with preaching considered to have a more subjective, emotional impact than teaching.[93]

It is not always true that the market-driven or oriented churches are always evangelistic, but they certainly tend to be that way more than congregations where the household of faith type of preaching is carried on week by week.

Preaching Issues

Before you can honestly make a decision about where you will place yourself on this continuum, it is important to give serious thought to the following questions.

1. *How will you define preaching?* Of course, there are as many definitions of preaching as there are teachers of preaching and perhaps even as many definitions as we have pastors. Let us give strong consideration to Roger Greenway's definition which certainly has merit. "Today we have a more restricted understanding of preaching: we mean by it the exposition and application of Scripture by an authorized and ordained minister under the supervision of the elders. Charisma has become office. In the New Testament, evangelism was understood as bringing good news with a view to conversion and was not a subject to be debated and endlessly defined. It was as natural as eating and breathing. . . . The question of evangelism never came up. The heartbeat of the church was in missions and evangelism."[94] It would certainly be advantageous for at least the pastor to define preaching and to communicate that definition to the congregation.

2. *How does preaching fit into the nurturing of the congregation?* Once the definition of preaching has been formulated in a suitable way for everyone involved and before every sermon is preached, the question will need to be answered, how does this sermon help fulfill our church's philosophy of ministry? No doubt this basic question will change a lot of sermons.

3. *How will you face with the tension of dealing with the unsaved*

on one side and the seemingly spiritually but overfed people on the other side? As you seek to be evangelistic, are you weakening the nurture of the seasoned believers? Eugene Peterson said it is not difficult in such a world to get a person interested in the message of the Gospel. It is terrifically difficult to sustain the interest.[95] Roger Greenway would remind us that many pastors and their congregations have wrong views about what ought to happen in sermons anyway. "First, the people of God, believers, and their children gathered for public worship are always a mixture of the spiritually mature, the immature, and the unconverted. Therefore, the milk of the gospel must never be missing. Second, the spiritually mature who can be fed spiritual meat but who complain when the ABC's of the gospel are proclaimed thereby call into question their maturity."[96] People will tend to commit themselves to a congregation for a longer period of time and be more greatly content once they understand exactly what the purpose of the Sunday morning service is.

4. *Are you defending yourself by saying that the people are not responding to the preached word because their hearts are hardened when in fact you may not be speaking words that they can hear or understand?* One of the valuable assets of having your church go through an evaluation by the Institute for Church Development is to help the pastor find out if he is addressing the language and content level of his congregation. Questions about preaching are segmented into demographic categories. Each groups specifies what satisfaction level they have with the pastor's preaching. It is not a bit surprising to find that many pastors feel they are addressing certain levels in the congregation, when, in fact, they are not addressing that segment of the congregation at all. It may be that the Spirit of God is not moving the people because they are not even hearing the Word at their own level of comprehension.

5. *Have you told the congregation what you are trying to do and why?* Failure to do so may cause many members of the congregation to leave or to be seriously dissatisfied with their weekly spiritual diet.

The Sun River church in Sacramento has in their philosophy of ministry that they are a worshiping/teaching church, not a lobbying church. Tom McKee says, "We do not feel that we are an organization as a political caucus to lobby for the challenging of the civil laws."

Charismatic Tension—Charismatic or Noncharismatic

UPWARD TO GOD				
Charisma	Charismatic			Non-Charismatic

It appears that there is almost a universal desire that the Holy Spirit's presence would be felt in all our churches. The major question is what does that display look like and how do we bring it to pass? Leith Anderson talks about today's society looking for the supernatural. He says what exists today "is a far cry from the intellectualism of the 1950s and 1960s. We began the twentieth century with the ascendancy of rationalism and liberalism. We are ending the century with a new supernaturalism. They are looking for a supernatural experience. . . . People tell me they are looking for a church where they can meet God, where there is a power of the Holy Spirit, and where their lives can be radically changed."[97]

Few people can deny the fact that the fastest growing churches in America and around the world are quick to identify themselves in the signs and wonders movement.

Hiebert, no doubt, speaks for a majority of the world's charismatics:

> He traces the development of this Western world view back to the 17th and 18th centuries. Secularized science began explaining natural phenomena without reference to the supernatural. Religion was allowed to deal with cosmic forces, sacred ritual, and possible exceptions to the natural order, but it has little to do with the problems of everyday life. And religion was regarded as unscientific. Our Western world view became highly conditioned with what many Christian leaders today are calling secular humanism.[98]

Wimber would suggest that the origin of the special work of the Holy Spirit dated much earlier. He says:

> One of the earliest of the church fathers to acknowledge the working of the Holy Spirit in his day was Irenaeus who lived about A.D. 140-203. He wrote: we do also hear many brethren in the church who possess prophetic gifts, and who through the Spirit speak all kinds of language, and bring to light for the general benefit the hidden things of men, and declare the mysteries of God, whom also the apostle terms "spiritual."[99]

He further shows that other early church leaders like John Wesley, D. L. Moody, R. A. Torrey, Arthur Pierson, Hannah Whitehall Smith, and A. J. Gordon saw the wonders of God displayed in mighty power in their meetings.

It is not uncommon to see controversy surrounding any seemingly special movement of God. It is interesting to note that during the upheaval on our college campuses in the sixties and seventies, there was also an upheaval in our churches over the tongues movement which soon seemed to blossom into the signs and wonders movement, which is a broader issue. Churches all across the country were splitting, members were transferring, and others were attracted or distracted to these congregations. Obviously, we have not yet seen the end of the division among Christians in America over the signs and wonders issue.

Those who have identified themselves with the charismatic movement on the extreme would be individuals who speak in tongues and participate in signs and wonders in public and in private. Those who do not do so are strongly taught and coerced to do so or at times are even asked to leave the church or volunteer to leave of their own volition, sometimes causing churches to split over such issues. Those who classify themselves as noncharismatics would be at the other end of the tension and would teach that tongues and signs and wonders are not for today. Many churches find themselves somewhere between those two extremes. This was expressed recently in a Presbyterian church where I was doing a consultation. They asked their congregation a special question about whether they spoke in tongues privately and believed that tongues were for the church today. Thirteen percent said they did. Sixty-three percent said they felt that tongues could be given to others, and only twenty-three percent said that they did not believe that tongues were for today.

Dr. David Hubbard of Fuller Seminary raises another issue that both sides need to address. He says on both extremes, "no 'miracles now' or 'miracles whenever we program them'—do not seem to reflect a biblical pattern. But finding that pattern—which appears to lie somewhere between the two extremes—and applying it to the life of the churches in our day is no simple task."[100]

It is more and more common to see churches declaring openly where they stand on the charismatic issue. They will either state it in their doctrinal statement, or often it will be reflected in their philosophy of ministry statement.

Charismatic Issues

Because the issues are so complex and it would take volumes to present all the theological positions and to reflect all the hermeneutical and exegetical studies on the topic, I will simply cite two issues which are worth your serious consideration. I was impressed with a number of the pastors who spoke openly about the fact that they read extensively on both sides of the issue so they would be certain to be honest in the position which they had taken. They, like you, needed to consider whether there is healing in the atonement. Many believe that there is healing in the atonement of Christ and that the healing ministry of the church should not cease after Christ's death. Another issue has to do with the exorcism of demons. Peter DeWitt quotes George Eldon Ladd saying, "The exorcism of demons is proof that the kingdom of God has come among men." He goes on to say, "Ministers, laymen, and theologians forget the fact that the Savior means healer. He who makes us whole."[101] If you have heard of George Eldon Ladd you will recognize quickly that he interprets the kingdom of God as having roots in the Old Testament. Thus the interpretation of Old Testament passages do apply to the New Testament as well.[102] We cannot study the issue very long without having to come to grips with whether or not the Bible presents a dispensational view of God's economy. Other major issues which need to be addressed are whether or not gifts have ceased. How you view the many different kinds of gifts and how they are categorized may readily put you to one side of the spectrum or the other.

> Category A: Social Signs or Signs Applied to a General Class of People. (1) Preaching good news to the poor, (2) proclaiming release to the captive, (3) liberating the oppressed, and (4) instituting the year of the jubilee (acceptable year of the Lord).
>
> Category B: Personal Signs or Signs Applied to Specific Individuals. (1) Restoring sight to the blind, (2) casting out demons and evil spirits, (3) healing sick people, (4) making lame people walk, (5) cleansing lepers, (6) restoring hearing to deaf people, (7) taking up serpents, (8) raising the dead, (9) speaking in tongues, and (10) drinking deadly poison with no ill effects.

Peter Wagner speaks for the charismatics who outline the gifts into major general categories. He says:

> Category B: By signs is generally meant signs and wonders may be done by the holy child Jesus (Acts 4:30). They were also done by Stephen [and] the apostles. The main function of category B signs is to draw public attention to the power of God in order to open unsaved people's hearts to the message of the Gospel.[103]

I will let the *Bible Knowledge Commentary* speak for those who would represent the noncharismatic movement (as quoted by Peter Wager): "On the other hand, there are large groups of believers that say healing is not for today. James 5:21 is translated by Walvoord and Zuck in the *Bible Knowledge Commentary* (Victor Books: 1983), 'Actually there is no reason to consider "sick" as referring exclusively to physical illness. The word "asthenei" literally means "to be weak." He further goes on to show how that view better fits with the context of James.' "[104] If the Spirit of God comes at His initiation and if truly these are gifts from God, then it would appear that He would come at His own bidding and not at the bidding of the people. The question then remains, do you want the Holy Spirit to display His work in your life, and how is it that you would have Him to do so?

Those who hold to the charismatic position believe that the church growth movement has been extremely influenced by the signs and wonders movement.

"I hold that among vast populations, divine healing is one of the ways in which God brings men and women to believe in the Savior. Some Christians believe that God has called them to engage actively in healing the sick, exorcising evil spirits, and multiplying churches. They deliberately use the vigorous expressed faith in Christ that abounds in a healing campaign to multiply sound churches or responsible Christians."[105]

Jack Hayford's church in Los Angeles apparently has taken a moderate position for their corporate worship. On Sunday morning any member of the congregation who wants to prophesy must first speak to one of the elders before they are given permission to speak publicly. Tommy Barnett would approach the same issue with a little different twist. He has trained his congregation, like many other Assembly of God churches, not to practice the speaking of tongues in the morning worship service. He tells them to act as if the president of the United States were in the audience every Sunday morning.

Here are some passages of Scripture that need serious study and preparation for making a decision in your philosophy of ministry about the charismatic movement: Matthew 10:7–8; Mark 16:15–18; 17:17; Luke 4:17–18; 24:49; John 20:20; Acts 1:8; 2:5, 8, 10; 1 Corinthians 12:8; Galatians 3:1–5; and Ezekiel 34:4.

Participants Tension—Inclusive or Exclusive

UPWARD TO GOD					
Participants	Inclusive				Exclusive

One day in a church growth class at the Seminary, an older student spoke up strongly about the fact that church was for

Christians and non-Christians were not expected to be in church. For a while that student stood alone on his position which, of course, raised a great deal of discussion. Most people would not state their case so strongly, but it is not uncommon for me to hear in subtle ways from board members and other long-time Christians that church is for born-again people. After non-Christians get saved, they should come and be part of the congregation.

The people on the exclusive side of this tension would say that the church was intended for Christians. It is a place for worship, fellowship, and equipping people for ministry. The word "equipping" carries the idea that people who are in the battle of life will come and be equipped for life and ministry. They will have their broken bones set, their nets mended, and the storehouse of their ship filled before their journey of the week. They would say that if you do not know and love God, you would not come to church to worship Him to begin with. If that is not the central part of your worship service, then you are not honoring God's Word.

Those who take the inclusive position would say that if people see God as Isaiah did in Isaiah 6, they would fall down before Him and worship Him. The plan here is to lead the service in such a way that non-Christians would come, see, and feel the love of Christ among the members and want the Christ whom they see in the people of the congregation and that they hear talked about from the platform. Many people in these churches would call themselves seeker-sensitive or seeker-friendly. They pray and plan for nonbelievers to be there each week and are doing what they can to help them come to faith in Christ.

This was not much of an issue back in the '50s in America. Then Americans called themselves a Christian society, and at least Christians and church life were respected and valued by American society. Now that we are in a growing non-Christian, or at least a non-churched society, this decision is much more critical. Some denominations were very closed or exclusive by the very nature of what they believed and practiced even then. Today it is still common. Now they would not keep these people out of their fellowship, but these visitors probably would not find themselves at home if they were to come to the services.

This issue will be dealt with more in chapter 9 under the "Target Tension—Seeker-Driven or Family of Faith Church" heading. That tension has to deal more with evangelism. This one has to do more with the theme and goal of the worship service.

The exclusive church is not so concerned about having a

professionally run service. They are more interested in everyone's participation. The quality of the solo and the way that Scripture is read is not as important as it is to make sure that the people who are a part of the body of Christ participate in the various acts of worship. On the other hand, the inclusive congregation is often critical of the staff because it appears to them that the leaders are watering down the message so the visitor will be certain to hear the plan of salvation. Regular attendees want to hear a good old-fashioned expository message that will give them something new and exciting to think about.

Participants Issues

What really needs to be considered is who is in church. George Barna might help us to think through the issue if our congregation is a typical church. He says, "Among adults who say they are Christian and who attend church regularly, the majority are formal members but are not born again. There is little difference in spiritual commitment between members and nonmembers. Formal members: born again, 48%; not born again, 52%. Informal members: born again, 44%; not born again, 56%."[106] Since the congregation has a much broader mix spiritually than in previous generations, they may be willing to give consideration to what kind of message is being communicated.

Douglas Webster agrees with that lack of commitment and therefore is very interested in seeing the church "down-sized." He talks about the baby boomers wish list. "There is an inherent conflict of interest in the expectation and aspirations of baby boomers. They long for personal intimacy and friendship, but cling tenaciously to autonomy and self-interest. They want the experience of meaningful community but resist whatever restricts their personal freedom and fun. Their desire for independence and anonymity conflicts with their felt need for companionship. They have high expectations of what they deserve, but struggle with feelings of inferiority and low self-esteem. They expect the best from institutions like the church, but feel no personal obligation or institutional loyalty. A generation that sets its heart on immediate gratification guarantees spiritual dissatisfaction. The 'we-expect-more-of-everything' attitude generates a disillusioning tension with the pursuit of a more meaningful life."[107]

In the exclusive congregation, there tends to be fewer public conversion decisions. The congregation is often not accustomed to seeing or hearing about people being saved. So what may be out of sight may be out of mind. Members no longer feel the excitement or the burden of introducing people to the Savior. They believe that conversion should occur outside the church services because believers are penetrating society with the message of salvation and seeking to introduce people in the market place to their Savior. Recently, I heard an interesting comment from some long-standing members of a church located in a strong recreational community. Because the church had turned more to a seeker-friendly or inclusive congregation, many members no longer showed up on Sunday morning regularly because they sensed it was no longer a service for them. Somehow the goal of the service was not sufficiently clarified, and they no longer felt ownership.

The key for an inclusive congregation is that the philosophy of ministry needs to be clearly stated, prayed over, and owned so everyone participates in a different way. They do not come just to get their mind fed; they come to worship God and to be part of a congregation that introduces others to the Savior.

Rick Warren and the Saddleback congregation have addressed this issue by defining five segments of a congregation. The first two, *community* and *crowd*, are classified as people who are moving toward Christ but have not yet identified with Him. They definitely want these two groups of people in the worship service. In the context of the church, they conduct special services and programs to get these people to move toward Christ. The last three circles (*congregation*, *committed* to maturity, and *core* ministry people) are part of the church. Special events are conducted for each one of these groups as well in hopes that as they go through this equilibrium, they will move closer to the core ministry which eventually helps them to become the mission *force* (no longer just the mission field). By doing so, they have addressed individual needs and have given each person a sense of movement toward Christ. Each person would be able to identify where he or she is in his or her pilgrimage. The Saddleback congregation can now justify having Christians and non-Christians within the church service.

Chapter 8

Inward to His Body

P aul would not let us forget for a moment that Christ has great ambitions for His body, the church. The whole book of Ephesians is devoted to that idea. He "pounds the pulpit" in 4:15–16 to emphasize his point: "We will in all things grow up into him who is the Head, that is, Christ. From him the whole body, joined and held together by every supporting ligament, grows and builds itself up in love, as each part does its work."

Authority and Leadership Tension—Laity or Clergy Control

INWARD TO HIS BODY					
Authority / Leadership	Laity				Clergy Control

It appears that nearly every church today is tinkering with authority and the power structure of the church. Consequently, it has become a very hot issue in ecclesiastical circles. In my journey among churches, it appears that this is one of the two most critical issues in today's church. The other critical issue is the role of women in the church. This, of course, has to do with divorce, remarriage, women in leadership, and so forth. Isn't it intriguing to notice how closely these two issues are related?

In a laity-led church, the church belongs to the congregation but primarily to those who are in leadership positions. The pastor tends to be seen more as a teacher/shepherd. He administers the ordinances, seeks to build the congregation into unity, and is a pastor/teacher in the most traditional way. The board runs the church and often sees the staff as the employees of the board.

In a clergy-run church in the most extreme situation, the pastor sees himself as the boss or leader of the congregation. He usually is chairman of the board and sets the agenda for the board and the congregation. Of course, most clergy would see themselves as shepherds and pastor/teachers across the entire spectrum.

Callahan would define a more moderate position on the continuum by calling the pastor the facilitator or charismatic inspirer: (1) The nature of leadership is understood as being a charismatic inspirer. (2) One's philosophy of life is focused on dealing with whatever apocalyptic events are currently decisive. (3) One's perspective of the culture is that it is essentially fallen. (4) One's theology of the church is basically that of a covenant community. The missionary pastor is not the only leader in the church's mission. There are many leaders in that work. The key point is that the missionary pastor functions primarily as a leader and more than simply a manager, boss, enabler, or charismatic inspirer.[108]

The following diagram is an effort to try to show how leadership moves from a strong pastor-led church to a strong laity-led church. This might help you visualize where your church would be on the continuum.

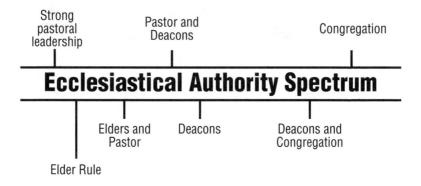

Here are some facts you need to know and some issues you need to consider as your church addresses the tension between a pastor-led and a clergy-led congregation.

It is fascinating to listen to church boards talk about the structure and listen to a congregation talk about its church board members. At times, you would think the organizational structure of the church is the ultimate, rather than the means to an end. This is an important reason why it is so critical to have a vision and a philosophy of ministry statement constantly held up before the congregation. These statements should help the leaders to put the organizational structure and the decision-making process in proper perspective.

Most authors who write about church growth are quick to say that the pastor is the number one institutional factor in the growth and prosperity of the congregation. Peter Wagner speaks for many people when he says, "We know that in local church leadership, the senior pastor is the number one institutional factor in the growth of the church. It is the number one. It is not the only one, but it is the number one. So I teach strong leadership, but strong leadership can be exerted through many different styles. So keep that in mind."[109] The same ideas are more fully explained in Wagner's book, *Leading Your Church to Growth*. The book advocates strong pastoral leadership to equip the laity for ministry and shows how this can be developed into a positive growth factor.

In taking an honest look at a pastor, it is important to face the fact that his role in the church and his position in society has changed dramatically in last few decades. It is far more difficult for both the congregation and the pastor to understand his or her role. "This change in responsibilities has produced considerable confusion among the clergy. Clearly by the end of the sixties and the early seventies this confusion had taken its toll. Ministers were filled with doubt about themselves and also saw their standing in society plummeting. They began to suffer serious anxieties over their status. The power that inward calling had once exerted on private consciousness—the sense of 'standing' before God, of doing His work by making His truth known—apparently was not enough. How, then, would ministers not only gain control over the market, but recover some standing as well? Since the seventies, the answer has been to become a profession."[110]

The idea of their becoming professionals has greatly changed the way pastors are evaluated by both society and their congregations. Unfortunately, along with that professional stance Guinness and Seel suggest that all the trappings of being professional come with the package such as being a specialist, having a career, being a manager, finding one's niche, being fired, and being totally at the mercy of the clientele one serves. In this paradigm shift has come the change in the pastor's role. "In 1934 the pastor was seen to have five roles: teacher, preacher, worship leader, pastor, and administrator. A study done in 1980 found that these roles had almost doubled to nine . . . and by 1980 another study found that the expectations of the pastor had expanded still further to 14 roles."[111] No wonder pastors have had a difficult time pleasing the average congregation!

1. Styles and Temperaments

Bennis and Nanus help us to understand the difference between being a leader and a manager. This tends to be an extremely important distinction in today's leadership. He says, "Manager means 'to bring about, to accomplish, to have charge of or responsibility for, to conduct.' 'Leading' is influencing, guiding in direction, course, action, and opinion.' The distinction is crucial. Managers are people who do things right, and leaders are people who do the right things. The difference may be summarized as activities of vision and judgment effectiveness versus activities of mastering routines, efficiency."[112]

The fifteen leaders whom I interviewed were quick to identify themselves as leaders more than managers. They would agree with George Barna's statement that says, "User-friendly churches invariably had a strong pastor leading the church. 'Strong' means that the pastor was in control and was a true leader. 'Pastor' refers to one who understood the needs of the congregation and the target audience and provided the necessary vision and spiritual guidance. A strong pastor is one who takes charge of the church without breaking the spirit of those who wish to be involved."[113]

Everyone I interviewed also talked strongly about the importance of understanding who they are. Often, that meant understanding their temperament. Randy Kinnison speaks for the group when he says, "I believe much of my philosophy of ministry is based more on who I am as a person, not necessarily the ministry I find myself in. I am more concerned about finding ministries that match up with what I am committed to than for me to try to change and evolve to match a ministry. Therefore when I went to Portland, I was very specific about my philosophy of ministry and what I was going to be doing." Two instruments which prove to be very helpful in getting a grip on one's temperament tendencies would be IDAK and the Chem Match.[114] As the leaders got to know who they were, they were able to bring in other staff people who would support their areas of weakness. It also enabled them to carve out a philosophy of ministry which was consistent with their own personality and giftedness.

Over the years, I have had the privilege of working with many leadership teams. Church staff procurement and team building exercises have been a delight. I have learned through those experiences to see how important it is for a leader to truly understand who he is. The use of temperament tests have proven valuable for the following reasons:

1. You can better understand the normal way you tend to behave in a given situation.
2. It will help you avoid getting yourself into certain situations which may bring out the worst in you because you can anticipate your natural response in most given situations.
3. It will help strengthen a team ministry by bringing an awareness of the need for a balanced approach to temperaments on the team.
4. It will make you aware of the potential conflict with other people on the team since you will know the potential conflict with other temperament types.
5. It will be a reminder to you that one type is not better than another; it is just different. Therefore you should be kept from being critical of those whose temperaments are opposite from yours.
6. You can better understand your particular tendencies to sin since you tend to sin within the expression of your temperament.

Rick Warren talks about how he understands himself and how he helps his team to comprehend who they are. He uses a simple acronym—SHAPE. He says these things make up who you are: S=spiritual gifts; H=your heart (that is, I love to do certain things); A=ability (things that I can work with, such as my talents); P=personality (makeup of my different temperament components); and E=experiences (such as education, vocation, spiritual team experiences).

Jeff Giles saw himself somewhere in the middle of the leadership continuum as he pastored Bear Valley Church. He would classify himself as one who causes disequilibrium. The church newspaper sets forth that idea for us:

> Ronald Heifetz, a recognized authority on leadership, contends that exercising leadership is not the same thing as being an authority figure. To illustrate, Heifetz says the auto mechanic is an authority figure. We take our problems to him, he decides how the problem will be fixed, and he fixes it. A leader, on the other hand, does not fix problems. Rather, he or she mobilizes others to face, define, and solve the problem.
>
> This leads us to the crucial point. Authority leads us to the crucial point. Authority figures are comforting and their function is to maintain equilibrium. Leadership does the opposite. It disturbs, provokes, and forces people to deal with problems they would rather avoid. For example, at BVC, I am committed to disturb, provoke, and force people to face the implications of

hassle-free, comfortable churchianity when our society is in serious peril. I would agree with Heifetz that the leader's role is to generate disequilibrium. Disequilibrium will create an atmosphere for authority figures to rise up, meet the challenge, and to right the ship bringing things back to an even keel.

Who are the authority figures at BVC? Various staff, especially the executive pastor, function as authority figures. Most of our authority figures are people involved in ministries. As a leader, my job is to create an awareness of the need. The awareness causes disequilibrium. Then God raises up people to minister, and they become the authority figures. They provide solutions for that need and restore equilibrium. But by the time authority figures have restored equilibrium, a good leader will have created more meaningful chaos elsewhere.[115]

2. *Laity Control*

Don Bubna helps us to keep in mind a balance between laity and clergy by saying that good leadership is not getting things done through people as the world often sees leadership but getting people done through things. After observing him as a pastor in two of his congregations, he seems to hold that balance in a very beautiful way.

Understanding who you are in the leadership/management matrix is extremely important because if you do not understand who you are, then you will be trying to do things that you are not gifted to do. There is nothing that causes burnout more quickly. This might be one of the quickest ways to determine your own personal burnout.

Once the church and the pastor struggle through this issue, they will finally determine how many people the congregation can potentially minister to. Here, again, it is important to apply one's temperament. Some temperaments which give themselves more to the intimate, the personal, and the small detail find it difficult to try to minister through other people. They would rather do it themselves. In order to keep this tension in perspective, it will be important to keep in mind how contrary to our nature it is to be a servant. Gary Inrig says, "We will still have to overcome a tendency in humans not to serve. This will necessitate much training. This comes out of spiritual maturity. 'Service for the public good was honored, but voluntary giving of one's self in service of one's fellow person is alien to Greek thought. One's highest goal was the development of individual personality.' That last sentence is strikingly contemporary and is mindful of the fact that a culture that is focused on self-actualization in self-fulfillment will find little value in servanthood."[116]

As we move from the idea of a pastor-led church to a laity-led church, Bruce Larson and Ralph Osborne remind the American church that these are marvelous days for the laity to be involved. "One of the main blocks to the renewal of the church is the clergyman who does not trust God enough to allow the laity to be ministers. A church program which is limited to the vision, insight, and approval of one person is destined to remain one-sided and ineffective."[117] Perhaps if the apostle John were with us, he might remind us about the danger of one serving his or her own interest, rather than that of the congregation. "So if I come, I will call attention to what he is doing, gossiping maliciously about us. Not satisfied with that, he refuses to welcome the brothers. He also stops those who want to do so and puts them out of the church" (3 John 9–10).

It is generally believed that if you are going to give the laity a sense of respect, then a mission statement for that particular task seems to be quite important. Randy Pope from Perimeter Church in Atlanta describes it as a difference between a job description and a mission statement. A job *description* describes the minimum for staying on staff, and a job *mission* focuses on growth-directed performance. The goal should not be to enhance and reward growth or just to clearly spell out and define the minimums. Articulate your mission expectations, and the right person will not only grow into the job but leave a larger one than he or she found.

Another way to deal with the relationship between clergy and laity is to think about how the team operates. In Appendix 5 there is an exercise on staff analogies which helps you to think through six different models of teamwork. It is important to think about the flow of authority and who the leader is. If you can define those two, then you can quickly figure out who is really in charge.

In busy Los Angeles, Rick Warren has discovered a meaningful way to keep equipping his leaders and at the same time remain in touch with them. Every month he dictates a cassette tape which he gives to all his church leaders. Many of them listen to these tapes as they commute to and from work. Rick Warren's idea has real merit since people can more readily apply one new idea to a leadership situation at a time rather than trying to apply numerous things they learned in a crash course.

If you really understand the nature of servanthood, then you will quickly come to the conclusion that everyone in the church needs to be hugged, have their hands held, and be made to feel spiritually fulfilled. The difference between a rancher and a shepherd is most succinctly defined at this point. A shepherd sees the need to hold everyone's hand and to hug everyone, while the rancher (servant leader) envisions doing that himself but more often gets it done through other people. Both persons want to effectively impact other people as a shepherd, but some see themselves as shepherding shepherds rather than shepherding each individual person in the congregation. George Barna speaks to that:

> A difference was evident between growing and stagnant churches. Growth-oriented churches had the attitude that it is the job of the church to prepare leaders to gain personal fulfillment through service to others. Stagnant churches were more likely to have the attitude that unless new leaders were trained to fill critical spots within the church's ministry, the church would suffer.[118]

If the laity perceives that they have the power to lead the church but do not have meaningful goals to accomplish, it is quite likely they will abuse the power that they have. One of the greatest places where the clergy and the laity can work together is in the setting and the accomplishment of the goals for the ministry of their local church. Hersey and Blanchard speak strongly to that issue: "The extent that individuals and groups perceive their own goals as being satisfied by the accomplishment of organizational goals is the degree of integration of goals. When organizational goals are shared by all, this is what McGregor calls a true 'integration of goals'."[119] I have noticed over and over again that everyone in the congregation does not have to be directly engaged in the accomplishment of the ministry goals. They ought to at least know the goals and be able to identify with the accomplishment of them because they are in the context where part of the body is ministering in a way that is satisfying to everyone.

One of the ways that Rick Warren keeps the goals before the congregation is to reward those who are making significant strides toward the accomplishment of these goals. Every month he gives out what he calls a giant killer award for people who are doing an outstanding service among the congregation. This gives him a chance to emphasize the goals plus reward these people who are toiling in a labor of love. As it is not possible to separate goals from power, it is also not possible to separate authority from responsibility. When people are given responsibility for ministry, they need to have the authority if they are going to carry out that ministry to its ultimate effectiveness. George Barna noticed this was true in growing churches: "In the growing churches, the pastor demonstrated sufficient trust and confidence in his people to allow them to make important decisions without his input."[120]

Bear Valley Church in my study group is one of the most explicit demonstrations of that principle. Most respective ministries in BVC's "Church Unleashed" philosophy are given the authority over the ministry which they have launched. These people are loved and encouraged and supported in many ways, but the failure or success of each respective ministry is in the hands of the leader. Kennon

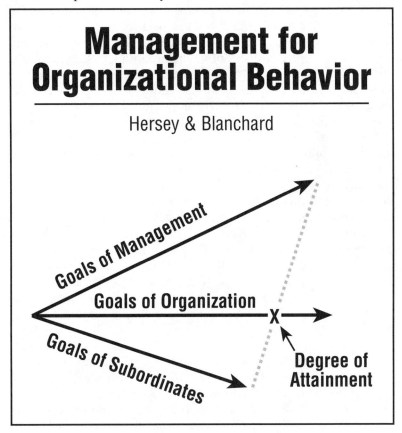

Callahan noticed that was generally true in effective churches: "Never give people responsibility unless you are willing to give them the necessary authority."[121] It is certainly a strong biblical principle to train and equip people for their respective ministries before giving them the responsibility and authority. Failure to provide that training could readily discourage the people, and they will generally not follow through with the responsibility for their respective ministries.

Before you can make a decision about where you are going to position yourself on this authority tension, you must come to grips with a proper translation of Ephesians 4:11–12. This is, in the opinion of most commentators, a key passage that deals with this tension. Christ has given to the church "some to be apostles, some to be prophets, some to be evangelists and some to be pastors and teachers) to prepare God's people for works of service so that the body of Christ may be built up." There is a specific order outlined in the text. Christ has given trainers to the church, and those trainers are to be about the business of equipping saints so that the saints will do the work of ministry. Inherent in the passage is an order of leadership. Christ gives leaders to the church who in turn equip the saints or, as it is more properly translated, "direct the spiritual exercise of the saints." That implies a managerial idea.

It is amazing how many times I hear pastors use that text as if they were following their biblical role of leadership by preaching sermons as the primary process of equipping people. If you hear carefully the word "directing," then you will come to understand that equipping implies the preached and taught word which leads the congregation to participate in ministry. It not only says that we ought to teach them the Word, but it says that we ought to guide them into and through the use of their spiritual gifts. If you are to come to a proper balance on this continuum, you must understand and operate properly within the framework of Paul's guidance here in Ephesians. Ray Anderson warns us about the complexity but provides some additional guidelines to help you make the proper choice.

> The minister must really serve. . . . A disunited church or a compromising church not only denies the character of God and loses its testimony to the world, but cannot adequately fulfill God's purpose for its own members. For each member to grow into the likeness of Christ, the relations among the members ought to be right. God designed the church to be a true family; the eternal blood ties of Calvary are even stronger than human blood ties. It is in the context of this *koinonia* or loving mingling of life that God does his work of building Christians into the likeness of Christ (Ephesians 4:11-16). This is no superficial, Sunday-club relationship. God intended an intimate sharing of life on the pattern of the character of God, the Trinity. To have such family solidarity, there must be discipline. Fellowship without purity of faith and life is flawed at its core. Unity and purity are interdependent

elements of a single relationship. Just as it is in the family, so it is in the church that where either love or discipline is missing, the children will be greatly handicapped.[122]

One of the great struggles that clergy have in releasing the laity for ministry is that they find so many of the laity who are not spiritually mature enough to take the role of leadership. Using the Institute for Church Development data base, I find that 61 percent of the people who attend evangelical churches feel that they are committed. George Barna provides some additional insight about the maturity level of church attendees. "Among adults who say they are Christians and who attend church regularly, the majority are formal members but are not born-again. There is little difference in spiritual commitment between members and nonmembers. Formal members constitute forty-eight percent who say they are born-again; fifty-two percent say they are not born-again. Of those who classify themselves as informal members, forty-four percent were born again, and fifty-six percent were not born-again. Those kinds of figures send shudders up and down the backs of lay and formal church leaders. How do you dare give them responsibility when they are not mature enough spiritually to serve as Christian leaders?"[123]

The Church on the Way in Los Angeles has what they call their Board of Shepherds. This board is made up of people who are mature, committed Christians and who are recommended to this board of approximately 400 by another mature Christian. When the church is going to take a vote on any major issue, it is the Board of Shepherds that takes that vote. They do not feel that the rest of the congregation is mature enough to take ownership for a significant vote in the church life. Maybe the same would be true for leadership positions.

Leith Anderson also speaks to that issue and provides a different system for dealing with immaturity in leadership. He challenges us to "think of these shopping-center churches as funnels. They are very wide and open at the top, but the farther a person goes in, the tighter the circumference becomes. The first experiences are broad and anonymous; the later experiences are focused and identified. The key is that the person, not the church, decides how deep and how far to go into the life of the church—much like the shopping mall."[124]

If the church leadership team is not seriously discipling people (which should lead them to spiritual maturity), then it is in grave danger of choosing leaders off the surface of the funnel who may not be capable of leading the congregation in a mature fashion. This perpetuates immature leadership in the congregation and gives the congregation a false sense of maturity. The congregation is only as mature as its leadership.

The leadership of the church will strongly reflect their position on the continuum by evaluating where they use their most valuable commodity—time. Managers look at and use their time in a substantially different way than leaders do. The percentage of time given to the five classes of people will quickly tell you whether or not you are a shepherd or rancher pastor, or whether you are a leader or manager. Ask all the leaders to designate how much time they think the pastor ought to spend with the five categories of people. After making a composite or an average of those scores, you might quickly tell whether or not they think the pastor ought to be a shepherd or a rancher. Keep in mind that these scores and this decision will greatly impact other facets of ministry. The groups of people are: (1) very teachable people, (2) very important people, (3) very needy people, (4) very demanding people, and (5) very enjoyable people.

Leaders will spend their time with very teachable and important people, while shepherds may spend more of their time with the other three categories. This exercise will be so critical since "pastors no longer have any way to judge how their time should be spent. In fact, they are entirely at the mercy of the clientele they serve. Thus their clientele's expectations have become so bloated that no mere mortal can any longer satisfy many churches."[125] When a church and its pastor fail to clarify these expectations, it could readily lead to his early departure, as it does in so many cases. Tom McKee's philosophy of ministry states, "We are a lay ministry church, not a staff-centered church. In our church, as we grew and grew, the temptation [grew] to hire a lot of staff people, but one of the things we really gave ourselves to was that every staff person had to be an equipper."

As you continue to walk the tightrope between too much power and not enough, you will be flirting with totally shutting down the congregation. Lyle Schaller addresses this when he says, "Canter makes the point that in large organizations, powerlessness tends to corrupt. A lack of power tends to attract persons who are more comfortable guarding their own turf rather than encouraging creativity. The entrepreneurial personality frequently oversteps the boundaries of that office and gathers the power and makes possible the mobilization of the resources necessary to implement that new idea."[126]

It is my observation that all the pastors interviewed were not in churches where there was a power vacuum. Listen to Russ Rosser who gives us an example of how he deals with that kind of tension:

You can develop a philosophy of ministry everybody is comfortable with. Working through, rather than walking away from, the marriage/divorce issue was a vital consideration for us at one time. At our church there are three to four different views, and I am probably the most liberal. We took the issue and laid it out on the table. One wrote a thirty to forty page paper. We studied it, and it came to a point where I had to make the decision. One pastor doesn't have to perform weddings of divorced people—I am comfortable with that. I don't ask him to compromise his moral convictions, but do ask him to consider different views that could lead others to believe differently. The same with the women's issues. Some are hierarchical, some moderate; and we are going to license a woman at our church— not to ordain. We won't split the church on an issue like that. Unity is key for us.

This should bring you to the place where you are now ready to define a role of leadership that the pastor will play in your church's philosophy of ministry. Ronald Osborn provides for us historic titles used for clergy during the last three centuries. As you analyze the strengths of the pastor, the needs of the congregation, and the culture in which your church is located, you may be able to best define the role of the pastor by studying these various titles: "18th century—saint, priest, master, awakener; 19th century—pulpiteer, revivalist, builder, missionary; 20th century—manager, counselor, impresario, teacher."[127] Listen to a word of caution from Willimon as he helps us to think through which title and role would be most appropriate for your church:

> See why I am concerned that two of the most popular writers on ministerial spirituality today are Henri Nouwen and Thomas Merton? We pastors are community persons—body people, not monks. We are called to tasks that are ecclesial, relational, functional, and pastoral not personal, professional, or universal.[128]

Discipline Tension—By Organization or Organism

INWARD TO HIS BODY				
Discipline	Organization			Organism

The phrase "church discipline" elicits a variety of reactions from Christians. To some it conjures up images of medieval inquisitions, of fanatical cults torturing the erring members. To others the term is relatively meaningless since church discipline has not been part of their church experience. Today's society tolerates flagrant sin more than ever before. Unfortunately, sin has walked boldly through the front door of the church, and most churches have moved away from dealing with it since it is so prevalent. Though church discipline often is misunderstood, the concept is found in many passages in the New Testament (1 Cor. 5:1–13; 2 Thess. 3:1–18; Matt. 18:15–18; 2 Cor. 5–7; 1 Tim. 5:19–24 and Gal. 6:1). The big question now is how is your church going to follow that strong biblical mandate and still have some members left in the congregation?

Carl Laney provides an understanding of what church discipline looks like. He states, "John Wesley emphasized in Methodism what the New Testament calls *koinonia*, a 'sharing in common' (Acts 2:42). Biblical *koinonia*, a word usually translated 'fellowship,' is much more than punch and cookies after church. Biblical fellowship involves watching over one another in love, advising, exhorting, admonishing, and praying for one another. Church discipline, I believe, is simply the practice of biblical *koinonia*. We may define church discipline as the application of Christian accountability in relationship to a brother or sister struggling with sin."[129]

The extremes as stated on the continuum might be defined as follows. The term "organism" refers to letting the body of Christ deal with Christian discipline as naturally as possible. You might hear folks who take this position say something like, "Since the Holy Spirit abides within the church and He wants us to do what is right, we will trust the Spirit or our conscience to deal with guilt and help us correct our sin problem." On the other end of the spectrum, people are referring to the organizational structure of the church and their responsibility to mete out church discipline. They will be the church board or the elders who are responsible to deal with this discipline in a formal way according to the church constitution and/or bylaws. They have been given the responsibility of keeping the church holy, pure and free from flagrant sin. They would not understand discipline to be truly negative or relating to a judicial matter. The church must do whatever it can to accomplish repentance, restore fellowship, and to make believers stable.

These two positions, like other continuums, are rather extreme. There appears to be a declining number of churches who take the organism-side of the spectrum in reference to discipline. If the church is a denominational church, then most of them would follow the rules which are set forth by their judicatory body. Church discipline is an item you will generally not find written about in the philosophy of ministry in any formal way. Yet, in a way it covers the church's philosophy. You should at least think it through carefully in preparation for concluding your philosophy statement. If you are going to think about discipline in a biblical way, you will want to see it through the eyes of Christian nurture. Some scholars would go so far as to say that if you do not deal with church discipline in a formal way, the church will lose its soul.

Space does not allow me to deal exhaustively with the exegesis of all the passages about church discipline. You are strongly encouraged to do so before designing your theology on this most critical issue. It would seem very difficult to make a serious decision about what nurture, preaching, and evangelism are all about without seriously taking into consideration the subject of church discipline.

1. Organizational Rejection

Recently, I had the responsibility of counseling a congregation in the San Francisco Bay area. During the time their multi-million dollar facility was being completed, the pastor was found to be guilty of immorality. Three of the staff members who knew about the situation made a choice not to deal with it publicly lest it might cause the church to go bankrupt or at least stop the construction of the facility.

It is not uncommon to find many congregations failing to deal with church discipline for fear it might split the church. At least, they feel it would discourage or frighten many prospective members away from joining or attending their respective congregations.

Oliver W. Price says, "Actually, just the opposite is true. Wise biblical discipline will unite the church, revive its spirit, and produce solid growth."[130]

Another factor that makes the congregation hesitant to deal with church discipline is the lack of commitment to their church body. This seems to be fostered by our mobile society. Some would say it leads to true consumerism. They feel that if you start to do that with the members of the congregation, many will move down the road to some more comfortable style of Christian love in another church. They might even go so far as to say that even if discipline is a biblical mandate, it is impossible to practice it in today's church. It becomes one of those *is* and *ought* issues, so many have decided to yield on the side of the *is* and not on the side of the *ought*.

2. Discipline Issues

It is going to be difficult to both keep the church pure and united at the same time. J. Robertson McQuilkin underlines that issue by saying:

> It is very difficult for the church to maintain unity and purity at the same time. It is much easier to go to a consistent extreme than to stay at the center of biblical tension. Whether in the local congregation or in the church at large, the church of Jesus Christ seems incapable of having both. The result is that the reflection of God's image is distorted, the evangelistic thrust of the church is blunted, and Christians are stunted in their spiritual growth. There is a great polarization between the professional unifiers on the one hand and the professional purifiers on the other.[131]

Many church leaders would opt out of dealing with church discipline since they do not have a formal membership. Therefore they have no set body of people for whom they are accountable. Some churches who recognize people as members after attending for a certain period of time feel that the membership is not very binding; therefore it does not permit discipline to be handed down. Even in churches where membership is a requirement, some congregations would be reticent to deal with discipline because they feel there are too many "seekers" who would not stay with the church if they saw such practices being carried out.

Still other congregations have difficulty because they feel there is a double standard given in Scripture. They believe that the leader's standard for holiness as expressed in 1 Timothy 3 and Titus 1:5–10 is much stronger than it would be for the normal Christian. They might, therefore, deal with *leadership* discipline but not *congregational* discipline.

The informal side would say that church discipline appears to be too much like legalism. They live in a suing society where legalism is so prevalent that they would argue that they should have an atmosphere of accepting people for who they are under the blood of Christ. They say, let the love of Christ and the inner working of the Holy Spirit in the body do His work.

When raising a child, all studies tend to show that developing self-discipline has the greatest and most long lasting effect on a child's maturity. Thus the child does not sense the strong, respected, unconditional love coming from the parent. When adults are being disciplined, they must know that it is being done in a redemptive context in order to accept that discipline and stay committed to the body. This is very difficult in a megachurch where there are not often sufficient systems to make sure that everyone is included in an environment of love and care. Small churches have the natural networking that makes it easy to have everyone under the watchful eye of the membership. Many people stay within the context of the family and faith environment because they do not like high systems and structures which at times seem to be legalistic. As a church continues to grow in size, it must have systems which provide for the strong, assuring love that makes discipline a possibility. If that is not the case, then discipline in the larger context without love will not be effective.

You might also hear the argument from many people that the practice of formal discipline among the members is rather unrealistic since we are all full of sin and the congregation is to be a place where love and forgiveness is constantly practiced. If God will forgive all who are under His blood, why would we need to discipline anyone? These people would conclude by saying that the power of Christ's spirit working among the believers will initiate all the discipline necessary.

The formal side will argue that there needs to be some specific guidelines for church discipline or it will appear that you are picking on someone for some hidden or obscure reason. If there are no rules written for church discipline, then it may appear that the congregation is like a bunch of junior boys playing ball and making up the rules as the game is being played.

Suburban Bible Church of Highland, Indiana, is one of numerous examples that I have seen of a church that has written guidelines for church discipline and distributed them to the congregation. An excerpt from their paper gives you a list of reasons for discipline: "There are some specific sins that are mentioned in the New Testament: doctrinal deviation (Gal. 1:6–8; Acts 20:28–30; 1 Tim. 1:18–20; with 2 Tim. 2:17–18); divisiveness (2 Thess. 3:11; Titus 23:10–11; Romans 16:17–20); undisciplined living (2 Thess. 3:6, 14; 1 Thess. 5:14); conflict between believers (1 Cor. 6:5, Phil. 4:2–3, Matt. 18:15–18); sins of the flesh (1 Cor. 5:11); sins of the Spirit (1 Cor. 5:11)." The booklet also includes discipline for church leaders and the procedure for discipline.[132]

The formal side will argue for tough love and will appreciate what Robert McQuilkin has to say on the issue: "Imbalance does not come from an overemphasis. It is impossible to have too much love or too much faithfulness. However, it is quite possible to have unfaithfulness masquerading as love. When God's people compromise through sentimentality or self-love, or for some other reason are unwilling to exercise church discipline, they are unfaithful though they speak much of love."[133] Most theologians would quickly agree that the church is to portray the character of God in both its holiness (Rev. 4:8) and its unity (Deut. 6:4).

Membership Tension—Inclusive or Exclusive

INWARD TO HIS BODY				
Membership	Inclusive			Exclusive

Fifty years ago in America, there was not much question in the study of ecclesiology and in church circles about whether or not church membership was an option. There tended to be a great deal of confusion about what constituted membership. In the last few decades, the whole idea of membership seems to be up for grabs by many leaders and churches. There is no question that churches understand Hebrews 10:24–25 as meaning that we ought to meet together as a New Testament church. However, the question is, do you have to be a member of the church to meet with that church? Membership affects many of the same issues that church discipline affects: autonomy, service, commitment, finances, maturity/ accountability, attendance, growth, service, recruitment, and others you might think are equally important. If you are concerned with any of these issues in your church, then you had better seriously look at the issue of church membership.

Those who identify with the inclusive side of the continuum tend to think that you must be a member to take any role of leadership in the church. You must go to a membership class, you must be discipled, or you must be baptized according to that church's definition of baptism. Even the issue of baptism is undergoing change among many denominational churches.

On the exclusive end of the continuum, membership is not important at all. In fact, most churches in this group do not even have such a thing as church membership. One's confession of faith and attendance is all that is necessary to be called a member of these congregations. In most cases, there is no vote by the congregation. If there is a vote, it is only on a limited number of issues.

The middle of the road position generally holds to some form of representative government where the congregation would vote on such issues as the purchase of property and the calling of the senior pastor. If you are familiar historically with the issue of church membership, you will be quite surprised to see the radical changes in the rules about church membership in American churches. There tends to be much less concern with rules by the baby boomer generation than the G. I. Joe generation that still holds to what they say is a strong theological position on church membership. These are issues which need to be considered as you determine whether or not your church will have membership as a requirement for

participation in that local ministry. No doubt some of this change
has to do with the reaction against the formalism of the church
which existed prior to World War II.

1. Membership Issues

One of the major issues to consider in this section is whether or
not the ordinances were given to the universal church or to the
local church. Many scholars would hold that the ordinances were
given to the local church. For this reason, membership in a church
naturally precedes communion. Since communion is a family right,
participants should first be a member of the family (Acts 2:46–47;
20:7; 1 Cor. 11:18–22).

Membership is a symbol of church fellowship. Being excommunicated
implies nothing if it does not imply exclusion from the ritual of
communion. If the supper is simply communion of the individuals
with Christ, then the church has no right to exclude any from it. For
a complete study of the issue of the ordinances in reference to
membership, it would be advisable to study Bruce Shelley's *The
Church/God's People* (Victor Press, 1978, pp. 79-81).[134]

From a psychological or sociological viewpoint, it is important
to think about church membership in reference to the commitment
of members to the body. Membership tends to tie people to a church
in the same fashion that marriage ties people to each other. Without
that commitment, the church may lose the commitment of its
members both to attending the service as well as losing control of
church purity. Without membership, there is no way to maintain
church discipline. Leith Anderson thinks that this issue is particularly
prevalent in the megachurch movement, which of course is rapidly
growing. He says:

> Many people do not want to formally affiliate. They may go
> to church but not join the church. They like the job but aren't
> interested in the labor union. They may not vote Republican but
> are registered Republican. . . . People are choosing churches not
> denominations. They view local churches more as networks than
> formal organizations. Many come and participate but never join.
> Those who do become members often insist that they may belong
> to that local church, but they do not consider themselves part of
> the denomination.[135]

On the other hand, there is another viewpoint which states that
people are looking for something to believe in, something that has
integrity. Kent R. Hunter speaks to that: "Growing churches have

been characterized as those that demand a lot from their members—one reason many sects have grown so rapidly. People are looking for a group of believers with integrity; they show interest in churches with backbone."[136]

2. Denominations

As Christianity spread west with the growth of America, the believers took with them churches with their denominational labels. They greatly appreciated the fact that the family could grow up in the same denomination that their grandparents did some years before. Denominations then and now continue to be built around theological issues. Most of the new denominations were splinters from an old denomination because of some theological issue. Now that theological issues are not as critical in our current subjective age, denominations have tended to go out the door in a less objective era of time. The *Reader's Digest* stated that "deeply religious Protestants who no longer feel at home in their own denomination are turning by the millions to more faith-oriented, nonpolitical churches—many of an evangelical strain. Significantly, 445 of the 500 fastest growing churches in the country are not mainline denominations."[137] A growing evidence of the lack of denominational affiliation is expressed in the "Challenge of the '80s Update."[138] "Antidenominationalism—57% of the people who move from one location to another end up joining a church of another denomination or association. The expansion of church options coupled with specialization have caused a great decline in denominational loyalty."[139]

There is a growing belief that denominations will have less and less visibility in America. They were ethnic and theologically based originally but in many cases have become no more than a regulatory agency. Early in their history they had theological enemies, and they became mission organizations. Now, in many cases there are no more enemies to fight, and the parachurch organizations have become the mission agencies. In a sense it is also believed that megachurches have almost become a denomination to themselves. Lyle Schaller believes that if denominations do not become strong mission agencies once again where they give high deference to the concerns of people, then perhaps they will continue to decline in popularity in the coming decades. [140]

George Peters gives us some additional insight as to the reason for the decline of the importance of denominations in American ecclesiology:

The major forms of church structure are a matter of history
and culture rather than of revelation and apostolic tradition. The
present-day reaction to organization and structure is not derived
from or motivated by the Scripture. It is a reaction, rather, to
over-organizing and over-institutionalizing the church. It is the
natural reaction of an organism to a mechanism that does not fit
it, to a machinery that stifles the natural functions and legitimate
expression of the organism. The organism will also react, however,
to the absence of structure and form. . . . sooner or later the
organism will suffer seriously, cease to function dynamically, or
progressively disintegrate.[141]

There are a large number of leaders who still hold strongly to the
belief that a church ought to hold tenaciously to its denominational
affiliation. Ken McGarvey argues firmly that it is still a very valid
position to hold. "The word 'independent' means 'not dependent'
or 'free from control.' It is an unfortunate choice of words. Of
course no Christian or church would claim to be free from
dependence on God or His sovereignty. We depend on Him for our
life, health, salvation, instruction, growth, and destiny. Our churches
rely on Him for their power and effectiveness. Independent churches
are not claiming otherwise so why use such potentially misleading
terminology? Independent is too easily read in our culture as a
justification for a myopic rugged individualism. . . . In 1 Corinthians
Paul urged believers to heal the divisions and function as one body.
Perhaps Paul would not require us all to be one organizational
entity, but the notion of any church in a community being totally
independent from the other churches clearly violates his teaching."[142]

We can all anticipate some continuing changes in the area of
church membership that are somewhat determined by a group's
position on church membership. If your church is going to be a
genuinely biblical church and also impacting society, then it will
need to give serious consideration to the issues relating to membership.

Nurture Tension—Intentional or Inadvertent Growth

INWARD TO HIS BODY				
Nurture	Non-directed			Directed Growth

Ever since Pentecost, the church has been one generation away
from extinction. Every church's ability to nurture will determine whether
or not it will be vital for the following generation. Raymond Ortlund
reminds us of how critical this is: "Both the Lord Jesus and the Apostle

Paul, as they were leaving this life, were careful to say, in essence, 'Now don't be the end of the line! You turn around and go make disciples, teaching them everything I have taught you' (Matt. 28:18–20), and 'the things you have heard me say, pass on to reliable men who will also be qualified to teach others' (2 Tim. 2:2). In other words, they both encouraged others to keep the chain of discipling going."[143]

Once again, we have to say there are numerous forms that nurture takes, but all of them will be found some place on the continuum between the intentional and the inadvertent way of developing spiritual maturity. The inadvertent group says that they expect spiritual growth to happen naturally as a result of the presence of the Holy Spirit in the church (John 16:13). Because churches have new birth, there are babies who desire the sincere milk of the Word. That in itself will cause spiritual growth to occur. Some would go so far as to say that new babes need to be fed for a period of time, but after that they expect growth will simply happen by listening to sermons and receiving teaching that will move them toward maturity. Certainly, no Christian can deny that the Spirit's presence causes growth. A vast majority of the people who are in spiritual leadership in the inadvertent camp are there because they are self-motivated. They believe, given the right circumstances, other people in Christ will eventually move in the same direction. These people believe a church can be too much like a school. It is then too legalistic. They would say that those who are really hungry for Christ and maturity will take the steps necessary to grow. They believe that the Holy Spirit causes growth; therefore you cannot program growth.

They would also be frightened about trying to program spiritual growth because the Sermon on the Mount teaches that the Christian life has so much to do with attitudes. I long ago discovered that the attitude and motivation behind Christian behavior is something that cannot be evaluated. These people would ask how those attitudes can be taught.

The people who appreciate high structure or are part of a high-structure culture may not appreciate the inadvertent approach to spiritual maturity. The people who attend Mount Zion Church with E. V. Hill in the Watts district of Los Angeles may find highly structured systems of spiritual development to be quite distasteful.

On the other end of the nurture spectrum is the intentional or directed growth process. These churches would appreciate structured programs and high levels of discipline and accountability to facilitate each member's growth in the body. There are certain parachurch organizations such as the Navigators who would strongly favor this position. These people would strongly emphasize passages of Scripture that teach hands-on accountability in the spiritual development process such as 1 Timothy 4:7–8, Colossians 1:28–29 and 2 Timothy 2:2.

1. Nurture Issues

Here are some of the questions which must be addressed before you can make an honest decision about where you will be on this tension. What role does the Sunday school or small groups play in nurture? Those who are on the intentional side would have clearly defined what they anticipate will happen in the growth process during both sessions. As well, they will expect everyone to be in programs like those to facilitate the spiritual growth process. These people will be more concerned about what will happen to nurturing in the megachurch movements where there are so few opportunities for growth in Sunday school or adult Bible study classes. They will also ask the question about what relationship does nurturing have to preaching. Some would say that preaching is strictly for encouragement or motivation rather than for spiritual development. The role preaching plays will make a difference in this tension.

John 14:21-24 teaches that God will reveal Himself to His people in proportion to their obedience to His Word. Consequently, spiritual development is concerned about orthodoxy as well as orthopraxis. For the intentional people, spiritual discipline will have a prescribed curriculum which will have an outcome-based set of goals that is deeply concerned about a changed life, not just a learning or prescribed curriculum.

In a couple of instances, I have come across churches that have designed lecture programs during the Bible study hour on Sunday morning. This program trains people specifically for leadership. They would be able to complete all the necessary courses to be trained as a leader somewhere in between two to five years of continual study.

Another key issue has to do with a biblical definition of discipleship. Fuller School of Church Growth has defined for us a progressive definition of discipleship which fits a more proper exegetical study of the Great Commission.

D-1: The turning of a non-Christian society for the first time to Christ.

D-2: The turning of any individual from non-faith to faith in Christ and his or her incorporation in a church.

D-3: The teaching of an existing Christian as much of the truths of the Bible as possible, helping him or her.[144]

People who are in agreement with this definition would generally not be in favor of teaching on two-stage conversion or the second work of grace. People who understand and own this position will find themselves being in disagreement with Bill Hull's words in the disciple-making church: "The idea that only mature people are disciples and all other Christians are immature converts appears nowhere in the New Testament. Acts 21:16, the last New Testament use of disciple occurs nearly twenty-seven years after Paul's conversion."[145] What many people normally define as discipleship is better described as nurturing or teaching the church to observe all those things which Christ has taught us.

Yet another key question which must be addressed has to do with how people actually are edified or nurtured. Bill Hull defines disciple-making as "the intentional training of disciples with accountability on the basis of loving relationships."[146] Those who speak for the inadvertent side would quickly remind people that there were no organizational structures in the early church that aided in the growth process of the Christians who went everywhere turning their world upside-down. These churches would have some structures and programs that would help people who would like to be engaged in additional disciplines toward spiritual maturity. You would not find a great many programs, nor would you find a tremendous amount of pressure brought to bear on people to be involved at some level in spiritual development. Often there would not be many Sunday school classes planned for adults nor a large number of small groups where everyone is expected to participate.

2. Nurture Models

There are numerous models in churches across America which are highly intentional. I will simply take the time to mention a few of them which have impressed me. Most of the people I interviewed are engaged in some level of discipling or nurturing. I will let Randy Kinnison speak for the rest about his involvement in discipleship.

> I have always been discipling somebody, and at the same time, I have always sought a mentor in my own life. I believe it is extremely important that for you to grow in Christ, you have to be. . . that double-edged sword always seems to sharpen the man of God. I have always had some men in one-on-one situations and always work with some kind of small group as well. A requirement for me to disciple anybody is that they must be willing to disciple somebody else. If after six months they have

shown they have no inclination to do this, then they are dropped from either one-on-one or small group discipling.

Rick Warren at Saddleback is leading his congregation in a very systematic growth process in what he calls the Family of Faith Church. This is the Saddleback model of intentionally moving people toward maturity in Christ. Here is a short summary of that process:

> We bring them in. We build them up. We train them for it. We send them out. First, we offer steps to help them investigate Christ. Come and see who Jesus is. Next, they are invited to

Saddleback
5 Circles of Commitment

© 1981 The Encouraging Word

Saddleback's Program to Help You Grow Through Christian Life And Service Seminars

AN OVERVIEW OF C.L.A.S.S.

100 LEVEL SEMINARS:
To lead people to Christ and membership at Saddleback

200 LEVEL SEMINARS:
To grow people to spiritual maturity

300 LEVEL SEMINARS:
To equip people with the skills they need for ministry

400 LEVEL SEMINARS:
To enlist people to the world-wide mission of sharing Christ

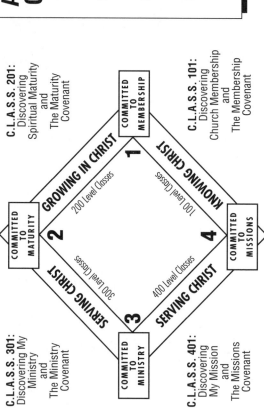

C.L.A.S.S. 201:
Discovering Spiritual Maturity and The Maturity Covenant

C.L.A.S.S. 101:
Discovering Church Membership and The Membership Covenant

C.L.A.S.S. 301:
Discovering My Ministry and The Ministry Covenant

C.L.A.S.S. 401:
Discovering My Mission and The Missions Covenant

GROWING IN CHRIST — 200 Level Classes

KNOWING CHRIST — 100 Level Classes

SERVING CHRIST — 300 Level Classes

SERVING CHRIST — 400 Level Classes

COMMITTED TO MEMBERSHIP — 1

COMMITTED TO MATURITY — 2

COMMITTED TO MINISTRY — 3

COMMITTED TO MISSIONS — 4

participate in certain events where the crowd is introduced to a relationship to Jesus Christ. Next, they are encouraged to participate in 201 classes which are geared to help build them up in their Christian experience. Our goal is to lead members to be committed to spiritual growth. We cannot expect them to come into a church, get on a roll, and that is it. We don't assume anything. Our church growth is intentional not inadvertent. We do it through intentional programs like small groups or discipleship groups. We think through what we want people to see. What are the qualities we want to see in people? Next, they are moved from the committed to the core. Next, they are invited to be in 301 classes where we help them find a ministry that makes them become what they want to be. The bottom line is not to plug programs. The bottom line is to develop disciples.

Yet another holistic church model is carried on by Don Jensen in Beaverton, Oregon.

Worship Service . . . . Pastoral application of the passage of truth being studied for the week.

Sunday School . . . . Personal involvement with group learning about the Sunday morning sermon topic.

Neighborhood Little Flocks . . Real core interaction between that week's portion of God's Word and people's lives.

Commentary provided . . . . . . A four- to six-page commentary is written each week to be read during the week by the congregation; provides pastoral care, keeps a unity among the group, keeps a focus on God's Word, trains teachers to apply the Word.

Don Bubna has undertaken the time-consuming task of visiting his entire congregation each year. Their spiritual inventory, they have found, has been very helpful in monitoring the spiritual growth of the people, particularly in the area of responsibility. "The goal of such a discussion is to find out about a person's spiritual life: where he has been, where he is now, and where he wants to go with the help of the pastor and church."[147]

There are three national programs which quickly plug into a baby boomer's mind-set. They desire individual and ultimate fulfillment. They are programmed into three new models of discipleship. Bear Valley Church has launched a program they call Spiritual Planning which is now used by numerous churches:

> "Spiritual Planning" affords us the flexibility to tailor-make an individualized plan for growth and is ministry-based on the unique package of resources and experiences represented in each disciple.
>
> These analogies are helpful to describe phases in this planning process. First, we serve like a financial planner. We ask each person to itemize the spiritual resources God has entrusted to them: spiritual gifts, natural talents. Resource management best describes the next step when we suggest potential ministry job descriptions based on our needs and available opportunities.
>
> Then like a career guidance counselor, we challenge the individual to write down a specific plan of action for the next twelve months. This spiritual plan includes feasible, measurable, and attainable goals for growth and ministry.[148]

Robert Acker has designed a program with Bob Logan which is now distributed through Fuller School of Church Growth. Their spiritual gift mobilization program is defined as "a place where every believer is being equipped by the spirit with one or more gifts. These are combined with their other natural talents that the Lord desires them to be using in ministry. We have invested energy and staffing to help people discover and start using their spiritual gifts."

There is still a third program called Networking, which is available through Fuller School of Church Growth and designed by the Willow Creek Community Church.

The following four books would be a very great help to you if you are interested in moving toward the intentional mode of discipling.

- Friedman, Matt., *The Accountability Connection* (Victor, 1991; Zondervan, 1989).
- Gangel and Wilhoit, *The Christian Educator's Handbook on Adult Education* (Victor Press, 1993). See especially chapter on Adult Sunday school by Westing.
- Hull, Bill, *The Disciplemaking Church* (Revell, 1990).
- Stranger, Mardelle A., *Spiritual Formation in the Local Church*.

Fellowship Tension—Directed Relationships or Anonymity

INWARD TO HIS BODY				
Fellowship	Anonymity			Directed Relationships

Something funny happened to Americans on their way into the '90s. A few years ago Americans went into their homes and shut the doors and started to complain about how unfriendly their neighbors were. I have found loneliness is felt in nearly every social level and in every corner of America. The more we move into the cities, the more we move into seclusion. In the 1950s, the small group movement had its rocky beginning as people lost their sense of belonging through the demise of the American family. By the 1980s, small groups really came into their own. For a great segment of America, people groups replaced the family. Often for the lonely, the megachurches played into the scene as well. Here is where they could find a common identity group if they wanted one but also could choose to be anonymous. About once a quarter in the *Denver Post*, there is a sample listing of around 1000 groups of every conceivable type and size which have found their way into society. They play a major role in helping to answer the inner craving for relationships.

During the last few decades, anonymity seemed to come out of hiding. At the same time, we heard cries from every rooftop about how lonely everyone was. A great public paradox seemed to come out of hiding, for on one hand we heard society saying, "I want your friendship," but then people quickly followed with, "Leave me alone." Subconsciously they were saying, "I don't want to pay the price of giving myself to you." Astute churches quickly saw a way to use the occasion to become evangelistic. They programmed all kinds of activities based on people's common needs and interests and then, in the midst of those activities, introduced them to Christ. It should be no surprise to find counseling programs sprinting onto the scene and dominating the American landscape. "There is reason to believe that there has been a steady increase, particularly since World War II, with three times as many Americans seeing 'mental health professionals' now as did twenty years ago."[149]

In many quarters, the church has come with its troops of counselors and small group leaders to address the loneliness gap in America. Elizabeth Shulin gives us a clue about that seeming dissonance seen in society's wanting relationships and at the same time anonymity. She says that it "is a unique combination of closeness and distance." The focus is really on one person, and there isn't a relationship outside of this circumscribed one. Yet it's a relationship with a very narrow and very, very deep nature. . . . It's a funny combination of business and closeness."[150] If that is what is happening in society, then we can expect some of the same to occur in the church and in its relationship structures.

Most congregations want to repeat the dynamic fellowship experience of the New Testament church in Acts 2 for the whole congregation. Churches are trying to make fellowship a meaningful part of their church experience, and it becomes especially hard for those who are socially passive or for other reasons want to retain their anonymity. Obviously, it will not happen in the same way for all, but it will be found some place on this continuum.

1. Directed Relationships

When the church becomes intentional in organizing groups and provides the trained leadership necessary, around 50 to 60 percent of the congregation will participate. There are a few isolated cases where more than 60 percent will participate. Dale Holloway's New Hope Church in Portland, Oregon, is a model of a church that has built the whole church program around the small group movement. It covers the Portland landscape in a highly organized fashion, using some paid clergy but mostly lay leadership. Many churches have followed their model or have designed a program which is somewhat similar.

The people on this side of the spectrum would say that relationships with no content are meaningless. They might say a body without a spirit is a corpse, but a spirit without a body is a spook. It is interesting to see that 15 to 25 percent of the American church will take the initiative and form their own small clusters once they have been around the church for a while. It may be these same people who identify themselves as multi-relational, which also number 15 percent of the American society. Perhaps there is a direct correlation between the two. On the right side of the continuum, the church acknowledges the human right to remain anonymous. They tend to have a strong belief that people will seek relationships if they feel they need them but will not be *pushed* into them in any way to participate. There are numerous reasons why people genuinely desire this style of relating and why leaders listen to their voices.

It appears that Willow Creek has put the word "anonymous" into the evangelical dictionary. They believe that since they are ministering to consumers, they have a strong responsibility to let people make their own choice rather than having it pushed upon them. In the shopping-center mind-set in the "urbs" of America, they would say that the newcomer must be given time to walk around through the church and check out what is going on before making any kind of commitment. Visits or phone calls to those people who have visited the church recently would not be part of the agenda for those who identify with the right side of the continuum.

Recently, one of my relatives went through a divorce. As I talked to her about what it was like to go to a new church with her sense of being wounded, she said that she did not want anyone to talk to her and was not interested in forming relationships right away. There might be time for that in the future. There are many people like her who would also express the same sentiment.

There is another group of people who are spectators to Christianity. They are not wanting anyone to push them. If, in fact, they feel pushed, they probably will not come back.

Still others understand that church people tend to be very transparent, particularly in small groups. They are reluctant to be involved for fear they might have to reveal some of their inner feelings which would not be very comfortable for them.

2. Consider These Issues

There is a serious misnomer that floats around, particularly in medium-sized and smaller churches. Many people there feel that the worship service environment ought to provide them an opportunity to build relationships. Knute Larson might help these people understand that the purpose of a worship service is for celebration and not for forming relationships. He said that "he sat in the Cleveland stadium once with Billy Graham and 87,000 people, and nobody there said, 'Oh my, we don't all know each other,' or 'This place is getting too big.' 87,000 of us sang 'How Great Thou Art.' It was a fabulous celebration!"[151]

People who do like to relate when they come to church are more committed to community than they are to committees. It becomes extremely important to form a small group ministry in order to retain large groups of people in some sort of meaningful relationship. Kennon Callahan speaks to that when he says, "Wherever the combination of relational and functional competencies is well in place, there will be a strong tendency for that program to emerge as one of the major programs in the life of a congregation."[152] He further goes on to say, "Most sanctuaries in cities and small towns become comfortably filled at approximately 80% of total seating capacity. There are four kinds of sanctuaries: uncomfortably crowded, comfortably filled, comfortably empty, and uncomfortably empty."[153]

Some studies done by Mansell Pattison suggest that a normal person "has from twenty to thirty relationships they can maintain. A psychotic has five. The neurotic has ten."[154] This ought to make us aware of the fact that putting more than 30 people in a group is quite unrealistic if we expect to build strong relationships among the people. Start noticing how common that is, especially in places like church choirs and Sunday school classes. You might even notice with interest that Paul gives greetings to 35 friends at the end of the book of Romans.

3. What Ought to Happen to Adults

There are some very strong biblical mandates for adult leaders to keep in mind as they design adult ministries. It has already been suggested that in Acts 2:42 a strong church will grow in fellowship. Here, the idea is that people ought to make a contribution to one another socially, physically, spiritually, and perhaps psychologically. Christ further modeled for us the extreme importance of having relationships in an accountability setting in Mark 3:14. If the Kingdom of God was to be accomplished, they would need to be accountable to him and each other. It is reasonable to expect that we would have the same kind of relationships in our role of kingdom building. Romans 15:1–2 and Galatians 5:25–6:2 strongly teach the importance of having someone in your life system to whom you can be accountable.

Christians are also taught that each believer needs to learn how to bear one another's burdens (Gal. 6:2) and to build strong love relationships with other people (1 Peter 1:22). As I studied Ephesians 4:15–16, I saw that Paul teaches us that Christ flows through the "joints in His body," the church. Consequently, Christ will not and cannot speak to and through His people unless they have those kinds of relationships.

If Christians are to practice the "assembling of themselves together" as they are reminded in Hebrews 10:24–25, then they ought to carry out the purpose for those gatherings. The passage teaches that they are to "spur one another." A real cowboy understands what spurring is. You spur the horse without breaking the skin, yet you get the greatest potential out of the horse for the race and sometimes for the task. In the same way, Christians are to spur one another so that they might get out of them "love and good works" without destroying their personhood. This is what Christian nurturing is all about.

One of the other serious guidelines for working with adults comes from a study of all of the "one anothers" in the New Testament. These "one anothers" all necessitate settings such as small groups and Sunday school classes because they are the only place in the normal church setting where this can be accomplished.[155] People who are not involved with other Christians in a nurturing setting may fail to fulfill the will of God for their lives (Col. 1:28–29). In large churches, it is so important to have cells, support groups, or discipleship groups to help people build relationships and to guide them toward their spiritual maturity. Both large churches and small ones have a great cadre of people who are not committed or not moving toward maturity. You will find Bob Gilliam's list of non-negotiables for a church which calls itself a disciple-making church in Appendix 4.

4. Structures

There tends to be a strong difference of opinion about the importance of Sunday schools or Bible study classes for adults in large churches where the small group or home model of education tends to be the norm. It is important to keep in mind that the average church will get 76 percent of the adults in Sunday school and approximately 25 percent in small groups with a maximum of 60 percent of the congregation in small groups.[156]

We need to listen carefully to what Knute Larson has to say about the importance of adult Bible studies and small groups. "I disagree with church growth people who teach that the church needs to offer only the large celebration and the small cell. Often they have based their teaching on the Cho model in Korea—a different culture, and a church that could use some 'congregational life' as adult Bible fellowships."[157] Knute Larson also suggests to us that there are some strong guidelines for getting people to commit themselves to small groups. "I understand that it is best when you first get people involved to have a terminal time—four weeks, and then they are done. Often the decision to go longer comes after the good initial experience."[158]

Anyone who is responsible for adult ministries in a church must understand that all groups eventually come to closure. Dick Murry underlines that fact when he says, "One of the most difficult things for many persons active in ongoing adult classes is to realize that their class will die. Unlike churches, adult classes by and large do not go on generation after generation, but instead have a life cycle of usefulness. This life cycle varies with different kinds of adult classes."[159] Once you recognize that reality, it becomes extremely important to keep launching new groups. Failure to do so could mean that the adult program will ultimately pass out of existence. The good thing about group closure is that trust and transparency and, consequently, spiritual development can better occur when a group is closed. Also, recognizing the reality of group closure can force you to keep starting new groups which in turn provide many new evangelistic opportunities for the church. Leaders need to keep graphing the attendance of all the groups so they can determine when closure has occurred and when new groups need to be started. Usually a group closes within a year to a year and a half.

Robert Acker says that the delivery system for all that his church does is due to the small group ministries. They also have a telecare ministry system where everyone gets a phone call at least once a month. They see it as a safety net. New Hope Church in Portland also sees that everyone gets a call each month, but they see it as such an important thing that they pay personnel to do the phoning. Both men recognize that adults will not relate in depth to more than one group at a time so they concentrate on building a group for every member of the church and then do not expect adults to identify with more than one group at a time.

Churches that give a great deal of attention to fellowship within a system are quick to work diligently to enfold or assimilate new people within their church. Steve Leas and Roy Oswald provide a helpful model of how one church has taken seriously the task of enfolding. See the appendix of their book called, "The Inviting Church."[160]

Don Bubna in Vancouver, British Columbia, has what he calls the pastor's welcome class during the Sunday school hour. The purpose of the class is to welcome and assimilate new converts, transfer members, and visitors. The class is taught in a cyclical fashion. On any given Sunday, all three groups of people will have a chance to meet other people who are eager to form new relationships and, at the same time, get to meet and to know the pastor more personally.

David Moore gives a video about his church to all the people who visit on any given Sunday. This allows people to go home and get a better look at what this church is all about.

Facility Tension—Modest or Stately

INWARD TO HIS BODY				
Facility	Modest			Stately

My wife and I were shocked with what we saw as we came up out of the subway in our visit to Moscow in 1991. The landscape was scattered with church spires. This is something, of course, we never expected to see. During some seventy-five years of bondage, the Russian people were constantly reminded of the history of the church in Russia. The buildings became a living memorial to a nation that once knew God and, no doubt, was a constant reminder to them that there is a God.

Many congregations are thinking about their facilities, just as the family thinks about the home. Which kind of home will they have, how lavishly will it be decorated, and how well will it be kept?

1. Modest

Both modest and stately are irrelative terms, so it has something to do with who you are and with whom you are trying to minister. Each class and culture hears different messages, but those messages are so critical because they will make a difference as to how effective you are going to be in the years that follow. The modest facility side of the continuum would generally be less ostentatious than the neighborhood in which it is located. There is a strong likelihood that money was not borrowed to build it and that they built something only the most conservative part of the congregation felt they could afford. Ron Sider speaks for these people:

> We are like the rich Corinthian Christians who feasted without sharing their food with the poor members of the church (1 Cor. 11:20–29.) Like them, we fail today to discern the reality of the one worldwide body of Christ (v. 29). The tragic consequence is that we profane the body and blood of the Lord Jesus we worship. Christians in the United States spent $5.7 billion on new church construction alone in the six years from 1967–72. Would we go on building lavishly furnished, expensive church plants and adding air conditioning, carpeting, and organs if members of our own congregations were starving?[161]

These people would want to say strongly to their society that facility is not the thing that is important. It is what goes on *inside* the facility that makes a difference.

E. V. Hill recommended to Mount Zion Church that the money they had saved for their new auditorium should be invested in a home for unwed mothers. That to him and to them was more important right then. Howard Snyder might speak for us by summarizing this position: "The gospel says, 'Go' but our church buildings say, 'Stay.' The gospel says, 'Seek the lost,' but our churches say, 'Let the lost seek the church.' "[162]

2. Stately

The people who stand at this end of the continuum would argue that God wanted the temple to be very stately and wanted it to commemorate the greatness of God. They believed that their church building makes a significant statement. Kent R. Hunter agrees: "Church architecture can communicate a church philosophy of ministry and should be carefully considered any time a congregation plans to build. Does the building suggest openness, mission, outreach? Or is it a foreboding, castle-like fortress?"[163] These people believe that storefront churches portray a transitory, cultic kind of faith and some place that you would not want to call home. When Doug Venezuela and Bruce Martin set out to build a church in the suburbs of Naples, Italy, for their growing evangelical congregation they wanted to build a large brick building because Italians are accustomed to associating God with their cathedrals. Although they did not want to build a cathedral, they wanted people to know that Christianity had roots. They planned on staying there, and it was something that the people could respect.

3. Facility Issues to Keep in Mind

There are two basic issues you need to keep in mind as you think about your facility. First, your facility will make a statement to your community whether you want it to or not. What kind of statement do you want it to make? Second, you must have a facility that will help you fulfill your philosophy of ministry.

Robert Webber reminds us of Winston Churchill's statement. He said, "We shape our buildings and afterward our buildings shape us." If someone walked into your home and declared, 'This is exactly the kind of house I pictured you living in', how would you respond? Is your personal space sometimes a prison because it improperly serves your interests and needs, or is it a haven with room for your growth, development, and comfort? If someone offered to build you a house that would reflect as clearly as possible the essence of who you are, what would you specify?"[164]

Don Bubna took that seriously enough so that when his church built their new auditorium, they built the pulpit into the communion table. They felt that the Word of God being preached is so closely related to the sacraments, they wanted them physically to be tied together so the people would think of them as one. I was equally impressed with how Randy Kinnison and his congregation implemented their philosophy of ministry by building their lavish recreation facility. It was because their philosophy of ministry tied so significantly into recreation, which of course is a significant part of our society.

I have followed with interest a parallel story which took place simultaneously with Gene Getz, Rick Warren, and Dale Schlafer. Each one of them was meeting with their congregations in gymnasiums or places other than a church auditorium. They all kept saying that the church facility was not important. In time, all three of them led their congregations to build new facilities.

Once again, Ron Sider gives us a concluding word to keep in mind as we think about our facilities.

> If we examine what the Bible says about economic relationships among the people of God, we will discover that over and over again, God specifically commanded his people to live together in community in such a way that they would avoid extremes of wealth and poverty. That is the point of Old Testament legislation on the jubilee (Lev. 25) and sabbatical years (Deut. 5), on tithing (Deut. 14:28–29), gleaning (Deut. 24:19–22), and loans (Deut. 15:2; 24:10–11).

When you start thinking seriously about building or remodelling a church facility, it would be wise for you to purchase and use C. Ray Bowman's book, *Church Buildings Source Book* (Beacon Hill Press, Kansas City, MO, 1982).

Traditional U.S. Church Paradigms

Paradigm	Primary Focus	Pastor's & People's Roles	Primary Target	Key Term	Central Value	Tools Used	Worship Style	Source of Legitimacy
Soul Winning	Evangelism	Evangelist & Bringers	The Community	To Save	Decisions for Christ	Visitation & Altar Call	Traditional Evangelism	Number Baptized
Experimental	Worship	Performer & Audience	The Crowd	To Feel	Personal Experience	Stage & Prayer Music	Charismatic	"The Spirit"
Family Reunion Church	Fellowship	Chaplain & Family Members	The Congregation	To Belong	Loyalty & Tradition	Fellowship Hall & Pot Luck	Traditional Evangelism	"Our Roots"
Classroom Church	Edification	Instructor & Students	The Committed	To Know	Bible Knowledge	Notebooks & Overheads	Pedagogical	Expository Preaching
Social Conscience Church	Ministry	Reformer & Activists	The Core	To Care	Justice & Mercy	Petitions & Placards	Liturgical	Number of Needs Met

An Alternate Church Paradigm

Paradigm	Primary Focus	Pastor's & People's Roles	Primary Target	Key Term	Central Value	Tools Used	Worship Style	Source of Legitimacy
Life Development Church	Balance of all Five	Leader-Equipper & Ministers	All Five Constituencies	To Be & To Do	Effective Christlike Lives	Development System	Seeker Sensitive	Changed Lives

Chapter 9

Outward to the World

The apostle Paul had tremendous passion to see the saints mature, but had equal passion to get the gospel out to those who hadn't heard it. But in reality, because of human nature, it's a tough pair (seekers or saints) to combine."[165] These were the words of Bob Thune, but the other three men in the Leadership Forum seemed to agree. Every congregation in America would express itself some place on the continuum between being an inwardly-focused or an outwardly-focused congregation. That is, they would either be a church primarily in existence for enriching themselves or seeking to penetrate the world with the purpose of impacting it with the gospel. The decision on this continuum is reflected in many ways throughout the life and ministry of the congregation.

As leaders consider the three major issues which are defined in chapters 7, 8, and 9, they feel that the theological issues in chapter 7, "Upward to God," should be first in order because these issues influence or drive the church's behavior about its concern for itself and the world which is reflected in chapters 8 and 9. The Peace Portal Alliance Church in Vancouver, British Columbia, expresses its preference in its philosophy of ministry by saying, "We will worship God for who He is and what He has done." They are attempting to express the fact that their being an outward church is driven, first of all, by the fact that they are a congregation that primarily focuses on the worship of God. On the other hand, there is College Avenue Church in San Diego under Gerald Sheveland's leadership saying just the opposite. Their philosophy says, "We exist to win, enfold, equip, and deploy faithful followers of Jesus Christ who experience and express His love and truth in San Diego and to the ends of the earth." After studying chapter 7, you should

161

have concluded what has the priority in your congregation's life: either to be worshiping God or to be expressing your concern for a lost world through some form of evangelism. Everything in this chapter primarily has to do with the biblical mandate to go into all the world and preach the gospel.

Outreach Tension—Seeker or Family of Faith

OUTWARD TO THE WORLD				
Target	Seeker			Family Reunion

Another way to express this continuum would be to say that you are a "closed" church or a "penetrating" church. "Closed" does not imply that you would not be a missional congregation, but it does express how you intend to go about the mission which Christ has given the church.

A church that would express itself in the extreme position of being a seeker-driven church could be defined as follows:

The church is in existence to penetrate the city, not to build the church. The church is a vehicle. Christians are trained and equipped ultimately to penetrate culture for Christ. It sees itself as a missional church where the pastor leads the congregation to make an impact on society. Church services are conducted in a more professional fashion that has the visiting unsaved person as a major focus. This then impacts the content and style of music and preaching which is more seeker-sensitive, felt-need oriented, and focused on the individual. Christian nurture would take place in services other than the Sunday morning worship service. Although membership is encouraged, a greater factor is a predominant concern for the salvation of those outside the church.

Congregations that would end up on that end of the spectrum would agree with Loren Mead and his presuppositions:

> We must come to see that the world, the nation, and the environment is no longer the same as the church. The former understanding no longer holds true. In some new way, we are conscious of the world as separate from [and] different from the church. (1) We can no longer assume that everybody is a Christian. (2) People no longer assume that the community is a unit of the religious world, living out values derived from the gospel. (3) We are returning to one of the features of the Apostolic Age. We now assume that the front door of the church is a door into mission territory, not just a door to the outside.[166]

Saved	Seeing your church's mission to the unsaved	Unsaved
FAMILY REUNION Guest		
	SEEKER SENSITIVE Accommodate	
		SEEKER DRIVEN Focused

The people who would position themselves on the family of faith end of the continuum believe that preaching is concerned with teaching the whole counsel of God in a faithful and relevant way. They see preaching as being effective in impacting evangelism and disciple-making. Music is an expression of body-life worship. Emphasis is placed on God-centered worship and prayer. The entire body is encouraged to be in small fellowship groups which nurture spiritual personal growth and accountability. The body understands mission in the context of the whole world. World Christians are committed to the global impact of the gospel. They are open to learn from the followers of Christ in other cultures and to pray for the impact of the gospel world-wide. Personal commitment to Christ is emphasized as the focus for membership. Each individual Christian is an integral member of the body of Christ and is expected to play a major role in one of its many inward ministries.

It is interesting to hear Pastor Paul Johnson making a switch from being a seeker church to more of a family of faith church. He would perhaps find himself and his congregation in the middle of this continuum. He said, "It wasn't long, though, before I realized my methods were restrictive. My passion for meeting people's needs was building a congregation with ever-increasing needs. The church grew because people came to have their needs met. But when I could no longer meet their needs, they could leave just as quickly as they came. I came to realize that if I didn't change these consumers into investors, before long they would distort the value of the church."[167]

He expresses clearly for us the kind of tension many leaders feel. Consequently new terms are being used to define various positions. Rather than being a seeker-driven church, many of them would say they are a seeker-sensitive church. They want to be aware of the needs of the people who need the gospel. Certainly various ministries in the program of the church would be directed toward the unsaved, but it would not be the primary or the focal point of the ministry of the church.

The major issue here is the way that the church sees the lost and the way they see society. The diagram on the previous page would express the three positions, but primarily the seeker-sensitive position.

Dr. Bruce Shelley exposes us to the historical position represented on this continuum. He says, "The colony exists because on their own the individuals could never survive as citizens in the hostile environment of a strange and alien land. So they work and live together. The colony is not yet fully established, nor out of danger. And yet, it is a haven of refuge, a community, a beginning. In the colony, citizens careful nurture the stories, values and customs of the homeland. They wisely introduce their young ones to a life-style that the surrounding culture neither understands nor respects."[168]

No one in America, Christian or secular, would disagree with the statement that our society is becoming more and more corrupt. Consequently the role of the church being in the world and influencing the world has become more difficult than ever before. You would probably agree with Joe Ellis who says, "The purpose of God in the world is evident in the nature of the church to reconcile a person to himself and to restore [his life] to working order, in harmony with His design. The church is both the product of God's purpose and the means for achieving it. The church is divinely energized in order that it may accomplish its God-given purpose and, conversely, it is divinely energized to the degree that it pursues that purpose."[169]

1. God's Passion for a Lost World

As you wrestle with where you will position yourself on this continuum, the following four kinds of issues will be important to keep in mind. First, you need to listen to God's passion for a lost world. Perhaps Alan Tippett can paint the best picture of God's passion: "The whole Bible vibrates with expectancy—from the psalmist to the evangelist and apostle and the Lord Himself. Of those engaged in the program of Christian mission today, obedience is surely required—but it is expected obedience. If the Bible still speaks to us, it surely speaks of the diffusion of the salvation experience, and the incorporation of the saved into a fellowship. . . . The New Testament has a rich range of picturesque imagery that shows growth is to be expected—both physical, numerical growth from outside and spiritual, qualitative growth from within."[170]

Most all of the major texts on the theology of mission talk about the passion God has for a lost world. Let Eddie Gibbs speak for those authors:

> We learn that church growth is on God's agenda, not simply through a few isolated "missionary texts" but through the long strands of teaching through the previous centuries of divine revelation recorded in the Old Testament. If such growth appears on God's agenda, then it should also appear on ours. He teaches us about all of the covenants which include the new covenant. It is also strongly implied in the fact that the Great Commission was given to all believers as well as being an expression of His harvest for a lost world. "The command to go and make disciples of all

nations occurs as a consequence of the ascended Christ having been given all authority in heaven and earth (Matt. 28:19)."[171]

If you as a congregation are genuinely serious about knowing and pleasing God, you will certainly listen carefully to His heartbeat for a world that is lost and on its way to hell. Once you hear that word, then you need to come to grips with how you will express that passion through the life and ministry of your congregation. You are challenged to come to grips with whether or not your congregation will express God's passion in being involved in the harvest or being a church that is in search of the lost. Church growth authors tell us there is a strong difference between the two, and it is beautifully expressed in the way people go about their mission. If you are in search of the lost, you are given to the idea of going everywhere and sowing the seed, not necessarily of seeking where they are most receptive for the harvest.

The idea of the search arose in the former, more discouraging era of missions in America. "Search maintains," says Peter Wagner, "that in evangelism, the essential thing is not the finding but going everywhere and preaching the gospel for which there is some excellent biblical authority." He goes on:

> We might say that seeking churches are aware of the lost, but not specifically focused on them. They do not have what is sometimes classified as "arovision." They are deeply concerned that the lost are not going to be with Christ eternally, but they are not proactive and intentional in evangelism. They are certainly seed sowers, but find themselves in that great tension of having to juggle the mandate of being a colony of believers who are in missions.[172]

Peter Wagner speaks for the church growth movement by explaining the harvest position:

> Mere search is not what God wants. God wants his lost children found. Let us examine the evidence. "God wants a harvest." Four kinds of biblical evidence nourish the conviction that God has a passion to find the lost. (1) Explicit statements of our Lord and his apostles are against the search position. In Matthew 9:37, seeing the responsiveness of a particular population, our Lord recognized the need for reapers. The whitened fields were God's. Simply walking through them proclaiming Christ's lordship was not enough. God wanted the grain cut (Matt. 10:14, Acts 13:51). (2) Our Lord's parables often emphasize actual finding. At the great banquet, the master did not commend the servant who

brought news that the invited could not come. He did not say, "Continue inviting these indifferent persons until they accept." He said to his servant, "Bring in the poor and the maimed and the lame and the blind." (3) The revelation of God culminating in Christ tells us that God himself is a searching, saving God. God wants people—multitudes of people—reconciled to himself. He was in Christ reconciling the world to himself. (4) Finally, we know that the New Testament church went where people responded, believing this to be God's will.[173]

A congregation that would take the harvest position would go to the fields that are most responsive. It would say that the best way to reach the world for Christ is to win those who are the most responsive first. It feels that they, in turn, will reach the unresponsive because of their relationships networking and their involvement in society with them. Robert McQuilkin adds to that by saying, "God is selective in His approach to men and has consistently involved His representative in that same process of selectivity. Responsive people, for their own sake and for the sake of [the] unresponsive, are always eligible for further light. Unresponsive people may in the grace of God continue to receive light. But (also in His grace) this light is normally diminished in proportion to the rejection of that light."[174]

Willow Creek Community Church, without hesitation, would classify itself as a seeker-driven congregation. Bill Hybels expresses that to his congregation as he gives them further teaching on their philosophy of ministry. In a message he said, "If this church isn't filled with believers who have a penetration mentality, that have a soldier mentality, that have an aggressive mentality—we need to get out and build bridges and establish contact and somehow rub shoulders with Harry and Mary so that some day we can give a witness to them. If not then this church is going to begin to die. Wasn't Jesus saying when he gave the parables in Luke 15 (the lost sheep, the lost coin, the prodigal son) that lost people matter? They matter enough to God to go and warrant a search."

2. Your View of Culture

Part of the subtlety of this tension has to do with the way a congregation views culture. Some churches are like scuba diver churches that have plunged themselves into the culture. They are *among* them, but not one *of* them. II. R. Niebuhr originally designed a taxonomy which expresses the various views that congregations hold concerning culture. Eddie Gibbs summarizes these and adds a sixth position. It would be advantageous to make a thorough study of these various positions, but they are best summarized for us by Gibbs:

> H. R. Niebuhr has shown the range of thinking with regard to the relationship between Christ and culture adopted by theologians from various times (1951). (1) Christ against culture. This view sets Christ against the world for the world is (in) the power of the evil one. (2) Christ of culture. Christ is regarded as the inspirer and perfecter of culture. (3) Christ above culture. Christ is the fulfillment of cultural aspirations and the restorer of the aspirations and the restorer of the institutions of true society. There is something that arises neither out of culture nor contributes directly to it. (4) Christ and culture in paradox. Christ is above culture but fails to achieve a workable synthesis. This leaves the believer to live with the tension of relating to the world. (5) Christ the transformer of culture. Culture is there to be converted rather than replaced by something entirely new. (6) God exists totally outside of culture while humans exist totally within culture. God chooses the cultural milieu in which humans are immersed as the arena for his interaction with people (number 6 was added by Kraft in 1979).[175]

If a congregation sees culture as being corrupt, it might tend to isolate itself from the world. However, if it sees that Christ could transform the culture through its own presence in the world, then it might be a congregation that penetrates society personally with the gospel. You may be surprised to find that your position on culture will predetermine whether or not you will be a seeker-sensitive or family of faith church. It has been fascinating to watch over the years how one's view of culture very seriously impacts and influences one's missional mandate and the church's effectiveness in its evangelistic ministry (see Appendix 6, "A Look at the Six Views of Culture," for a list of questions that will help you think through your cultural position).

I was interested to see an expression of this in my interview with David Moore. He said that he brought beer to one of the block parties they sponsored because he felt that was a way that he could better reach his neighbors. He testified that the next Sunday, the front row was filled with people from the party. David Moore went on to say that he felt that many people needed to be anonymous as they came to his church since they recognized the church stood for a cultural value system that may be somewhat different from their own.

Leith Anderson said that the church does not need to be ashamed or afraid to proclaim the gospel very clearly to people who visit on Sundays. "When I go to a restaurant, I expect to be served food. At a concert, I expect to hear music. In an art museum, I expect to see art. In the doctor's office, I expect there to be talk about medicine. I am never surprised or offended that these people and places present what they represent. The same goes for the church. Churches are people and places where God is expected to be present and his book is no surprise."[176]

When you finally sit down to make this decision, hear clearly a word from Elton Trueblood. The church is "always failing when it becomes an institution which is bent on saving itself. It cannot save the world if it demonstrates an obsession with material things."[177]

3. The Size of the Church

A question in the Institute for Church Development survey inquires whether or not a congregation wants to see itself grow numerically. It has been extremely educational for me to watch how significant the size of the church is in reference to its response. Congregations that are in the thousands often will mark that question with an average of 35 percent wanting growth. That percentage goes as high as 90 percent when the congregation is small and/or declining. I am not suggesting that the number of attendees in a morning service be the driving force for attendance, but it does have a residual effect on a church's ability or inability to be effective in its evangelism. Orlando Costas warns us about the danger here: "Numerical expansion is of utmost importance, but in order for it to take place, it needs the depth of qualitative and organic growth. Consequently organic and qualitative growth must lead to quantitative growth; and conversely, quantitative growth should be seen, generally speaking, as an indication of some form of organic and qualitative growth."[178]

People who argue strongly that the church should not be concerned about numbers are basically expressing a position that may suggest that Jesus is not interested in people. Of course there is always a great danger that the church is interested in numbers for numbers' sake, and it is easy to fall into that error. Numbers need to be studied because they do give a church insight into its effectiveness in reaching the lost world.

There are as many pitfalls in a small church as in a large church. For instance, two cell churches end up fighting. A church ought to have numerous groups or clusters to prevent that. On the other hand, large churches who adequately focus on celebration and cell can minister to thousands of people, while churches who are focusing just on congregation can only minister to hundreds. We need to be reminded that large megachurches can readily end up treating people impersonally. I am also reminded, however, that I have been in numerous small churches where at times people are treated more impersonally than in large churches. To be either a large church or a small church does not guarantee godliness.

Rick Warren, who pastors a megachurch, says from his point of view that megachurches can do a better job of ministry. He sees these four elements as being significant in a large church: (1) They are more salvific—they are like the churches in Acts; (2) they have more specialized ministries for a world that lives every day with many options; (3) they can attract believers because so many of them want to be anonymous; and (4) by virtue of their size and volume, they can have a greater impact on community.[179]

Leith Anderson, who often speaks for the megachurch movement, defines the megachurch:

> Megachurches have 2,000 or more people at worship services each weekend. They are large shopping malls, offering a broad array of services to enormous numbers of people. Megachurches have large staffs, require expansive facilities, operate on multimillion dollar budgets, provide an impressive variety of services, tend to be leader-led, and often have excellent preaching and music. . . . It is important to recognize that megachurches are not large versions of minichurches, just as a train is not a large car. They are different kinds of churches. They relate differently.[180]

It is my strong conviction that every church, no matter what its size, must ultimately think about planting another congregation. There are some serious dangers when you do not hold that position. You may eventually no longer be able to reach the unsaved because your facility is filled or because you have become so large you no longer have concern for a community around you that is without Christ.

However, it may not be advantageous for you to plant a church because there will not be enough of the critical mass remaining in your mother church. You could readily end up with the death of the mother by giving birth prematurely. More will be said about the size of churches and evangelism in the discussion of the next tension.

Evangelism Tension—Program- or Personal-directed

OUTWARD TO THE WORLD					
Evangelism	Program-directed				Personal-directed

In 1900 in America, there were 27 churches for every 10,000 Americans. In 1985, there were only 12 churches for every 10,000

Americans. Some place in America every day, an average of nine churches die.[181] These two startling facts ought to awaken us to the fact that evangelism and church planting is urgently needed in America. Obviously, the American church must return to the passion of the church in Acts. Roger Greenway underlines that ideal: "In Acts 8:1 we read, 'and all were scattered abroad except the apostles.' Therefore, according to the emphasis of this passage, those who went everywhere preaching the Word were everyone except the apostles. The term translated 'preaching the word' is from the Greek, *euaggelizomai*, which means, of course, to evangelize. Thus, in the early church all of the laymen went everywhere evangelizing. This is the lost ideal we are striving to regain."[182] All Christian leaders will quickly identify with that biblical mandate, but the major question is how will it be done? There tends to be a great division between those who feel that more programs will get it done, while others feel that it should be and could be done if individual persons in the body of Christ would take the initiative to evangelize those around them.

1. Program-directed

Those who would vie for the program side of that tension have a certain set of assumptions. They would say that all believers are not self-starters, but that they are better disciplined in the context of other people directing them through programs. They tend to be more motivated through groups. They would also say that a small majority of people have the relationship skills necessary to become evangelistic on their own. Just as each individual person ought to worship in a fashion which relates to his or her temperament, people ought to evangelize in the way that is fitting with their relationship style.

Jay Carty reminds us that approximately 85 percent of Americans need help in relating and in evangelizing. He says that 15 percent of Americans develop mono-relationships, that is, relationships which slowly but deeply are evolving over a long period of time. Fifteen percent of Americans are comfortable in multi-relationships, quickly developing many relationships but being content with relationships that are more shallow. Most of these people, when spiritually motivated, will witness on their own. Seventy percent of Americans tend to build relationships along common interest lines. That is, the need or the interest is the root or the relationship. Mono-relationship and common interest people are those who do need help in learning to relate and, therefore, need help to be active in evangelism.[183]

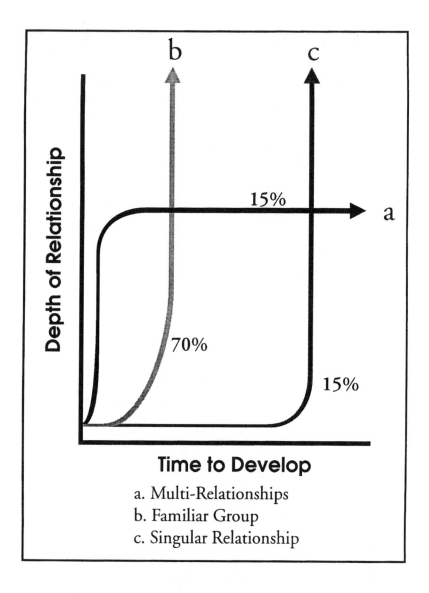

Depth of Relationship

b
c
15% a

70%

15%

Time to Develop
a. Multi-Relationships
b. Familiar Group
c. Singular Relationship

2. Personal-directed

Those who would identify themselves on the personal-directed side of the continuum would strongly believe that since Christians possess the presence of the Holy Spirit in their lives, that in itself is sufficient to lead them into a life of witnessing.

Those who personally agree with the personal-directed end of the continuum would say that Christians will be motivated and directed by the Holy Spirit to evangelize since the Holy Spirit is present in each Christian's life. They would use Acts 5:39–42 as the guide for this position: "But if it is from God you will not be able to stop these men. You will only find yourself fighting against God." They would further go on to say that the church does not need programs because the body of Christ is an organism that has infused the spiritual life. They would argue that a programmatic style of evangelism would tend to be legalistic in its nature and therefore not be as effective. If there is life within the body of Christ, then you do not need to prime the pump with programs. They would strongly say that evangelism was caught not taught. The average person can no more learn to evangelize in a classroom than he or she can learn to fly an airplane in the living room.

Myron Augsburger points out: "Some people assume that evangelism is a church-sponsored program that prescribes particular verbal formulas to be delivered at certain times. Inadvertently, perhaps, they compartmentalize life into times of evangelism: one or two hours on a weekday evening and times for other things. Evangelism for us isn't relegated to a time slot, nor to one or two types of activities. In short, evangelism is practiced as a way of life. It is not surprising, then, that barriers come down, and that people hear and believe the good news of the gospel."[184] Mr. Augsburger would certainly argue that the habit of witnessing ought to come with a spirit of spontaneity within a redemptive community because the church is a living organism.

As you read the late Ray Stedman, you quickly get the impression that during his long tenure as pastor, he moved from a more programmatic to a more personal form of evangelism and felt that it was more biblical. He wrote:

> The one clear conviction was derived from Ephesians 4, that the work of the ministry belonged to the people and not to the pastor. I was rather vague as to what that ministry was, but felt from the first that my task as pastor was to unfold the Word of God in its fullness (as best I could understand it) and leave to laymen the major responsibility for visitation of the sick, presiding at the leading church services, and evangelizing the world. We determined from the start that all evangelization would be done in homes, backyards, rented halls, or other public meeting places.[185]

Richard Halverson would certainly agree with the personal style of evangelism but would strongly suggest that community is critical to that personal witness when he says, "Community is the matrix of mission. A congregation without community cannot fulfill its evangelism mission, whatever is done to exhort or train. When there is community then it will happen spontaneously . . . people will be attracted. Community happened at Pentecost. That day a new, absolutely unique social entity was born."

3. Evangelism Issues

To help you reach the decision where your church should be on this continuum, you will need to consider the following issues. First, it is important that you have a proper definition for evangelism. Robert McQuilkin defines evangelism as "proclaiming the way to life in Christ in such a way as to give people a clear understanding of this good news so that they may choose to become His disciples and a part of His church."[186]

Orlando Costas amplifies that definition of evangelism by reminding us of what the essential ingredients of salvation are. Therefore in our witnessing, we need to lead non-believers to conversion which includes "a threefold meaning: (1) liberation from the power of sin and death (Rom. 8:1–2); (2) adoption into the family of God (John 1:12; Rom. 8:16–17, 29; Gal. 3:16, 26–29; 4:5b–7; 1 John 2:1–2); (3) participation in the reign of Christ (Eph. 1:2; Rev. 1:5f)."[187]

4. Agents of Salvation

In the process of making this decision, it is important to do your theology about the role of God and the role of man in evangelism. Psalm 21:27 says that unless the Lord builds the house, its builders labor in vain. We are reminded in this text that it is possible to build a church without God. At the same time, it suggests that unless God is active with man in the building of the church as fellow workers (1 Cor. 3:9), then it will be an exercise in total futility. Ask yourself, "Have I ever seen a church that God built all by Himself?" Certainly we have seen many that men have built by themselves. Not only do men play a major role in the building of the church, but believers have an important responsibility in selecting their target for evangelism.

May I suggest that praying for God's wisdom in the selection of your target is extremely essential? The final responsibility lies in our hands, however, not only to discover the responsive group of people but to go in the direction of the ripe harvest. If we do own the idea that we are to go to the most responsive people, then we may find ourselves ministering more in the suburbs than in the urban communities since there tends to be a greater response to Christ in the suburbs than in the inner cities of America. Robert McQuilkin teaches that God's selectivity is based upon people's response (Gen. 6:3; Rom. 9:11–18). He believes that the unresponsive might be won by the responsive. Consequently God expects His agents to participate in selectivity (Matt. 7:6; Acts 18:6–11; 1 Cor. 16:8–9).[188]

Mission Hills Baptist Church would demonstrate that selectivity principle by targeting their evangelism to the middle-class society of the suburbs of Denver. At the same time, however, they are sending personnel and finances to the city under the supervision of Mile Hi Ministries so they can continue to encourage people in the inner city to come to Christ in their own setting. It is critical that you do your theology carefully in dealing with these issues. A study of these works will help you make decisions about targeting and receptivity: Eddie Gibbs, *I Believe in Church Growth* (Eerdmans, 1981), chapters 1 and 2; C. Peter Wagner, *Understanding Church Growth*, 3rd edition (Eerdmans, 1990), part I; Robert McQuilkin, *How Biblical Is the Church Growth Movement?* (Moody Press,1973). See Appendix 7 for a further list of helpful material on evangelism.

5. Lordship Salvation

The interfacing of the kingdom view of evangelism and lordship evangelism are other major issues which need to be addressed in determining the agents and targets of evangelism.

There has been a great deal of argument as to what a new inquirer needs to know before he or she makes a decision to follow Jesus Christ. What entails the most meaningful decision? The First Evangelical Free Church of Rockford, Illinois, felt this was so significant that they included in their philosophy of ministry a statement about what Lordship salvation looked like. They followed the guidelines as they discovered them in the book of Acts and in the Great Commission. "These traits were the ones they saw in New Testament disciples: (a) open identification with Christ; (b) students of the Word like the Bereans; (c) prayer was the primary activity; (d) they spent time with each other in community; and (e) they were engaged in evangelism and service."

One of the most comprehensive statements about Lordship salvation was made in *The Pasadena Consultation*. I include the lengthy statement to help you make a clear and clarion call to those who come to Christ.

We agree that to preach the gospel is to proclaim Jesus Christ in the fullness of His person and work; that this is to "preach the kingdom" which embraces both the total salvation and the total submission implicit in gracious rule of God, and that it is always wrong to preach Jesus as Savior without presenting Him also as Lord, since it is precisely because He is the supreme Lord exalted to the Father's right hand that He has the authority to bestow salvation and the power to rescue sinners from sin, fear, evil, the thraldom of spirits, and death. We agree that in what has been called "lordship evangelism" we must not isolate from one another the separate parts of Christ's commission, namely to "make disciples," to "baptize," and to "teach"; that the Christian nurture of converts is indispensable because Christian growth is not automatic; and that daily repentance and daily obedience are necessary parts of Christian discipleship. We agree that the call to repentance must always be faithfully sounded; that there can be no repentance without ethical content; and that the precise ethical issues will vary according to each situation.[189]

Eddie Gibbs reminds us that too simple a view of salvation or cheap grace may be a big danger to the church. He says, "Mission is not simply self-proliferation, for the church is not the kingdom. As Rene Padilla cautions, 'To speak of the kingdom of God is to speak of the purpose of God of which the empirical church is little more than pale reflection (Padilla, 1975).' He goes on to say if Christians see their spiritual vocation in life simply in terms of making other Christians, many areas of life can be conveniently overlooked. Their light may shine with a narrowness of a laser beam rather than provide the illumination of a beacon."[190]

6. Evangelism of Children

It is alarming that so little is being said and written about the evangelism of children since approximately 50 percent of the converts in American churches are children.[191] My years of study and observation of the church in reference to the evangelism of children teaches me that there is little study and thought that goes into the church's program of the evangelism of children. It is quite likely that many children prematurely come to faith in Christ without a solid foundation and understanding of what commitment means; therefore, later on in life they practice little of the commitment which tends to be expected by their Master. If salvation includes a commitment of one's life to Christ, then they ought to be old enough to make a lifetime commitment to show their genuine desire to follow Jesus Christ.[192] Maybe this is the major issue in what is often called the age of accountability.

7. The Evangelizers

Forty-two percent of those people responded saying that they personally participated in an evangelism endeavor in the last six months. It is noteworthy, however, that in those churches, they only saw 0.02 percent of their congregation coming to Christ per year during the last decade.[193] You might find that surprising since the findings of Fuller School of Church Growth suggests that in the most highly active evangelistic churches, only ten percent of the people are actively involved in the programs of evangelism in their local church. Obviously, a high percentage of this 42 percent saw their participation in evangelism as teaching Sunday school class, inviting someone to church, or making a friend of an unsaved person at work or in the neighborhood.

Further evidence of the seeming lack of evangelism in the local church is reflected in the fact that only 18 percent of the people in our church data base at the Institute for Church Development reflected that they came to Christ through the ministry of the local congregation where they currently attend. This, no doubt, has a great deal to do with the fact that transfer growth is so high in evangelical churches, plus the fact that parachurch organizations sometimes have more effect on evangelism than local churches.

It is important to keep in mind that the longer people have been Christians and in the church, the more difficult it is for them to have the necessary friendship contacts that produce potential converts. The chart on the next page reminds us that 70 to 80 percent of the converts come through the contacts they have with nonconverts. Bonding among adults usually takes place between new attendees and members in the church within a period of 12-18 months if it is going to happen. As they move into the community they soon do not have time or space in their lives to make connections with other non-Christians whom they used to know in the world. It takes a great deal of time to maintain church friendships. If the church does not continue to have new converts, they very shortly will not have those potential contacts in the world that are needed for a growing evangelism program. Great effort must be given to help the new Christians constantly bring their friends to Christ if the spiritual/psychological growth system is to keep bringing people into the context of the gospel and the church.

In a recent survey the Evangelical Free Churches of America discovered that the pastors played a far more significant role in evangelism than the laity. The following chart shows that the larger the church, the more important the pastor's own evangelism emphasis is in terms of encouraging and empowering participation by members.[194]

New churches have a higher evangelism rate than older churches. The exception is the church that is 5-15 years old.

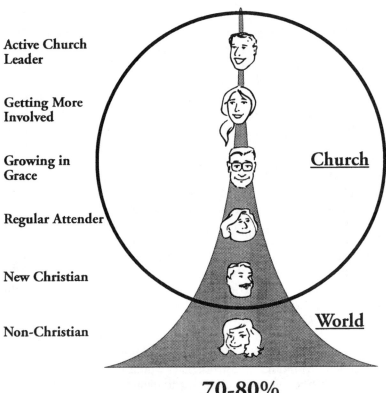

Active Church Leader

Getting More Involved

Growing in Grace

Regular Attender

New Christian

Non-Christian

<u>Church</u>

<u>World</u>

70-80%
Friends and Relatives

Evangelism and Church Age

youngest	9.6
young	6.8
older	7.7
oldest	7.7

rate = # persons won per hundred members.

1. In the average Evangelical Free Church of America, it takes 99 layman and 1 pastor per year to win 8 persons to Christ a year and retain 6.2 of them as attenders. Senior pastors average winning 3 persons a year to Christ and retaining 2 of these as attendees.
2. The average church wins 9.8 persons to Christ per year and retains 6.2 as attendees.
3. Of those won to Christ,
   10% are pre-schoolers and 80% of them are retained
   33% are elementary age and 67% of them are retained
   41% are adults and 60% of them are retained

   It should be noted here that childhood conversions are not well recorded.
4. Of all persons won to Christ, 48% are won by the senior minister alone!
5. Seventy-three percent of those won by the senior pastor are adults.

Church Size and Correlation

Largest	+.67
Large	+.56
Small	−.04
Smallest	−.03

As you give further thought to the target of your mission and the receptivity of that target, it is significant to see who has played a major role in the conversion of those in church: the preacher, 21 percent; Sunday school/VBS teacher, 13 percent; friends and relatives, 14 percent; own search, 7 percent; parachurch, 3 percent; media, 1 percent; other 8 percent. This study, along with others, validates what has long been believed; recent converts are the ones who have the greatest potential to reach people for Christ. They still have their connections in their old society and have the greatest potential of introducing them to Christ. The longer a person is in the church, the less connections he or she has with society.

Calvin Ratz is quick to remind us of the church's failure to train people for evangelism which perhaps accounts for their ineffectiveness in evangelism, when he says:

> Whether it's IBM or Disney World, growing companies spend lavishly on training. They've learned that taking a person off the job and sending him through a training program not only increases his productivity, it also builds confidence and morale. Training costs are an integral part of annual budgets in successful companies.[195]

8. Equipping for Evangelism

The church really has no excuse today for not being involved constantly in training its people in evangelism. There are numerous home videos and a great variety of courses which can be used either in church or at home, plus classes and courses offered by parachurch organizations and local training institutions in most major cities. Perhaps the major problem is not a lack of sources for training but a lack of motivation to do so. The workers analysis suggests that the average church ought to have at least 10 percent of its congregation engaged in some form of evangelism.[196]

It is noteworthy that more and more congregations are hiring ministers or directors of evangelism. It is important that they take into consideration the only major text that deals with such a role. Ephesians 4:12 suggests that "Christ has given to the church pastors, teachers, and evangelists so that the saints might be equipped so that they might do the work of evangelism" (paraphrase). I have observed in numerous churches where there is a director of evangelism that often the work of evangelism tends to be isolated in that office and under his or her supervision. It may be noteworthy to see that the Ephesians text suggests that the pastor/teacher has the role of directing other's activities in evangelism and not doing it alone.

The Mission Hills philosophy statement departmentalizes all age groupings of the congregation and gives each one of them the responsibility of leading their respective groups in worship, missions, stewardship, and shepherding. In their philosophy statement they suggest, "Therefore in all areas of our church life, we will seek to motivate, train, equip, and organize people to do Jesus' ministry."

The Evangelical Free Church of America suggests a means to

get everyone in the congregation involved in evangelism. "It is not wise to ask people in your church if they want to be involved in evangelism because evangelism is everyone's responsibility. Instead, ask them how they want to start being involved and give them three options: (1) Be a 'teller' of the gospel. Ask them to choose one of the several options for evangelistic approaches in your church; (2) Be a 'bringer.' Ask them to specify to which evangelistic activities they will bring an unsaved person. They, then, become a part of that team for a year; or (3) Be a 'pray-er.' Ask them to specify one evangelistic approach to pray for, and feed them prayer requests and answers weekly."[197]

9. Programs of Evangelism

Those churches and leaders who are afraid of facilitating their evangelism by programmatic means are often afraid the program, rather than the Holy Spirit, will empower the ministry of evangelism. It is important, however, to keep in mind that any structure such as preaching, teaching, counseling, evangelistic training programs, and the printed page could be seen as programs of evangelism. It is noteworthy, however, that often programs tend to run themselves. Therefore those who move in that direction could err very quickly at that point. They must constantly give themselves to seeing that they are working together with the Holy Spirit in the ministry of evangelism.[198]

10. Target Ministries

Most churches in America that have had a certain amount of success in evangelism have built multiple approaches to help them reach people who have common needs or identify with common groups. Of course, what is advantageous is that 70 percent of the people who best relate to common interest groups are those who have the greatest potential to minister to these various "target ministries." Tommy Barnett's church in Phoenix, First Assembly of God, has more than 40 target ministries. E. V. Hill talks about the 60 or more target ministries which his church carries out in the Watts area in Los Angeles.

It is fascinating to see the list of the hundreds of kinds of target approaches to evangelism. Most of them arc owned by the people yet are carried out under the auspices of their local church. I have only space to list a couple of creative ways of approaching target evangelism. A trained team of people from Foothills Bible Church of Denver recently went door to door and offered professional landscaping advice to the new home owners in their area as a means of showing interest in their new neighbors. This was one way to make a connection with these people and then invite them to their church. Steve Speichinger (who was the pastor in Goodland, Kansas, during the farm crisis) had a "Farm Crisis Recovery" seminar. Of course, these were held within the church facility. As he linked up with city, state, and national farm agencies, he found a tremendous receptivity. In that context the people were offered spiritual guidance and counsel which would aid them through their current crises.

I have also seen recently that a number of churches are using the ever-increasing dinner theater held in their local facility as a means of inviting their community to participate in their church's programs and ministry. Trinity Baptist Church of Mesa, Arizona, is one of those churches which has had a most effective means of reaching their community through the dinner theater. Many gifted people in their congregations have found a great deal of pleasure and fulfillment in this endeavor.

Pastor Bard Marshall of Bethel Baptist Church in McMinnville, Oregon, has seen thousands of people come to Christ through evangelism tapes which are personally distributed to interested people in their community. This is one of numerous means used to introduce people to Christ in the comfort and security of their own home.[199]

Whether you leave it up to each individual to allow the Holy Spirit to work through him or her or you design programs and strategies to utilize the laity in evangelism, be aware of this final caution: "Some people assume that evangelism is a church-sponsored program that prescribes particular verbal formulas to be delivered at certain times. Inadvertently, perhaps, they compartmentalize life into times of evangelism—one or two hours on a weekday evening—and times for other things. . . . Evangelism for us isn't relegated to a time slot, nor to one or two types of activities. In short, evangelism is practiced as a way of life. It is not surprising, then, that barriers come down and that people hear and believe the good news of the gospel."[200]

People Tension—Homogeneous or Heterogeneous

OUTWARD TO THE WORLD				
People	Homogeneous			Heterogeneous

One of the most emotionally charged issues among American church leaders has to do with the issue of leading a congregation to become a heterogeneous or homogeneous church. Periodically, I have encountered lay people who are concerned, but for the most part, it is a theological and church leadership issue.

1. An Homogeneous Unit

Peter Wagner and Donald McGavran have pioneered the idea of the homogeneous unit principle within church growth literature. They would summarize their idea by saying that there is a section of society in which all members have some characteristics in common. They believe that people most often do not come to Christ when they have to cross ethnic, linguistic or social barriers. They strongly agree that the church ought to remove as many barriers in their relationship with society as possible. These might keep people from coming to Christ. Therefore it is easier for the unsaved to come to Christ within the context of their homogeneous unit. In their opinion, this approach is a means to an end and not an end in itself. They see that culture has integrity and validity, and it need not divide the church or the fellowship within the church. They say that the barriers to the acceptance of the gospel are often more sociological than theological. Thus, they feel that people reject the gospel not because they think it is false, but because it strikes them as alien.[201]

2. The Heterogeneous Position

The people who own the heterogeneous position believe that the church should seek to evangelize and cross the seeming barriers which society has established such as geographic, ethnic, linguistic, social, educational, vocational, economic, or a combination of these and other factors. They should seek to do so because the church is to be a unity, and that maturity ultimately reflects that unity. They would suggest that if certain peoples are won to Christ in an homogeneous unit context, then they would be called to a faith and practice that is not biblical.

You would hear these people strongly emphasizing such texts as 1 Corinthians 9:22 as a plea for the unity of the body. "I have become all things to all men that by all possible means I might save some." Thus they are suggesting that the New Testament church was totally integrated. If we are going to be a biblical church today, then we need to be a totally integrated church. Those who take the extreme position would say that Christ demands unity in the body and that unity implies the potential of all believers worshiping together. The people on this side of the issue work very hard to integrate the church services and programs as much as possible. They would seek to model unity and integration as much as possible.

3. Commonness of the Homogeneous Unit Position (HUP)

By and large the majority of churches in America are homogeneous churches. Schaller, however, suggests there are two major exceptions to that rule:

> The homogeneous unit principle is the most controversial statement in contemporary evangelistic efforts. Literalists have assumed this means pluralistic congregations cannot experience numerical growth—and that often appears to reflect reality. There are, however, two major exceptions to the homogeneous unit principle. First, many highly pluralistic congregations do experience numerical growth if a sensitive, systematic, and continuing effort is made to manage congregational life to accommodate and affirm pluralism. Second, highly pluralistic congregations that fit the behavioral model often experience numerical growth. Frequently, the only characteristic the members of the behavioral church share in common is an appreciation for that nurturing style of congregational life. . . . they place a high value on nurture, even though they may differ in many other ways.[202]

It has been interesting to note that many more churches think they are HUP churches when, in fact, they really are not. They may say they believe in it and teach it, but in fact they practice just the opposite. For instance, they might have a strong singles ministry but say in fact that they are a homogeneous church. They realize, however, that if you are going to reach singles for Christ, you need to do so with a singles ministry.

It is important to keep in mind as you search through this issue that churches are more neighborhood-type churches than the average person realizes. The average person simply drives six miles and 12.1 minutes to get to church. Of course, many people drive longer distances, but the average is closer to the church facility than the anonymous leader realizes.[203]

4. Preaching

Grouping of adults for fellowship and education plus preaching are the two places that most readily express a congregation's commitment to heterogeneity. Lyle Schaller provides for us some insight about the difficulty of preaching across ethnic and cultural lines when he says that "content analysis of black preaching and white preaching suggests black preachers are more likely to emphasize Old Testament texts and to stress visual imagery while white preachers tend to rely more on New Testament texts and to verbalize abstract concepts."[204]

As a student of figures from church surveys, I have noticed with keen interest how difficult it is to preach to people from widely differing educational and cultural backgrounds. In the Institute for Church Development's data base, there are questions which speak to a congregation's ability to hear and appreciate the pastor's message. The categories in the survey often show that both ends of the spectrum do not have the same appreciation for the pastor's message. In fact, over a period of time one group tends to stay with the preacher, and the others will often move on to another church where they feel they can be more adequately fed.

5. *Working with the HUP*

One of the best ways to understand the need for or difficulty of working with one of the two groups is to take a look at what Ralph Winter has defined as the three evangelism targets. They are defined as, "some common grounds culturally: (1) E-1—You have a head start in evangelism, (2) E-2—I understand only partially, and (3) E-3—includes all those people beyond any significant common ground of language and culture, people totally strange to us."[205] Most church leaders will readily tell you that evangelism is much easier at the E-1 level and becomes increasingly difficult as you move to E-3 level.

When a church finds itself in a transition neighborhood and the congregation is substantially different than the neighborhood in which the church is located, the congregation generally faces a real crisis. Will it move to a neighborhood that is more like the church, or will it try to reach the community that is moving in around them? If it is going to do that, then it needs to take on a missional mind-set as is best expressed in John 12:24: "Unless a kernel of wheat falls to the ground and dies, it remains only a single seed. But if it dies, it produces many seeds."

John suggests that if missionaries are going to produce many seeds, they need to change their culture to more readily identify with the people they are trying to reach. Many missionaries who have the right heart and desire find that change extremely difficult as they go to other continents and cultures. There are very few people in congregations who have the desire and the ability to make that kind of transition. Most churches who cannot make that kind of change end up eventually in the church burial grounds.

Midway through my daughter and her family's first four-year term in Italy as missionaries, my wife and I went to pay them a visit. As good parents, we both readily identified with the traumatic change she was going through as she was trying to become Italian when, in fact, our daughter was raised as a strong Anglo. It was simply her sheer determination and the abundant grace of God that enabled her to eventually make that transition. While we were there watching her suffer through that cultural death and transition, we came to understand what it means to be a missional church in a changing society. If a congregation is serious about ministering to its changing neighborhood, then it needs to take this biblical principle to heart.

If you have watched groups on both extremes, as I have, you will see that they both have mental traps. Evangelism can and does take place within a heterogeneous congregation, but because it is much more difficult and often growth comes slower, there tends to be a greater level of discouragement. I have found that people sometimes assume a holier-than-thou attitude because they feel they are taking a more righteous position that enables them to continue in their pursuit of that kind of grouping. On the other hand, the homogeneous crowd faces the danger of becoming ingrown and exclusive, therefore showing little concern for other groups of society. Russ Rosser has led his congregation to a beautiful expression of the blending of heterogeneous and homogeneous principles. His church has five different congregations that meet separately each Sunday, but often have the Lord's supper together to celebrate their unity in Christ.

Listen to him talk about his church in Flushing, New York: "We are committed to becoming one congregation—one church with one body and one staff—oneness with diversity. We are committed to heterogeneity and/or homogeneity. The mature believers are committed to a heterogeneous body. The new believers are usually more comfortable being homogeneous with their own. We are committed to team, unity, and being homogeneous. These are three important things for us."

If a congregation holds strongly to the HUP position, then it has a far greater responsibility to send missionaries, perhaps even from its own congregation, to other groups who are not like that church in its own city.

For further study about this tension, I would recommend reading works by Shanks, Schaller, and Wagner.[206]

Morality Tension—Creation or Redemptive Theology

OUTWARD TO THE WORLD				
Morality	Creation			Redemptive Theology

No Christian I know seriously questions whether Christians ought to be involved in the world. We are already in the world, like it or not. We vote, buy, sell, and eat in the world. Our religious actions and beliefs have sociological consequences and vice versa. So the question is not *whether* we should be involved or concerned politically or socially; but the question is *how*.

Churches have been struggling with this issue since the beginning of the New Testament church. Denominations have split from other denominations, and individual churches have split over the issue.

1. Redemptive Theology

"Jesus came to seek and save the lost" (Luke 19:10). Picking up the biblical mandate of Christ, the church is to seek and save the lost. Bruce Shelley defines this position well. He says the way the evangelistic church "faces the challenges of their changing world is . . . clearly focused on 'eternal life' rather than on 'social action.' It is concerned over the deterioration of traditional standards of personal morality, but is persuaded that the conversion of a significant number of individuals is the best way to change the world."[207]

Yamaguchi warns us about the dangers on both ends of the continuum. "Although this is neither a completely accurate nor a universally valid characterization, it is fair to say that in the last fifty years theological liberals have tended to stress social issues to the exclusion of the preaching of the Gospel to individuals, whereas theological conservatives have done the reverse."[208]

2. Creation Theology

These people would strongly emphasize wholistic salvation. The people who are on the extreme end of this position would say that the ultimate will of God is to change society. They might even go so far as to say that working toward the wholistic redemption of society is, therefore, strong evidence that they are born again. Bruce Shelley also gives us a definition for this group which he calls the activist position: "They are most common in theologically liberal churches where they have been taught that God is concerned about the unjust structures of society and that the ministry of the church is advocacy of the cause of every 'oppressed minority' within society. Jesus was not so much a divine Savior as a social liberator."[209] Peter Wagner would add to that definition by saying:

> The specific content of the cultural mandate is awesome. God expects a great deal of those to whom he has entrusted the earth and all of its goodness. Distribution of wealth, the balance of nature, marriage and the family, human government, keeping the peace, cultural integrity, liberation of the oppressed—these and other global responsibilities rightly fall within the cultural mandate.[210]

Liberation theologians would strongly identify themselves with this end of the continuum because they have held to the idea that Jesus is a social liberator.

As you start to struggle with where you are and where you want to be on this continuum, take a look at the taxonomy provided in the Lausanne Mission statement: (1) The mission involves the cultural mandate only; (2) they prioritize the cultural mandate over the evangelistic mandate; (3) they give equal weight to both mandates and refuse to prioritize either; (4) they prioritize the evangelistic mandate over the cultural mandate; and (5) they hold the pre-Lausanne view that mission is the evangelistic mandate.[211]

I have conducted consultations in churches that represent both ends of the continuum. This has forced me to study why they have taken the position which is represented in their philosophy of ministry. In doing so, I have come to see how you can readily choose either side of the tension. Maybe the Lord knew how quick we would be to polarize around one side or the other to the exclusion of the opposite position. The following set of questions, when they are honestly answered, should help you to determine your position on this continuum.

3. What Is Morality?

Dietrich Bonhoeffer suggests that we not concern ourselves with "'How can I be good, and how can I do good,' but he must ask the utterly and totally different question, 'What is the will of God?' . . . The aim of ethical reflection is, then, that I myself shall be good and that the world shall become good through my actions."[212] Webster says that morals are "doctrines, principles of conduct based on distinction between right and wrong."[213] Morality always has to do with absolutes. For the Christian, of course, there are biblical absolutes about behavior, and we must be totally honest about our living by those standards.

On the other hand, ethics are defined by Webster as dealing with "a system of morality; a system of the study of moral action." In that study of morality, ethics involves a unitary character of truth in the universal validity of moral norms.[214] That leads us to think about the authority of Scripture and our translation of God's law.

4. Is Your Hermeneutic Honest?

It is extremely critical that you carefully do your theology with an underlying biblical hermeneutic on each one of the tensions. Probably none of them is more critical and more difficult than this one. John Stott says, "One's deep uneasiness about the current ecumenical writing is basically hermeneutical. It concerns the treatment of Scripture, both Old Testament and New Testament."[215] He further addresses the idea by suggesting that the liberation of Israel from the Egyptian oppressors is often used to teach the liberation of people in Christ. Some people's hermeneutic takes them from that to its seeming application in Luke 4:18. Here Stott says:

> Material poverty, physical blindness, and unjust imprisonment are all conditions which in different degrees dehumanize human beings. They should provoke our Christian concern and stimulate us to action for the relief of those who suffer in these ways. My point, however, is that deliverance from these things is not the salvation which Christ died and rose to secure for men.[216]

It is easy to see how one's interpretation of texts seriously impacts the style of a preaching/teaching and thus the ministry of a congregation. So it becomes increasingly important not only to determine what morality is, but to interpret its application to society.

5. Are You Dealing with a Personal or Corporate Morality?

The church must speak to the world and to its orders and systems, but how is that to happen? Are we to equip people morally in the church so that they influence the world as they invade its causeways, or is the church to speak corporately to society? Often churches are influenced here by their church's polity and its accompanying autonomy.

Martin Marty notes that "many of the mainline denominations have had more success relating to the public order than being the church."[217]

We must hear the warning from William Willimon that "the church is the central place of a Christian's moral formation, for only the church keeps this vision before us in this effective, habitual, social way. Christianity must not allow itself to become a moral system, with the religious reduced to little more than an emotional tinting, a vestigial accessory to an essentially humanistic ethical scheme."[218] Many would join Willimon and say that when the corporate body speaks, only the body speaks, and the individual loses its moral fiber and thus its potent voice in society.

Very quickly you will hear the people on the other end of the continuum saying that the church is the representative of Christ in society and therefore needs to speak to society. They would feel that the church as a corporate body will be heard more readily and has more influence as it speaks corporately. The rise and fall of the Moral Majority in society is a valuable case study and is worthy of consideration as people position themselves here.

While you are in the process of making this decision, it is important to keep in mind how social ethics are taught. Educators would be quick to tell us that social ethics such as values are more caught than taught. The church provides the models, the norms of the way we treat people and the way, as a congregation, we make decisions about society. The congregation has certain ways of treating the moral, the handicapped, the divorced or the divorcing, the poor, the adulterous, and the morally fallen. Children and adults learn their Christian ethics by observing the congregation living out its Christianity. Willimon agrees. He says, "We learn our ethics as we learn language, and incidental to growing up with certain people, not because someone sat down and taught it to us."[219] Some would be quick to say that since the values have been modeled in the congregation, they have been preached and taught. Now the congregation is ready to corporately speak to society about its biblical ethics, but it is reminded that it is possible that the church, by spending too much energy leaning over to speak to the world, sometimes may fall into the world. Carefully hear the warning of Willimon who says, "The chief political task of the church is not to provide suggestions for social policy but to be in our existence, a social policy. . . . the gospel call is an invitation to be part of a peculiar people, a colony, an institution that is struggling to create those structures that the world can never achieve through governmental power and balanced self-interest."[220]

So some are saying that Christian leaders need to change people through the ministry of the church so that they can speak to the world as they penetrate the world. Then the other side says that the church ought to speak corporately to society about its need to buy into a biblical morality. Willimon would want you to hear a precaution as you make the decision. He says, "The social activism of most liberal, mainline denominations sounds as if someone has asked us Christians to run the government rather than be the church. In so doing, we are unrealistic about our effect upon both the present political situation and the unsuspecting victims of an inadequate ecclesiology."[221]

Finally, a church needs to make a decision about what ethical issues the church will publicly address. Robert Schuller has decided not to take a stand on ethical issues, but other churches do. For some churches it is appropriate to take the stand on such issues as abortion, Operation Rescue, consumption of alcoholic beverages, homosexuality, divorce or remarriage, school prayer, nuclear energy, pacifism, and pornography. Churches that decide to make these kinds of statements to society need to put them in writing and should preach and teach them to the congregation, so they will be issues that are known and owned by the congregation. Tom McKee has led his congregation to this cautionary position by including it in their philosophy of ministry. It states:

> We call ourselves a worshiping/teaching church, not a lobbying church. We don't feel that we are an organization as a political caucus to lobby for the changing of the civil laws. Now we had a lot of people who didn't like this, and they wouldn't come to our church. We had a lot of people leave our church over this because they felt that we should be having petitions in the morning service and people out there demonstrating at certain kinds of marches. We basically said that if God calls you to do that as an individual go do it. In fact you probably should; but I felt that when Paul organized the churches, he never led the churches to demonstrate against slavery in the first century.

One moral question that every church in America faces is the divorce and remarriage issue. This is one of those issues that most often the church will need to deal with corporately. Although most churches would not put this in their philosophy statement, it most likely would be stated in the way they deal with divorced people and remarried people in leadership. Dr. Paul Borden's graph on the next page may help you see where you stand on this issue. You definitely will attract or detract many people to Christ and your church by the position you take on this issue. Give serious thought about it in reference to your targets for evangelism.

William Willimon would agree with the sacramental churches' statement because he feels that the "liberals decided that 'social

Divorce and Remarriage in Evangelism

by Dr. Paul Borden

Justice ———————————————————————— **Mercy**

	Closed	**Moderate**	**Open**
1. Different Positions Taken by Leadership	1. No divorce, no remarriage	purity of doctrine Traditional position – (John Murry). An act of immorality or desertion will allow for divorce and	current culture Most allow for remarriage
2. How Policies Are Implemented	2. Leaders usually discipline • Some publicly disciplined and some visibility • Disciplinary actions and position on divorce often	or remarriage Selective discipline – Church position often stated in	after divorce • Decisions often not handled with policies • Policies are not in writing • Each situation dealt
3. Theology of Church Governs the Church's Decisions	conveyed publicly 3. Churches are keepers of the Truth • Emphasis is on	documents Fluctuate between purity of doctrine and relevance to the	with individually Church viewed as an agent to penetrate the culture. The emphasis is

on relevance.
By the year 2000 20% of the children will be stepchildren and only 25% will be in a nuclear family.
Divorce drives most people into lower classes.
1,300 children each day enter into a stepchild relationship.

concern' meant the politics of power rather than the witness of the cross. We began improving the world rather than reforming the church. As a result, we have what the theologian Moltmann calls a 'chameleon theology' in which an acculturated church, baffled by its inability to have an impact on society, merely blends into society and becomes the victim of every passing fad, and politely waited, hat in hand, for something useful to do to help keep society intact."[222]

Not only is the church concerned about the demise of the moral fiber of our grand old America, but the political and social order is joining in the same parade. How will your church seek to stand in the gap and hold back the further flood of decay?

6. How Do You Maintain Balance?

If your church decides on a middle position and therefore agrees about the balance between a redemptive or a social/creation theology position, then you need to recognize how difficult it will be to maintain that balance with a high level of integrity. I raise that question because I heard of one church in particular, and have heard of many others, who acknowledged the fact that when they became involved in numerous target ministries, the people became so involved in meeting the physical needs of society that they failed to bear a witness to the world about its need to receive Christ as Lord as well as Savior.

John Stott would help us through this dilemma by suggesting that there are three ways to look at this balance: "(1) Some regard social action as a means to evangelism. This makes social work the sugar on the pill. (2) It regards social action not as a means to evangelism but as a manifestation of evangelism. Social action becomes the sacrament of evangelism, for it makes the message significantly visible. And (3) social action is a partner of evangelism. As partners, the two belong to each other and yet are independent of each other. Each stands on its own feet in its own right alongside the other. Neither is a means to the other, or even a manifestation of the other."[223]

The leaders who framed the Lausanne Covenant were well aware of that difficulty and tried to state a way for churches to think through that balanced position.

> Although reconciliation with man is not reconciliation with God, nor is social action evangelism, nor is political liberation salvation, nevertheless we affirm that evangelism and socio-political involvement are both part of our Christian duty. . . . The message of salvation implies also a message of judgment upon every form of alienation, oppression, and discrimination; and we should not be afraid to denounce evil and injustice wherever they exist.[224]

All the churches in the study had certain social services available in and through the congregation, but they did not always use them in the same way. I would not even say that they had the same intention in their use.

I saw the Phoenix Assembly of God Church in action having 1,000 people sign up to each bring a turkey and give it to the poor who had come to visit their church and hear the gospel on Thanksgiving in 1992. It was impressive to see their strong ministry to people in wheelchairs and other handicapped in society. They built apartments across the street for people who formerly lived in poverty but now had found Christ.

Every day E. V. Hill's church serves food to the street people for fifty cents per person in their food kitchen. They have two tents on their property to care for the poverty stricken. But then again, we need to hear that caution: what the world sees in the American church is not a people who are converting the world but another organization that is trying to preserve peace in the world.

E. V. Hill's message to the Lausanne Conference was one of the finest addresses I have ever heard on the moral issue for the church. He saw the church's mission like a baseball game. He suggested that everyone needed to go to salvation's first base before going to social concern's second base. To him, third base was becoming a servant. He was very insistent that you must go to first base before you can go to second base. Then if you want to get home, you have to go through third base.

As you finally come to make your decision, you may want to study these texts of Scriptures and these authors as further guides to you in the decision-making process. Here are some texts that need to be considered in determining where you are on this continuum: Leviticus 19:18; James 2:15–16; Matthew 5:13–16; John 3:19–20; 12:47; Luke 4:18; 1 John 3:17, 18; Acts 6:1–6; 10:39–42. Excellent books to study for further understanding of this issue would be: (1) George W. Peters, *A Theology of Church Growth* (Zondervan, 1975); (2) Bruce Shelley, *Consumer Church* (IVP, 1992); (3) John R. W. Stott, *Christian Mission in the Modern World* (IVP, 1975); (4) Peter Wagner, *Church Growth and the Whole Gospel* (Harper and Row, 1982); and (6) William Willimon, *What's Right with the Church?* (Harper and Row, 1985).

Stewardship Tension—Mission Removed or At Home

OUTWARD TO THE WORLD				
Stewardship	Removed			at Home Mission

Missions is bodies, bucks, and bricks. Whether it is at home or abroad, the question always remains, "Where does the first dollar go?" It is one of those seemingly necessary evils—really an honor— which we are not able to escape.

Those who hold to the mission removed or abroad concept believe that God blesses a church with a mission budget that gives a high percentage of its monies to foreign missions and tightens its purse strings on its budget for its own home front causes. This would mean limiting facilities, programs, and staff so they can be more generous in helping foreign mission causes. Raymond Ortlund has a succinct description of a church like that. "Some churches consider themselves 'mission centers.' These churches raise an extensive amount of money for missions. They have world maps in prominent places with lights twinkling on them, and the people talk a lot about 'fifty-fifty budgets' and hear numerous missionary reports from their pulpits."[225] These people take as their commission Acts 1:8: "But you will receive power when the Holy Spirit comes on you, and you will be my witnesses in Jerusalem and in all Judea, and Samaria and to the ends of the earth." These people see as their highest priority the spreading of the gospel through the entire world, and they will not only want to get their parishioners to participate in that bodily, but they will also want to see as many of their dollars as possible invested in foreign mission causes.

These people will quickly tell you that the greatest churches in American history are those that have put a very high priority on foreign missions. They can show you signs of that by the number of youth who have gone from their midst as missionaries around the world. Further, they will tell you how their own church has prospered financially and spiritually, and they will quickly attribute that prosperity to their investing in foreign mission causes.

1. Missions at Home

The people who represent this end of the continuum would argue that if they were to give a greater percent of their budget to their own staff, programs, and facilities for the nurturing of their own congregation, then they would ultimately have a greater dollar amount to give to foreign missions. They believe that their own community is their mission field. Since most Americans no longer esteem church, God, and Christianity in their value system, their primary focus must be first to their own "Jerusalem." They see themselves living in a pagan society which is in great need of the gospel. In fact, to them it is more important than assisting the spreading of the gospel on other continents. These people are not opposed to foreign mission endeavors, but, in fact, believe the biblical mandate is that the whole world receives the gospel. It is a matter of priority to them to build a home base in an effort to ultimately have the greatest impact on the world.

They would say that their church has its priorities in order. First, to Christ, then to itself, and ultimately to the world. You might hear them referring to the teachings of Christ in John 15 as their orderly guideline. In verses 1–11, Christ says, "Remain in me." This is the mandate for worship. Verses 12–15 emphasize "Love each other." Here Christ is praying that their joy might be full through their fellowship within their body of Christ. In verses 16–27, they are admonished to "testify about me that the world may know me." That pertains to the third priority of international missions.

These people would agree with Alan Mead who says, "We are returning to one of the features of the apostolic age. We now assume that the front door of the church is a door into mission territory, not just a door to the outside."[226]

The neutral ground between these two groups would converge at the point where both would say that a large percentage of their budget ought to go for evangelism and another large section ought to be given to nurture. The question remains, "Where does the first dollar go and what percentage goes to each?"

2. Stewardship Trends

I was amazed to find how few of the pastors in the study group talked about money. It was not a big issue with them, but vision was far more important. It appears to them that if the congregation sees and owns the church's vision, then members will quickly invest their dollars in God's ministry bank. In my study of progressive church philosophies there appears to be an increasing number that refer to priorities in the ministry without directly talking about finances. Of course most of those items are heavily freighted with financial obligations. These leaders seem to be right when they say that where people's hearts are, their money quickly follows.

E. V. Hill provides an excellent model of that at Mount Zion Church. A great percentage of this church's budget goes to help the people in the Watts area in Los Angeles. If there is money left over, then it goes to staff and facilities. Anyone who studies the economic condition in America these days is aware of the fact that budgetary items will be an increasingly difficult issue in church ministries in the coming decades.

If you study the budgets of boomer churches, you will rather readily discover that a strong majority of them identify with the missions-at-home position. The people at the Leadership Network say that:

> Many studies of the giving of Baby Boomers indicate that
> while they give at levels equal to or even surpassing that of older

church members, there are significant differences in the motivation and expectations of Boomer giving. They are much more pragmatic givers and will not be motivated to give out of guilt or by tradition. They demand a higher degree of accountability in the use and effectiveness of their money than do older members. To the Boomers stewardship must be personalized, especially giving to foreign missions. There is more inclination to support local, more tangible, mission efforts and ministries.[227]

Some research done at the Institute for Church Development has pointed out a very interesting correlation between the percentage of money given to missions and the growth of that church. There tends to be an inverse correlation between the volume of money given to foreign missions and the growth of the church. A study of the following table shows that when giving externally remains at 15 percent or lower, the decadal growth of the church is more substantial than when the volume of money going to foreign missions increases. Then the growth of the church tends to decrease. It is assumed that adequate church staff can help the church grow. If monies are given to missions and not staff, then the growth is somewhat hampered.

Impact of Budget Ratios on Church Effectiveness

Given Externally	Foreign Missions Budget	Decadal Growth
0-14%	10%	81%
15-19%	15%	57%
20-24%	14%	39%
25-30%	21%	29%
31+%	26%	15%

Rules of Thumb

1. Churches averaging 0-200 in attendance can give 10 to 15% externally.
2. Churches averaging 200-1000 in attendance can give 15 to 30 % externally.

Five Symptoms of Giving Too Much Externally

1. Church is understaffed (less than 1 staff/150 attendees, *plus* 1 more staff).
2. Church has inadequate quantity or quality of facilities.
3. Church is doing a poor job in evangelism itself.
4. Church is numerically plateaued or declining.
5. Church is spiritually slumped.[228]

First Baptist Church of Flushing, New York, has made a decision that illustrates this. When Russ Rosser went to Flushing, he encouraged the congregation to cut back on their foreign missions giving so they could invest more money in missions to the city of New York. Their willingness to participate in that change encouraged him to come and be their pastor. Since that change occurred, the church has grown substantially. Currently, they are able to give more dollars to missions than previously. Some churches see the extension of this principle by investing money to plant churches in their area. To them, that is a wise investment of their mission dollars.

A study of the goals of churches in the study group revealed that many of the goals were tied to finances, but in nearly every case, the local ministry item took preeminence over the budget item. The rationale is that if a congregation sees the need for the mission item, the budget will readily follow. I heard Randy Kinnison say, "I spent a great deal of my time helping people visualize the ministry that would happen in the new facility which we were currently building." Don Bubna challenged his congregation to provide space for the people in their community whose needs were being met in Christ and who were moving into their congregation. This was the one string on his fiddle that he kept plucking to encourage his congregation to give generously to the Peace Portal Alliance Auditorium Fund.

Another interesting trend is the return of strong missionary dollars from adult Sunday school classes or adult communities. This, I think, tends to reflect the trend toward close association with those to whom you give. In the large church, it is difficult to maintain any level of intimacy necessary in commitment to mission dollars.

Stan Perea spoke of another major trend that concerns him. He identified the American churches in three concentric circles that move outward from the inner city: (1) the inner city—10% of the American city churches, (2) the deministerized zone—65%, (3) the suburbs—25%. This large group of middle class Americans who attend what he calls the deministerized churches are the group of people who attend churches in the physically declining landscape between the suburbs and the inner city. For the most part, these are the churches that are struggling to reach their communities. Often it is because they have tight budgets and limited leadership. He sees that it is easier to raise dollars for struggling churches in the inner city than it is in the churches in the deministerized zone. Unfortunately, these churches, like the inner city churches, are the struggling, declining churches that need a great deal of attention and leadership but are often overlooked because of the great demand for dollars in the inner city missions and churches. Every congregation will face increasingly difficult decisions about where to invest its stewardship portfolio as America faces the economic, moral, and physical decline of its cities.

3. Sociological Norms on Finances

Once the American society began to move away from a corporate to an individual mind-set, there were some significant changes in the commitment of mission dollars. Kennon Callahan summarizes that by saying, "People give to people. Next, to purposes. Then to causes. Fourth to programs, and finally to paper."[229] One of the interesting indications of this is that congregations who are following the lead of a strong pastor are very reticent to give to additional programs, staff, and facilities when they sense an uncertainty about the tenure of the pastor. Some churches have gone so far as to put an insurance policy on the life of the pastor in fear that he might transfer to glory at some unexpected time!

William Easum points out a number of interesting factors which need to be kept in mind as you plan for ministry expansion. "Asking for money encourages growth. When people become honest with their money, the church grows. . . . The best thing a pastor can do for the people is to encourage them to be honest with their money. One-sixth of every word from our Lord is about money. He knows our basic sin-love of money. . . . Over the years, I have been impressed by the fact that 20% of the Christians I have known possess 80% of the enjoyment and satisfaction of being a Christian. They know they are happier when they reach out to help someone. . . . Do not ask people to give to the church or tell them the church needs their money. Ask people to give to God rather than to a church or a budget."[230]

In studying churches across the country, I sense that the faith promise approach to budget is increasing in rapid proportions. Easum points out the importance of that particular approach to budgeting in these days. "Budgets of growing churches should never be more than 70 to 90% underwritten by pledges. If the entire budget is underwritten by a pledge drive, increase it immediately."[231]

More than ever before, people are voting with their feet and with their pocketbook. Kennon Callahan reminds us that money follows mission and not the reverse.[232]

4. Budget Issues

The Institute for Church Development has been watching carefully the dollars given to the local church and those which go to parachurch organizations. More than two percent of the money is given outside the local church. Also, it indicates that 58 percent of the people who responded to the questionnaire were satisfied with their church's stewardship program. George Barna provides some additional insight to parishioners' giving. "While most people who attend a church on a regular basis donate money to that congregation, the data indicates that among adults who call themselves Christians, about one-third (31%) also donate money to Christian ministries other than churches in a typical month. This generosity is especially likely among people forty-five or older, people earning $20,000 per year or more, married adults, born-again Christians, and adults who regularly attend church."[233]

"When decisions are made about the financial part of a philosophy of ministry, the following issues need to be considered: the total debt the church incurs for a building program should not exceed an amount equal to three times the last twelve months' income of the church. The payment of the debt service should not exceed one-third of the church's income."[234]

The staff budget should consist of around 40 percent of the total church budget. Some churches give more of their budget toward staff for one of two reasons. Either their facilities are paid for, or they are stretching themselves by adding staff in anticipation of having additional funds through the ministry of the staff. William Easum gives us another important tip. "An increase in worship attendance results in an increase in giving. Income toward the budget in a healthy church should exceed $1,080 for every person in attendance at an average Sunday worship service. If your church has two hundred in worship, your income toward the budget should be over $200,000, not including foundation money or borrowed funds."[235] Another way to look at the budget amount was provided by John LaRue. "The median annual budget amount per worship attendee was $701.00, and the median annual budget amount per member on church roll was $551.00 in 1991."[236]

5. Biblical Teaching on Stewardship

Here are some important biblical texts to keep in mind as you think about where you will put your missionary dollars: Proverbs 13:11; 14:20, 31; 17:16; Ecclesiastes 5:10; 7:12; Acts 4:34–37; 5:1–4; 1 Corinthians 16:2; 1 Timothy 6:10; 2 Timothy 3:2; Hebrews. 13:5; James 4:13–14; 1 Peter 5:2.

Chapter 10

Security Levels and Paradigm Shifts

When word reached me that David Willis was leading a six-day pack trip into the Sierra Nevada Mountains, I wouldn't have been surprised if he was still in high school, for then he was genuinely hooked on climbing mountains. However, I was shocked that he was able to do so now because only a couple of years before he had lost his fingers and toes in a personal climbing expedition on Mt. McKinley. Now he was leading a group of crippled and blind people on what seemed to be an impossible venture, but they went for it! Better yet, they succeeded. Summit Expedition takes on the challenge of getting someone in a wheelchair up an 1,800 foot rise, a three-mile vertical train, or a fifty-foot high rock wall.

Since his first trip, he has been helping the handicapped "go for it!" It almost seemed as if he were taking a page from the life of Paul in 2 Corinthians 4:8–10: "We are pressed on every side, but not crushed; perplexed, but not in despair; persecuted, but not abandoned; struck down, but not destroyed. We always carry around in our body the death of Jesus, so that the life of Jesus may also be revealed in our body." What Dave and his friends have faced in the physical realm could have led them down the path of despair. They could have become human vegetables who ceased to have a mission or any sense of dignity or accomplishment, but they saw it only as a temporary roadblock to their ultimate goal.

A church pilgrimage looks very much like David Willis's dilemma and accomplishment. There is a vision that is deeply ingrained in one's heart, many seeming obstacles, and a confidence to go on in spite of overwhelming odds. Etched on every heart is a desire for greatness. You can see it every day if your eyes are open to see it. When you mingle among the congregation you ought to be in touch with that reality. If your people could only express themselves, they would tell you that is why they come. How can that be released in them? We all want to climb the mountain, but so many are in chains and can't be free to even get started. They need to hear the voice of God saying, "Then you will know the truth, and the truth will set you free."[237] People flock to churches where that is encouraged, permitted, and provisions are made for it to happen. I watch the flow of people who leave churches because they feel the death pull of degeneration in their previous churches. I am not condoning the actions of church tramps; I am only saying that this is what is happening.

The Revision of Type Principle

Over the years as I have gotten acquainted with many congregations, I have concluded that many are like trees and others like posts. Both come from the same source, but one is growing and the other is dying or rotting. Some are like "David Willis trees" in their richness of life. Their lives are constantly producing an abundance of fruit in spite of unbelievable storms that blow against them. They are respites for many on life's journey. Others are hollow. They drain people rather than feed them. They may have a beautiful façade when viewed from a distance; but upon further examination, you find they are hollow-like posts, weathered by time and frustration. Churches can and do grow weary and fall short of reaching their goals. They become posts instead of trees.

"David Willis churches" have learned to stay alive while they are living. I have been in that kind of church. What a breath of fresh air! These people have come to recognize that there is a law of sin and death that pulls them down and wants to make those trees into posts. Henry Drummond tells us about the law in the universe that explains that process. He says that God really has only put one set of laws in the universe. Even though there are both spiritual and scientific natural laws, there is basically only one set of laws. In his book, he discusses such laws as biogenesis and conformity to type and environment. We can get a beautiful insight into those spiritual laws by studying the laws of nature.[238] There is no doubt what Paul had in mind when he stated in Romans 1:20 that "the invisible things of Him [like the laws of nature] from the creation of the world are clearly seen, being understood by the things that are made, even His eternal power and Godhead."

Another one of those unalterable laws is the law of degeneration. It basically says that you are either growing or dying. Drummond defines the law of degeneration by saying, "The natural law by which such a change occurs is called "The Principle of Reversion of Type." If we neglect a garden plant, then a natural principle of deterioration comes in and changes it into a worse plant. . . . Now the same thing exactly would happen in the case of you or me. Why should man be an exception to any of the laws of nature?"[239] Then we also need to ask, "Why would the local church be an exception to the laws of nature?" They, too, have life by the Spirit in them. Of course the universal body of Christ will not die, but local congregations can and do.

It is very hard for many congregations to face the fact that if they are not becoming all that Christ wants them to be, then they are moving toward death. Pierre Berton gives us a clue about what those churches look like. "So many Christians have learned all the answers to all the key questions. They have inversion reasoning—that is, they no longer have a broadening perspective, but a narrowing one. Life narrows down to simple answers. They have made all the friends they can possibly keep up with. They have arrived at their positions of power in the church. They think they have faced all the key issues, and now they are in the comfortable pew. Now there is no world to conquer, and now the process of post formation is at work."[240] No church can remain stagnant very long before decay begins to set in. There are many congregations that are only one generation churches. The other frightening reality is that 85 percent of the churches in America are in decline or standing static. Church history is strewn with the wrecks of churches and entire denominations that lost a sense of purpose. When people are selfish and self-centered and there is no vision or passion for the world, the church will soon die.

If you listen to Pastor E. V. Hill talk about his congregation, he keeps saying that they want a church that "makes a difference." They, like many, have come to see the fact that the Lord wants them to strive with the Holy Spirit in helping His church to grow. "We proclaim Him, admonishing and teaching everyone with all wisdom, so that we may present everyone perfect in Christ. To this end I labor, struggling with all His energy, which so powerfully works in me."[241] As you visit with Dr. Hill you quickly understand that his congregation feels a heavy responsibility to carry out God's work in the Watts area. They know that they are accountable to Him for that work. They have come to see what all Christians need to realize. Success is not just an American value; it is *Christ's* value for the church. He wants success in the harvest. If Christians do not buy into that, the church may be in trouble.

We are in a conflict with Satan and his forces. We must succeed to win the world and to aid Christ as "God's fellow workers"[242] in building His church. God does not seem to be happy with that kind of middle ground. It appears that there is no place for it in His mind. He says, "You are lukewarm, you are neither hot nor cold. I am going to spit you out of my mouth."[243] Yes, the law of degeneration is at work there as well. We must come face to face with the bold reality. We live daily in the church where the revision of types is at work in our midst. It is part of the sin nature in our world. Many tend to think that if they do not see any outward satanic work among their congregations, they are doing fine. However, just to sit there and do nothing is, in a sense, part of satanic influence in today's world. Hear Christ talking about His desire for His church. He says we ought to speak "the truth in love [so that] we will in all things grow up into him who is the Head, that is, Christ. From him the whole body, joined and held together by every supporting ligament, grows and builds itself up in love, as each part does its work."[244]

Another important passage which gives both aspects of the law of degeneration is Matthew 25:14–29, the parable of the talents. The soul of the church, in its highest sense, has an immense capacity for God. It is as if the soul is a vast chamber which has elastic and contracting walls that can expand when God is present and contract when He is absent. The central thesis of this passage zeroes in on the fact that some people are going to lose what they had. They are going to lose their talent—their presence with God. Is God going to be the big ogre who will take it away like a spoiled brat because He didn't get His way? No, they will lose it because they neglected to keep the talent active. God is going to give those talents to the one who keeps using them—the one who keeps holding back the law of degeneration.

A vision and a philosophy of ministry says very loudly to everyone, "We are going to fight the law of degeneration. We want to make a difference in God's world." They say, "This is where we want to win and this is how we plan to do it step by step." If the church does not have that big picture, it may just dabble around in doing unrelated and often unimportant things. The people become very active and seem very busy, but they are not as productive as they could be.

Sermons, programs, and ministries in dynamic living churches are all moving toward that end. Sermons are preached because they will help the church get where they want to go. The body wants to grow spiritually which then, in turn, takes the church into a corporate invasion of the world. They hear the thundering tension of organism and organization which they just cannot escape if they are going to minister through the American church to the needy world. They must fight to maintain the organism while all the time dealing with the worldly structure of the church. "The organization's flexibility to change and adapt to new circumstances and external demands is its only prospect for sustaining itself over several generations."[245]

A philosophy of ministry can aid in the fight against the law of degeneration. Such a philosophy document can be called a paradigm. Joel Barker defines a paradigm as a "pattern or a model; it is a set of regulations, established boundaries. These rules provide the edges and borders within which people can solve problems. Paradigm acts as a filter that screens information entering the scientist's mind."[246] You see a philosophy statement then as your vision. It is the way you see ministry, and consequently the way you as a congregation will go about doing ministry. It is almost so strong that it forces you to see things through your paradigm. As culture changes, your paradigm may need to shift to a new way of thinking so you can be kept from a reversion of some type.

The leaders at Faith Community Church in Covina, California, have given us a clear and simple illustration of a paradigm shift. They call their children's Sunday school Honey Creek University. The new approach is a replacement of their traditional children's Sunday school and is a continuous flow of activities from 9:00 a.m. through 12:00 p.m. on Sunday. The goal of Honey Creek University is to provide a creative and enjoyable learning experience that adds to the children's spiritual, relational, personal, and emotional growth. Learning segments at Honey Creek are no more than thirty minutes long, and include such activities as Amazing Discoveries (science illustrates Scriptural truths through demonstrations and learning experiments), the Honey Creek Band (children participate with their own variety of instruments), Acts Alive (dramatic vignettes of biblical stories are portrayed in modern settings; children both watch and participate), Power Breaks (one half hour of games and activities which teach cooperation and team work), and a Bible Discovery session (teachers creatively teach one insight from Scripture).[247]

An helpful way to determine if degeneration is happening in your congregation is to study their life cycle. There are differences of opinion as to how long the average life cycle is, but it is generally thought to be around thirty-eight years. One of the more interesting studies of life cycles is the one done by Saarinen. He states:

> . . . that growth and decline progress from stage to stage. Experience has indicated that once in the growth phase, a congregation will progress from infancy, adolescence, and prime. Similarly, once a congregation is in the decline phase, it will pass from maturity, aristocracy, bureaucracy, and then to death. Second, development and decline do not progress uninterrupted from stage to stage. Movement from one stage to another is marked by a cyclical process of dying and rising again in which the "energy" forces predominate in the growth phase and the administering forces in the decline phase. Third, growth may be aborted and decline may be arrested at any stage in their respective cybernetics. Growth may be aborted by succumbing to the seductive forces of presumption ("that couldn't happen to us") or despair (burnout).[248]

He tells in detail how a mission or vision for the church can keep renewing the congregation so that it will not be overtaken by death

The Joy of Dealing with Spiritual Energy

Martin Saarinen's reference to "energy" has to do with the presence of the Holy Spirit in the congregation. It is such a delight for the church to have available to it the energy of the Spirit as its aid in the ministry. At times, that energy seems to come without any effort on our part. Then there are times when it seems to come to the people of God as they establish the environment for His energy to be active.

You will be able to apply the wisest kind of energetic direction for the congregation if you know where you are in your current life cycle. A picture of how children learn will help you to understand how a congregation can grow. Visualize a child as an inverted pyramid or cone. Children start with the most fundamental piece of information. Every time they develop a new skill or learn some new knowledge, it germinates the pieces that are already in the mind. This becomes an expanding pyramid of knowledge. They have an ever-expanding horizon to draw from as they move through life. It is almost like seeing a brick wall being built. New experiences are fused with new knowledge which, in turn, gives a basic new capability. As this happens, you would say to the child with a great deal of excitement, "My, how you have grown! Look at all the new things you can do."

You hear the same pattern: "Train yourself to be godly for physical training is of some value, but godliness has value for all things, holding promise for both the present life and the life to come."[249] Here Paul is saying to Timothy that he needs all of his lifetime to keep moving toward a new capability or a new position in his godliness. There is a clue here about how you can tell where you are currently and, therefore, what cycle you are in as a congregation. He says, move to a higher stage of godliness. This suggests that you ought to grow to a new position. That might suggest that you have a new capability or skill and an accompanying knowledge base.

In observing the spiritual growth in believers, I have noticed that growth is almost always associated with one's security or insecurity. You are comfortable and secure at one level of trust but not at the next. The next step of growth seems to introduce fear or insecurity. There are numerous reasons why you might fail to move into that new level of trust, but nonetheless, you are stifled right there. Now, defining what the next level of trust is may quickly suggest where you are currently because that engenders a strong feeling of insecurity.

Educators suggest that those are stages of classification in a taxonomy. A taxonomy is a progressive set of stages that lead chronologically from the lowest level to the highest level of maturity. Here is what a trust taxonomy looks like:

> (1) Trust God to forgive us our sins and to give us new life; (2) understand who Jesus is and trust Him as our leader; (3) trust God in public identification to win people to Jesus; (4) trust Christ in assuming a responsible place of leadership in family or movement, and trust Him to govern our lives; (5) trust God for the eternal above all temporal matters in separation to Christ from the world; (6) trust Christ to work in other members of the body; and (7) rest in the sufficiency of the risen Christ and begin to trust Him to use you to reach the world.[250]

Can you tell how strong your trust is? For instance, you might say you are comfortable with a leadership role in your church. You know that is where you are. If you have a hard time trusting God to work through other members in the church, this is the next step.

The key factor here is understanding the chronological stages you go through in any one of the areas in your philosophy of ministry. There is great danger in trying to get the congregation to become proficient at a level that is two or more stages beyond where it is currently. You can see in the illustration on page 209 that this growth produces a great deal of emotional pain or insecurity. You are not sure that you want to trust God for it. You have not done it before, and you feel insecure about moving into that arena.

The church needs leadership that applies wisdom in leading the people forward to new stages of spiritual growth with the least amount of pain, but at the same time keeps them in the pain threshold. Here is a taxonomy that shows how to lead a church to new heights of ability and to deal with the issue of ministry to the poor. Notice that each stage introduces the congregation to a new stage of difficulty which may feel painful.

1. *Partial knowledge:* All church board members can verbalize the meaning of the church's role in caring for the needs of the poor of their defined community.
2. *Corporate knowledge:* The A.M. attendees can verbalize what the church's responsibility for the poor looks like on a day-by-day basis.
3. *Financial commitment:* There is a healthy commitment of the congregation's budget toward financing ministries for the poor.
4. *Guided commitment:* A vigorous commitment of time on the part of the congregation to work with programs for the poor.
5. *Personal initiative:* A sizable percentage of the congregation will take initiative to launch a specific caring ministry for the poor.

I have watched so many pastors fail as leaders because in their preaching and leadership they have tried to get the congregation to move to where they themselves are personally, rather than to the next acceptable level of the congregation's security level. The pastor and congregation both feel great frustration and failure but for different reasons.

Congregations ought to be able to see their knowledge and experience levels growing, but they need someone guiding them and interacting with them so they will know what is going on. There is nothing that will encourage them more than that. They will probably be like little children experiencing new capabilities for the first time. Then they keep saying, "Let me participate in some growth ministries." Building blocks of our experiences germinate one another and expand our horizons in Christ. That is what Christ is saying to us when He tells us to "grow in the grace and knowledge of our Lord and Savior Jesus Christ."[251] No wonder Paul is saying to Timothy, "Friend, there is profit for this life and the life to come." You feel the joy of experiencing that new energy in your life, and you know you will be rewarded for its activity when you get to heaven.

Trying to get in touch with the feelings of the people at Mt. Zion, I found that they spent their building fund budget for a cause different than that for which it was intended. They had been working for years to build a new auditorium. Pastor Hill called on them to invest instead in a home for unwed mothers, which was a growing need in the community. If they had just thought about themselves, they might have felt cheated; when they thought about Christ's kingdom and the girls they were helping, then they felt they had been rewarded. Christ does that to kingdom builders.

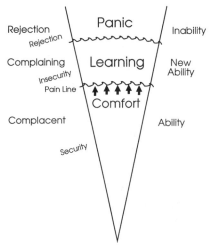

You can figure out rather quickly where the congregation is if you do a written evaluation which helps define where they are in their thinking or in their performance. The same can be done by conducting a group interview. Great caution needs to be exercised in the kind of questions asked. If not, you may end up trying to take them to a stage beyond their capability.

On the other hand, if you do not do an evaluation, then it could also be dangerous because of the terrible insecurity which could cause some sort of rejection because of our psychological reaction. That is why it is called the pain level on the stretch cone. The whole growth process shuts down when there is too much pain. You can often see that in a body of people. Their ability to tolerate emotional pain is very vital to their performance. You hear about it in athletes all the time. Their physical pain is too great, and they finally sit on the bench. Most of you would quit long before they would. You had better understand where the congregation's pain line is because people will just sit down in their spiritual growth without any warning. There will be no more money for new projects, no volunteering, and no new missions. They cannot handle that much pressure. They need to be made to feel insecure but not to the point that will cause rejection.

Randy Pope suggests that you do not talk about change because even though people like to grow they resist change. For instance, he talks about the fact that his church was going to be a bigger church, even a megachurch. There was going to be great growth but all the time they would still be a local congregation. The home base was just going to be a great deal larger than it currently was. Further security was assured because they would all belong to smaller "flocks" in which their identity would be maintained.

Many congregations feel they are growing in Christ just because they want to do so. They talk a great deal about growing and how they are to grow, but think very little about honestly judging whether or not they are growing. Maybe it is because they are actually afraid to test whether or not growth is taking place. In the same way, you hear a cancer patient talk about how healthy he or she is because it is too difficult for him or her to think about dying.

You must never forget in this whole process that Christ promises to be with you in your growth. It is His Church, and it is His keenest desire for His church that you will "in all things grow up into him who is the Head, that is, Christ."[252]

Another way to think about the process of defining one's comfort zone or pain level is to call it one's paradigm position. When you are going to move the congregation into a new paradigm, you would call that a paradigm shift. When you start to shift a paradigm, it is necessary to go back to ground zero and start the thought process all over again. This is healthy because you have to stop and evaluate again just what you are all about. Why are you doing what you are doing? It is the same question raised in an earlier chapter. Who are you trying to reach, and how are you going to reach them? Will this change move you another step along in this process? Well, it ought to do so!

Lean into the Pain

The phrase above does not sound very enjoyable—maybe not at first. Keep in mind that it is a biblical tenet. Also keep in mind that growth does not come without pain. In fact, we are told in the Timothy passage that we ought to "exercise ourselves" or inject pain into our lives if we want to grow. Then we are also introduced to the fact that Christ brings pain into our lives so we can grow. "Consider it pure joy, my brothers, whenever you face trials of many kinds, because you know that the testing of your faith develops perseverance."[253]

You cannot have a greater maturity until you have suffered, until you have faced stress, or are willing to lean into the pain. That is the same thing Paul was telling Timothy in 1 Timothy 4:7–8. Paul is getting Timothy ready for leadership. He does not want him to be spiritually flabby. There will be hard times for the church, and he needs to be ready for his task in the work of the ministry.

Paul is saying, train yourself so you can form a higher standard of godliness. The difference between a post and a tree resides in those words, "exercise yourself to be godly." Exercise is the same root word that is used for "education" or "discipline."

The great producers in this world in various fields or endeavors have succeeded because they kept stretching their capacity to perform greater physical and mental tasks. The great spiritual, servant leaders in every culture have succeeded by constantly exercising or stretching their biblically mandated capabilities. Great churches are no different. If they would try to do that all at once, it would cause too much pain and insecurity. At seminary we call that "syllabus shock." That usually comes the first day of school when you get all of the quarter's assignments during the course of one week. It looks impossible because somehow you think that you are going to need to do it all at once. If you have been there, you know the feeling and can understand why many students drop out the first week.

You have to get your congregation comfortable smelling the manure so it can enjoy the roses. People want the roses but not the manure that makes them grow. Leaders are learning that it is healthy for a congregation to feel insecure. James Stockdale reminds everyone that "all leaders are astonished to learn that peace, not war, is the destroyer of men; that tranquility, rather than danger, is the mother of cowardice, and that not need, but plenty brings apprehension and unease."[254]

Tommy Barnett seems to understand this principle. He saw people moving out of their comfort zone as he challenged them to do something great for God. He sees himself playing a major role as a motivator. He keeps asking his congregation to do things that the average pastor would not begin to ask a congregation to do. "When they see great results from their service they are driven to do more," he said. Every Christmas he finds hundreds of people willing to put on thirteen Singing Christmas Tree pageants because they use it as a means to introduce many people to Christ. He makes sure that they see the effect of their ministry.

Be sure you understand why a reasonable amount of pain or insecurity is in every situation. Remember, it has to be the median amount of insecurity that the congregation feels, not the amount that the strongest or most mature member can accept. It might be very easy to push the congregation too much and then become like Demosthenes. He disciplined himself so much that he became totally ineffective. He wanted to be a great orator, but he was not physically made for that. He was a man with stooped shoulders and spoke as if he had rocks in his mouth. Again, the warning is to make sure that the new level of godliness you are expecting of your congregation is reasonable for it. Do not bring them to an early death, rather to a healthy new stage of life. Keep the words of Proverbs in mind as you lead them to new spiritual heights. "A prudent man foresees the difficulties ahead and prepares for them. The simpleton goes blindly on and suffers the consequences."

Disciplining Yourself to Do the Next Step

The tension point in life is between the excitement or the expectation of doing and the cost of doing it. That is where the pain is for everyone. Dr. Brand suggests how important that pain is to your living and being productive for God. "Christian physicians have a responsibility to put pain into perspective. We need to help patients get rid of the idea that pain is in some way a punishment, and thus something to be hidden."[255] Doctors have discovered that the reason leprosy patients injure and then lose their limbs is that they fail to feel pain. He says, "If I had one gift I would give to people with leprosy, it would be the gift of pain."[256] See pain then as a friend in the growth process.

Hans Selye has invented a word for the beauty of stress. He calls it "eustress." The prefix is taken from a Greek word, "euphoria," or "euphonia." Therefore, we have the word, "good stress." Good stress is that which keeps life alive and growing. Without it, your whole life may go to sleep. He says that you can convert negative stress into a positive experience.[257] A church is like a limb. It will soon go into atrophy if it is not used. Then the pain will be so great most of the people in the congregation will not be able to stand the insecurity of the situation. The trick is knowing how much pain to prescribe for the congregation. Too much pain may cause panic and tissue rejection.

It is my opinion that natural change will not occur in many churches that have not had any change for a number of years. They have worked hard to live in peace and tranquility. Conflict has been avoided at any cost. "Don't rock the boat" has been the eternal model. People like to be comfortable. The trouble is that they have been thinking all the time about conflict, not disequilibrium. Make people think through the issues of life. Jesus did not call us to a life of ease. "Do not suppose that I have come to bring peace to the earth. I did not come to bring peace, but a sword. For I have come to turn a man against his father, a daughter against her mother, a daughter-in-law against her mother-in-law—a man's enemies will be the members of his own household. Anyone who loves his father or mother more than me is not worthy of me; anyone who loves his son or daughter more than me is not worthy of me."[258]

We were driving through Williams, Arizona, when we stopped for lunch in a small town along old Highway 66. Recently, they had finished a new freeway that bypassed the town. We immediately felt that small town atmosphere where everyone knew each other. The sign on the pole on the old Highway 66 dated back to the '50s or so. These people had memories that bonded them together. There were new motels and restaurants going up at the interchange. I asked myself if that restaurant would make it. The progressive entrepreneurs would build the restaurants at the interchange, and their businesses would survive for some time to come. The restaurants in the town had to figure out how to meet the needs of the community so they could do well financially for a few years. The others would die eventually like the thousands of others we had seen in small towns all across America on Route 40. Many churches are like that because they will not move to where society is traveling. They have the food for people who are passing through society, but they have not learned to go where they can feed the hungry souls of the weary travelers. Bill Hull gives a clue about what those churches look like. "When people find their niche in a church and stay there, they enter the comfort zone. Nothing challenges their fears, confronts them with their weaknesses, or asks them to expand their strengths. The key word is sameness, and the patron saint of the comfort zone is Walter Mitty."[259] Let's learn to lean into the pain.

Chapter 11

Leading the Church Through Creative Change

Barnabas was seemingly the first one to say to Paul, "Yes, you are okay. You have great potential to help plant the church of Christ." Here is the first case of cybernetics in the Bible. Barnabas continued to play out his role with Paul as a "son of encouragement." He played a vital role in establishing Paul as a bonafide servant of God. Throughout this book I have been seeking to play a Barnabas role with you and your congregation. You are free to be a great witness for Christ and thus to bring glory to Him in the world. You have been given all the ingredients you could ever ask for to build a super church. First, a great unshakable foundation has been provided in Christ. "For no one can lay any foundation other than the one already laid, which is Jesus Christ" (1 Cor. 3:11). It would be foolish to build on any other. He has also provided all the ingredients necessary to build on the superstructure. I call these ingredients the functions of the church. These building blocks are the only ones to be used in its construction, but you have been given freedom to use those ingredients in a way that best reflects who you are.

When we built the house we now occupy, we took the foundation plans from a home that was built in another place in our neighborhood; but no one has ever guessed that we have the same floor and foundation plans. Our home is a true reflection of the people who live there and of all our values and tastes. The same can and ought to be true of the church Christian leaders build.

When our house was finished, we moved in and invited our friends and neighbors to come and see what we had created. In retrospect, we were wanting them to tell us that what our minds had created was an outstanding house. We already knew it, but we needed that extra "It's okay" from the respected others in our lives.

I have given you the encouragement and instructions about how to build a church that honors God and reflects His image in you. Now let me encourage you to glorify God by being creative in the construction or remodeling of your church. Lest you feel you do not have any creative genes, let me encourage you with the thought "that [every] person has imagination; not all of us have creativity, which is only a function of imagination. Creativity results in art. The result of imagination might be art, but it could just as easily be something practical."[260]

One of my greatest delights in life is to see the expressions of people's imaginations. I see it in a new way that the road-builders go about designing and laying pavement. I see it in marketing schemes and in children at play. I find it in art galleries and in shops and factories. I enjoy how families find a special way to worship God together. I see it at work in the classroom and in television programs and commercials. These people are the ones who have opened their eyes to see how they can use the ingredients that God has provided for them to make life most productive. What a boring life it would be were it not for the mark of *imago Dei* (image of God) in everyone, part of which is the imagination. "It marks people as God's human creatures. It helps us know God, receive His grace, worship Him, and see life."[261] It appears to me that the greatest leaders in our world are the ones who learn to see things as others do not. The reason for the great variety of products offered to us as Americans is that each person is allowed the freedom to use his or her imagination in the marketplace. When my wife and I were visiting the former Soviet Union in the winter of 1991, we saw the blight of an economy that was not given that freedom. I praise God for the varieties of churches we have in America. It gives everyone a place to respond to God in a way that is fitting to his or her own uniqueness.

One of the things that amazed me in the study group of pastors was the outstanding work of God's *imago Dei* in them. Each one saw the facets of the church in a little different way, often to the amazement and delight of the local body of Christ. Unfortunately, at the time their gifts may not have been appreciated. There were some who could not see outside of their cramped perspectives. I saw them working with those ingredients like a potter on the potter's wheel who worked with the clay to form a piece of art in worship, discipleship, fellowship, evangelism, etc.

The Bear Valley leadership team created their spiritual planning model, and Don Bubna saw the possibilities of bonding people while others saw those new folks as a bottleneck to fellowship. Russ Rosser saw air space as building potential while others just saw dirty air. The leaders at Perimeter Church in Atlanta saw dirty diapers as a sweet means of bringing mothers to Christ, not just a smelly nuisance in the church basement. Let me check your imagination. Take a look at the squares before you on this page. How many squares do you see? (See endnote 262 for the answer.)

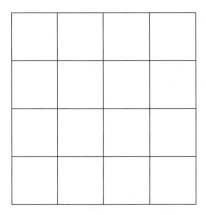

To know God is to know the creator of imagination. "He shattered ordinariness with the incarnation of His Son. We just haven't gotten the message yet" about the God of imagination.[263] Study God as a communicator, and you will get a peek at His crafty ability with problem-solving in communication. Let your mind skim through the Old Testament, and see how God sought to get different people to listen to Him by using things and events. You see Him using kings, shepherds, children, priests, prostitutes, donkeys, plagues, clouds, snakes, and on and on it goes. He always chooses the appropriate object or person to accomplish His mission. You can almost see God sitting at His desk and designing a creative means of getting Pharaoh to let His people go. It took ten different designs before it worked. The burning bush made a pretty good mouthpiece to catch Moses on the run. Now who would have thought of the use of a whale to catch Jonah in flight? Well, these are just a few instances. Maybe the growing use of drama has a real place in our sanctuaries after all!

Think of imagination as the ability to make new, valuable combinations and worthwhile relationships growing out of the uniqueness of the individual. Again, you can see God's display of that imagination in His universe. See how simple imagination is. That may set you free to do your own thing. God's imagination arranged all that you see in the universe by simply rearranging 100 natural elements and two phenomena, matter and energy. All the words that have been spoken or written in English are just a rearrangement of 26 letters. Think of it! All of the 14 million or more books that are in the Library of Congress are just a rearrangement of those few letters. When you are going to create a book or a document, you can do anything you want as long as you use those letters and stay with the dictionary. The rest is all fun and games. All the music that has ever been written is just a rearrangement of twelve notes. The most amazing is the endless new innovations which have come out of the computer that are just the realignment of the on and off button. The sky is the limit as to what can yet be done as long as the engineers understand the limitations of that button, and they have only figured out a very limited amount of things that can be done with that button.

God has given us the functions of the church and His foundation to build a church that will express His attributes to this world. Now it is time to go to work and to do our multi-layered thinking to build His church. There is no need to do things the same way again. I heard that in what Gerry Sheveland was saying. "The reality is that I like innovation and tend to get bored with maintenance ministry. The fact is that I have always been fascinated with new ways, new ideas, and creative approaches." Why can you not be like a true artist who wants to express God's glory to a world that may be blind and deaf because of the communication saturation in this noisy world?

The use of your imagination and creative skills is necessary because of the law which says that "the higher the predictability, the lower the impact." That is why the advertising industry is telling us that we need to say everything at least six times before anyone can hear. You will need to catch the attention of the world with the best message they can hear. Maybe you don't like the "John 3:16" signs that keep appearing on T.V. during athletic events.

Well, that has probably caught the attention of more people than you have with your communication skills. People who live by predictable patterns and in cloistered houses shouldn't throw stones. You have all the necessary ingredients to get the job done. You just need to learn how to make Christ the foundation of the fifteen different functions mentioned in this book. They will help you see how you can make novel combinations of these ingredients in order to build a unique church that speaks to today's culture.

Ray Bakki told of one church in the ghetto that started a small business in the context of the church to help the neighborhood people learn self-respect and productivity. The church leaders got the neighborhood's attention all right, and of course these folks finally came to hear about the real Carpenter who could give them true meaning in this life and everlasting life as a bonus. These churchmen saw possibilities others had not seen.

I was equally impressed with another set of eyes that saw as others had not and rearranged the ingredients as others had not. The Harley-Davidson Motorcycle convention was coming to town. Everyone just heard what? Noise—and lots of it! This man saw an evangelistic opportunity. He set up his welcome booth alongside the road with free lemonade, a friendly greeting, and a written and oral word about the Christ who was the way to life for weary and dusty travelers.[264]

Think about the innovation of the people who brought the lame man to Jesus in Mark 2. "Bold ingenuity brings people to Jesus, Mark 2:4 states. Since they could not get him to Jesus because of the crowd, they made an opening in the roof above Jesus, and after digging through it, lowered the mat on which the paralyzed man was lying. The text literally states, "They unroofed the roof." Luke's account mentions that they took the tiles off first, while Mark adds that the men dug away at the mud that was under the tiles. The four did not give up. They used their ingenuity. They knew that the paralytic needed Jesus."[265] All three of these illustrations tell us very clearly that a true vision for the needs of people drives the imagination. That is the first step to jump-starting the imagination.

The second principle states that imagination can be developed when you are willing to go back to ground zero and design ministry with the basic ingredients. Most of the ministry training institutions in this country are given to training the left and dominant side of students' brains. They learn language skills and mental reasoning very well. The books and papers never seem to end. Certainly some of that is needed in training for effective ministry, but the problem is that the right side of the brain (the nonverbal, emotional, 3-D perceptive, rhythm and pitch, and the creative problem-solving skills) is left dormant for all those years of training. Educators have not listened enough to the science of hemispherisity. They say to strengthen the muscle of the right side of the brain if you are going to solve the real problems of society. Today's society needs men and women who will use the creative muscle of the right side of their brains to express their "organ of meaning" or their imagination, which the Book of Common Prayer calls society's means of grace and their hope of glory.[266]

There are numerous expressions of creative training programs that are being developed in this country. All these programs have leaders who have gone through a paradigm shift in their thinking. They have gone back to ground zero and worked with the basics. That is, they have taken the basic biblical elements of training people for ministry and have started all over with the program design rather than trying to rearrange all the various parts of the program which the institutions have accumulated through the years. All church leaders who are going to be imaginative leaders must learn to work with the basic elements which are the functions of the church. At times it seems like an impossible task to bring a congregation to that place of desired change. If they cannot give up the "form barnacles" which have clung so tenaciously to the functions of the church, then they never will go through that enriching paradigm shift which will allow them to be the church of the 21st century.

A third guideline for developing your imagination is to make sure you have exposed yourself to an adduced amount of raw material. This will enable you to make new, valuable combinations that are referred to in the definition of imagination. "When you focus on creativity in another field, people say, 'I can suddenly make connections.'"[267] The pastors in my study group all seemed to read broadly. They were able to draw from the widest range of material possible. David Moore mentioned that he reads all secular literature on the field of communication so he could better communicate to the secular mind. When your audience lives in and among the secular world all week long, they need to be moved into the spiritual realm when they start thinking about the abstract, spiritual Word of God. You must start where they live! That means reading in the fields such as physical science, business, history, political science, sociology, psychology, literature, and mass communications.

I cannot imagine that you could be a creative leader in ministry if you were satisfied with the status quo. There has to be an insatiable desire to solve problems in your mind if you are going to be creative. That basically means that you cannot stand things to be done in a second-rate fashion. It means that you cannot stand to see the needs of people go unmet. You cannot stand a dying ministry idea or program. You will either bring it back to life or put it to rest.

I can remember years ago hearing the late Dr. Henrietta Mears discuss a list of seemingly unsolved problems that she had on her desk when she first went to Hollywood Presbyterian Church. I am sure that she had a list of things that she needed to finish each week and month just like all of us do. She discovered, as all of us do, that people tend to forget those problems which they feel they can never solve. By putting them down on a list, they keep the problems before their eyes. The problems are on the frontal lobe of their minds where they are always nagging at them for attention. The problems become their prayer list. Then someone wakes up in the middle of the night with a magnificently creative solution to one of those problems.

That is the way I see imaginative leaders. They have that restless desire to solve those mighty problems of ministry. I saw this in Russ Rosser who says, "I'm not patient, but I'm stubborn. I'll stick to something until it's concluded, so I don't lose hope. We keep working on a different arrangement of services until we find a solution."

"Chicago was built with no thought of fire. Even the sidewalks were made of resinous pine. The great fire of October 8–10, 1872, killed only 300 but incinerated three and one-half miles of central city and left 100,000 homeless. Local moralists, comparing the disaster to the destruction of Babylon and Rome, called it a "modern apocalypse." A new Chicago arose speedily. It was the first American urban renewal. The years ahead would bring great architectural creativity and the birth of the skyscraper."[268] This is similar to the story of Randy Kinnison who took a church that had just gone through two splits. With his problem-solving determination, he became the imaginative change agent to the Portland suburbs. Now the church is attracting many people, and they are launching into a large, new building program as a meaningful part of the outworking of their new philosophy of ministry.

Management guru Tom Peters concludes that innovative people who are willing to risk failure by treading into uncharted territory lead infinitely richer lives. He says, "You will get more 'at bats,'

toy with more madcap ideas, laugh more, and enjoy the trip more."[269]
Let's say that the next important thing to keep in mind as you seek
to be creative within your ministry is to take the risk of failure.
Certainly this goes beyond the pastor's sermon into every facet of
ministry, including the bulletin announcements.

I was thrilled to hear Rick Warren say that in his staff meeting
they give awards for failures on a regular basis. He feels that is the
only way to encourage risk-taking. I hear much bad theology around
the church about failure. Somehow that always seems to be the
work of Satan. Well, it may be related to the fall, but it is more like
a true expression of our imagination to seek to solve the sin problem.
It should come from a genuine effort to get people to hear the good
news of being free from Satan's domain. God helps everyone to
laugh at his or her mistakes. Then people will be far more
encouraged to be risk-takers.

When you listen to an imaginative thinker, it is almost like
listening to a person from another world. They see things as no one
else does. Risk-takers see all kinds of opportunities. They work
hard on not taking the stereotyped view of the environment. Of
course that takes independent judgment and an ability to tolerate
ambiguity. I like to be with a gifted photographer and watch where
he or she positions the camera to take the pictures and listen to him
or her describe the scenery. I would pay for an architect's time just
to walk down the street of the city and ask him what he or she sees.
Even more important is the chance to walk through the church with
a creative ministry architect. What does he or she see when looking
at the people and the building, when reading the bulletin, and when
looking at the parking lot and even the storage bin in the dark
basement? Listen to these people and develop that same ability.
That muscle in your brain needs a great deal of exercise to get to
such a place.

Hear the story of a trained mind that sees the world the way you
ought to see it. This guy has to be a leader by now. I'll guarantee
you that your church will never be the same if you see the world as
he does:

> If you have ever gone through a tollbooth, you know that
> your relationship to the person in the booth is not the most
> intimate one you'll ever have. It is one of life's frequent
> nonencounters: you hand over some money, you might get change,
> and you drive off. I have been through every one of the seventeen
> tollbooths on the Oakland-San Francisco Bay Bridge on thousands

of occasions, and never had an exchange to remember with anybody.

Late one morning in 1980 heading for lunch in San Francisco, I drove toward one of the booths. I heard loud rock music. It sounded like a party or a Michael Jackson concert, I looked around. No other cars had windows open. No sound trucks. I looked at the tollbooth. Inside it, the man was dancing.

"What are you doing?" I asked.

"I'm having a party," he said.

"What about the rest of these people?" I looked over at other booths. Nothing moving there.

"They're not invited."

I had a dozen other questions for him, but somebody in a big hurry to get somewhere started punching his horn behind me and I drove off. But I made a note to myself: find this guy again. There's something in his eye that says there's magic in his tollbooth.

Months later I did find him again—still with the loud music, still having a party.

Again I asked, "What are you doing?"

He said, "I remember you from the last time. I'm still dancing. I'm having the same party."

I asked, "Look. What about the rest of these people?"

He said, "Stop. What do those look like to you?" He pointed down the row of tollbooths.

"They look like . . . tollbooths."

"Nooo imagination!"

I said, "Vertical coffins."

"What are you talking about?"

"I can prove it. At eight-thirty, like Lazarus from the dead, they re-emerge and go home. For eight hours, brain is on hold, dead on the job. Going through the motions."

"I'm going to be a dancer some day." He pointed to the administration building, "My bosses are in there, and they're paying for my training."

Sixteen people dead on the job, and the seventeenth—in precisely the same situation—figured out a way to live. That man was having a party where you and I would probably not last for a few days. The boredom! He and I did have lunch later, and he said, "I don't understand why anybody would think my job is boring. I have a corner office, glass on all sides. I can see the Golden Gate, San

Francisco, the Berkley Hills. Half of the Western world vacations here. I just stroll in every day and practice dancing."[270]

Probably the most frightening thing to a leader who starts using his or her imagination is that often some of the ministry designs start to seem illogical. An imaginative leader needs to develop a tolerance for ambiguity. It is almost like becoming an abstract artist. "Elijah was the epitome of godly creativity (1 Kings 18). While most people would have taken the easy way out and settled for a war of words on whose god was greater, the prophet proposed the "Match Light Barbecue Challenge." The god who set the altar sacrifice aflame would be declared the winner. You know the story. The Baal followers earned points for vocal endurance and aerobic fitness, but their efforts were fruitless. Elijah then arranged for the firewood to be doused with water three times before the God of Israel answered the prophet's call with fire from heaven. Illogical? Believe it. Effective? Certainly."[271]

This step is especially hard for the engineering type of mind who has to have it all in black and white. No, you cannot do that because some things are too complex. Some have contradictions and disorders that cannot be easily resolved. I have watched Clyde McDowell as a model of what other leaders are doing. He has launched out on a venture that has few answers in place, but a great vision of what might be. He has seen the largest counseling center in Denver come into place out of some very obscure vision of what might have been. Now his vision is for a training center for leaders and churches. The scientific types are nervous because there are so many unanswered questions. He is trusting the God of details to put the pieces in place as they move along during the next year.

When I started to develop my model for the design of a creative philosophy of ministry, I did not know exactly how my model would develop. I am confident that every mind will apply the principles in a different way. Some will not try because it is not a pure enough scientific process, but those who have worked in this fashion seemingly have been successful in their venture to draw people to God and His Kingdom. No, they have not moved outside the framework of God's absolutes, but they have rearranged those functions and principles in a distinct fashion that has expressed God's uniqueness. Count on it. They are guaranteed by Christ, the Chief Cornerstone, that the end product will be a dynamic church. Leith Anderson, Bruce and Marshall Shelley and Steve Rabey all communicate an urgent message that Christians need to create a new expression of Christ's church for the next century in America.

They are saying in their books, "The church must change or drift into cultural irrelevance. Although the challenge they describe is monumental, it is no more difficult than the challenge faced by the earliest Christians."[272]

My list of imaginative characteristics of leaders is not by any means exhaustive, but it will do for starters. If it is godly to be an imaginative thinker, then you can grow up into that image of grace in the same fashion I suggested in the last chapter. Lean into the pain, and you can grow up into righteousness. Keep in mind that there is promise in this life and in the life to come (1 Tim. 4:9) for those who learn to use that art form in building the church.

When you start using your imagination for creating new forms for the church, you will be faced immediately with the necessity of dealing with change because imagination and change are almost inseparable. The older the individual church, the more difficult the task will be. All authors who address the subject of the change of structures talk about the tremendously difficult task of getting people to face the staggering paradigm shifts which the church will need to go through in order to be the church for tomorrow. That requires the wisdom of Solomon and the power of God Himself. Orlando E. Costas reminds us "that if church growth, or for that matter any other missionary theory, wants to fulfill its missionary objective, it is going to have to interact theologically and sociologically with the phenomenon of change. Otherwise, it will neither be able to effectively penetrate the social structures of our world with the gospel, nor to intelligently discern and interpret the signs of the Kingdom in the secular structure of society, nor, consequently, to contribute to the expansion of God's reign in a heterogeneous and complex world."[273] Loren Mead goes even a step further to say that "every congregation will face a major stress in the coming decades, more or less. Power will shift. Financial systems will be affected. Relations with congregations will change. The basic framework may have to be redesigned. The old model of oversight will not be adequate. In many places, even today, it is in crisis or collapse already."[274]

If you listen to these men well, you will come to realize that every church leader who wants to lead the church where it really makes a difference will need to be a masterful change agent. Space will not permit the critical subject of change to be discussed at length, but there are a few salient suggestions that are critical for you to keep in mind as you become the change agent. For a more thorough study of the subject, it would be wise to study the works of Leith Anderson, Lyle Schaller, and Mike Tucker.[275]

If you develop your philosophy of ministry well, it will no doubt include some change. As you approach change, it is very important to keep in mind the "security cone" described in chapter 10. That is extremely basic to the change process. The following questions need to be addressed: "Where is the congregation secure?" "What is their next stage of insecurity?" and "Are they ready for this change?"

Your church's polity may not necessitate your taking issue with the congregation for change. Even if you do not need to do that, it is still wise to get them involved. That is especially important when it is some kind of ministry in which they need to participate. It may take longer, but their ownership in the process will be greatly affected by their participation in the change. Hersey and Blanchard state when that is most important:

> The participative change cycle tends to be more appropriate for working with individuals and groups who are achievement-motivated, seek responsibility, and have a degree of knowledge and experience that may be useful in developing new ways of operating. In other words, people with task-relevant readiness. Once the change starts, these people are much more capable of assuming responsibility for implementation of the desired change. Although these people may welcome change and need to improve, they may become very rigid and opposed to change if it is implemented in a directive manner. A creative change style is inconsistent with their perceptions of themselves as responsible self-motivated people who should be consulted throughout the change process. When they are not consulted and change is implemented in an authoritarian manner, conflict often results.[276]

It is so important if you are going to lead people through any kind of change that you earn the right to take them into the change. Kenneth Blanchard suggests that you can contract power with people from the very beginning. They will need to give you the right to do that anyway.[277] It could surely save a great deal of conflict in the future, so why not get their permission to start with? After all, you are going to be dealing with their lives. If you are unwilling to do this, then maybe the change is for you and not for them. That starts to look like anarchy. You certainly need to be aware that it may take years to gain the right to lead in any major change. That is somewhat determined by the tenure of your leadership, your age in contrast to their age, and how effective you are perceived by the congregation.

Randy Kinnison talks about having the confidence of the congregation.

> We launched groups using Church Alive material (including an on-site visit from a consultant), sent people to San Francisco for training, and eliminated our Wednesday night Bible study at the church in order to facilitate Wednesday night small groups. I believe the church responded to the willingness to let go of Wednesday night Bible study at the church, which they have held for years because (1) there was little interest in it, and (2) they had come to, I believe, trust me as their pastor. I had done my homework. I brought before them a well-researched program that I believed met the needs of our specific church, and I had just spent a week alone in prayer and solitude believing that the spirit of God had directed and brought a deeper sense of purpose and unity to my life.[278]

It appears that faith and confidence in the pastor are closely associated with having faith in the institution itself. Both of these things are of equal importance when it comes to institutional change. "The most crucial component of character when we talk of change is the motivation that comes from faith in the fairness of the organization and its ability to change. Unfortunately, these are the very beliefs executives destroy first when they try to motivate people to change by showing them the inadequacies of the old system."[279] You need never forget how precious the character of the church is to those who are members of the body of Christ. Their whole character and identity is tied up in their local assembly.

If you are really going to be a sensitive leader in the process, then you will want to take precaution to use the appropriate kind of leadership style. Here is a simple understanding of what Kenneth Blanchard calls situational leadership: "You will choose your style of leadership in reference to the current situation. This includes many things such as the willingness and ability of the congregation to change. Those styles change as those two traits increase." [280]

> R1 *Telling*, unwilling and unable
> R2 *Selling*, unable but willing
> R3 *Participating*, able but unwilling
> R4 *Delegating*, able and willing

In the early years of my church consulting, I learned that many of the things I would suggest that churches do to make them more effective were things they had done in the past but had failed to continue for one reason or another. It is much easier to go back and reinstitute something from the past that was effective than to try to bring about change. The event or idea may simply need to have a new coat of paint. Peter Drucker found that failure in major business ventures in America often came the same way. He said, "Results were achieved not by doing something different but by doing something everyone had been preaching—but only the few had been practicing."[281]

When you are going to lead any group through change, it is critical to understand what their culture is because that is basic to who those people are. Will you disconnect them from their history? You cannot destroy that because if you do, then you may destroy their identity. It is delightful to find that if you can introduce change within their culture, then they will be far more ready to accept the change. Drucker illustrates this so well: "Culture, no matter how defined, is singularly persistent. Nearly 59 years ago, Japan and Germany suffered the worst defeats in recorded history, with their values, their institutions and their cultures discredited. But today's Japan and today's Germany are unmistakably Japanese and German in culture, no matter how different this or that behavior. In fact, changing behavior works only if it can be based on the existing 'culture'."

The leadership of Mission Hills Baptist Church of Denver did their home work well in preparation to lead the congregation through another major change. They kept their harmony as they went through many changes in recent years. When leaders brought the idea of changing the name of the church to the congregation, they voted it down. To them the name Baptist represented their culture. That was the way they saw themselves. It represented their history and basically who they were. No doubt that change may eventually come, and if it does, that issue will have to be dealt with again. They might get a key insight into instituting that change by listening to Alan Wilkins who suggests that "rather than trying to dismantle the old character, grow on the strengths of the past. Identify what has worked well previously and what will continue to work. In reality, there is no alternative. People cannot simply cease to think and behave in old ways upon demand."[282] It appears that churches who change their name deal with that identity issue carefully.

One of the greatest tools to have in your change toolbox is a list of the reasons why people tend to resist change. In your dialogue, you will generally hear resistance phrases that will give you a clue as to how to address the group you are seeking to lead through change. Here are some of the major reasons why people resist change and one suggestion in each case as to how you may get them to make changes which are to their benefit:

1. They are very comfortable with the present. They feel that the future arrives just about the time they are getting comfortable with the present. This may take some time, but it definitely will necessitate presenting an adequate picture of how they will fit into the future. They must see themselves fitting comfortably into that new situation. Randy Pope learned that it was wise many times not to flag a change because that made them go into a resistance mode.
2. They find that their turf or vested interest is being attacked. In this situation they may need to be involved in designing the future constitution, name change, building plans, or philosophy of ministry.
3. They may have that inner fear of failure. This tends to be common among perfectionists. These people have to see all of the details and be shown the way everything in the change will work out for the better.
4. They may be ignorant of all the circumstances that are involved and therefore may be resisting the unknown. This may mean a group hearing or at least some dialogue where all of their questions are answered to their satisfaction.
5. They may be resisting the people who are leading the change because of a personality conflict or some unfortunate circumstances of the past. In these situations, the conflict must be discovered and then dealt with.

I had read the story of Michaelangelo's paintings in the Sistine Chapel with great wonder. When my wife and I saw them, we could readily see why this was what most critics have described as one of the world's greatest pieces of art done by one of the world's greatest artists. My imagination glands worked overtime while I stood with the crowds in silent admiration of these masterpieces. My imagination pictured the artist lying on his back for months on end, trying to create a view of what these angelic beings must look like. After numerous tries to stroke the glories of God on one face, he laid his brush down in frustration. Out of the corner of his eye he saw a small boy playing in the courtyard among the rubble left over from the construction. He hollered, "Son, come up here, I need your help." Without a moment's hesitation, the boy climbed the scaffolding and found himself at the side of the master artist.

"What do you want, sir?"

"Well, I'm having a difficult time getting this face to look like someone who is working and worshiping in the presence of God. You look like you ought to be able to help me."

"No sir, I have never painted, and I don't know what you are trying to do."

The master took his hand and said, "I need the freshness of your youth and your imagination. You go ahead and paint, and I will guide your hand." Soon the expression on the artist's face shown with great satisfaction. "Look, son, together we can do this work. I'm sure that God is pleased with our work. Thank you for letting me have your hands and your mind."

You can imagine the sense of satisfaction the boy felt as he climbed down from the scaffolding even though he didn't know that he was in the presence of the world's greatest artist.

You, too, can have that great sense of gratification as you climb the ladder of Christ's church and hear Him say, "You are God's fellow worker" with me in building my church.[283] Never lose the wonder of a child working hand in hand with God in building His glorious church in the rubble of a bleak and ugly world.

Appendixes

Appendix 1

Values Auction

This learning exercise should be used for a leadership team at the church. It would be best adapted for a leadership retreat. This should be used to help leaders corporately and personally discover where they put their highest values. Appoint an auctioneer to lead the leadership team in bidding on the following items. Each person is given $10,000 with which he can bid on any or all of the items. People are to make a values decision about the worth of each item they would feel worth their investment. The list is simply a suggestion and should be of assistance to you as you design a list of the values you want the leaders to deal with. This will be determined somewhat by the current position of the church in its history and its culture.

Be sure to add to the list things you may guess that people would choose for their own personal portfolio. The auctioneer will play a major role in getting the group to come to grips with the things they highly cherish. After all of the items are purchased, have them meet in groups of three to discuss why they chose to purchase the things they did. Next you could have the whole group list in the preferred order of importance the items that they would like the church to own.

_____ A new gymnasium for the church
_____ A director of evangelism
_____ 100 new converts
_____ A cure for cancer for the world
_____ A 95% turnout for a night of prayer
_____ The formation of 15 new discipleship groups
_____ A doubled missionary budget for next year
_____ A new group of people to form a new evangelism team
_____ Money and products to meet the needs of the city's poor for 6 months
_____ Getting the congregation to be faithful to all of the worship services
_____ A new organ
_____ A new library for the church
_____ A revival of the congregation which would lead the majority of the congregation to deal with personal sins
_____ A youth group doubled in size

(Add to the list the additional things you would have the group deal with.)

Appendix 2

Core Values of the Conservative Baptist Foreign Mission Society

Values create, shape and perpetuate the ethos of an organization. These core values assume a number of other commitments which are foundational to CBFMS such as doctrinal fidelity, missionary vision, dedication of life, personal holiness, and the local church as God's primary means of accomplishing His purposes today. In pursuit of our ministry objectives, the following underlying values characterize every aspect of CBFMS endeavor.

Individual Dignity

We diligently maintain and promote the dignity and worth of each individual within CBFMS ministries worldwide. People with a proper sense of spiritual and emotional well-being are freed for productive ministry that is committed to goal-oriented planning and team accountability.

Corporate Creativity

We encourage creative and innovative strategies directed by the Spirit of God and implemented through policies and structures which are characterized by mutual trust and cooperation.

Uncompromising Integrity

We adhere uncompromisingly to honesty and integrity in all matters pertaining to the mission enterprise whatever the consequences. This will always be manifested by biblical standards of ethics, morality and financial accountability wherever CBFMS personnel are involved.

Personal Development

We are committed at all levels of leadership to create an organizational climate conducive to continuing personal growth and development in missionary service. Management is implemented as a ministry of enablement and encouragement.

We believe these values have profound implications for demonstrating the new order which has begun in Jesus Christ. Their implementation in the life of the mission family will be reflected in our commitment to the glory of God through the fulfillment of the Great Commission.

—From Conservative Baptist Foreign Society literature

Appendix 3

A Study Sheet for Designing Your Philosophy of Ministry

Have your leadership team reach a consensus on these fifteen ministry functions after studying chapters 7, 8, and 9. Then mark on each continuum on the chart below what best expresses your church's position on each of the functions. The design of your ministries should be a reflection of those decisions. This will be a first step in designing your church's Philosophy of Ministry Statement.

UPWARD TO GOD					
Worship / Music	Contemporary				Traditional

UPWARD TO GOD					
Preaching / Teaching	Evangelistic				Exhortational

UPWARD TO GOD					
Charisma	Charismatic				Non-charismatic

UPWARD TO GOD					
Participants	Inclusive				Exclusive

INWARD TO HIS BODY					
Authority / Leadership	Laity				Clergy Control

INWARD TO HIS BODY					
Membership	Inclusive				Exclusive

INWARD TO HIS BODY					
Discipline	Organization				Organism

INWARD TO HIS BODY					
Nurture	Non-directed				Directed Growth

INWARD TO HIS BODY					
Fellowship	Anonymity				Directed Relationships

INWARD TO HIS BODY					
Facility	Modest				Stately

OUTWARD TO THE WORLD					
Target	Seeker				Family Reunion

OUTWARD TO THE WORLD					
Evangelism	Program-directed				Personal-directed

OUTWARD TO THE WORLD					
People	Homogeneous				Heterogeneous

OUTWARD TO THE WORLD					
Morality	Creation				Redemptive Theology

OUTWARD TO THE WORLD					
Stewardship	Removed				at Home Mission

Appendix 4

Philosophy of Ministry for a Disciple-making Church

Purpose: The purpose of _____ church is to glorify God by making disciples who *exalt* God, *edify* other believers, *evangelize* starting in their own locale, and *extend* disciple-making to all the world.

Non-negotiable Philosophical Principles:

1. We will at all times have an intentional strategy to accomplish each aspect of our purpose.
2. Evangelism (including pre-evangelism) is the starting point and indispensable catalyst to all disciple-making.
3. The purpose of every activity of our church is to produce and further develop disciples. We will evaluate every activity by its effectiveness in producing disciples and modify or discontinue activities that ineffectively do this.
4. We define a disciple as a believer who is becoming more like Christ by obediently growing in character, ability to minister to others, and in helping to make more disciples.
5. We will primarily make disciples as a team, as a church, not just as a collection of independent individuals.
6. The senior pastor's role and commitment is primarily to give direction, to train leaders, and be a model disciple. He should

    seldom perform ministries lay leaders could do unless it is absolutely necessary.

7. The church member's role and commitment is to grow as a disciple, to be trained, to use one's gifts, and empowered by the Holy Spirit to minister directly to Christians and pre-Christians. The church will encourage and empower gifted individuals to be creative, proactive, need-oriented, and decentralized in disciple-making, and will grant permission and give resources whenever possible.

8. We recognize servant gifts as being equally as important as leadership gifts in building a healthy, disciple-making church.

9. All staff, policy makers, and group leaders must be growing disciples committed to the church's philosophy of ministry.

10. Leaders will be recognized both by considering character and giftedness.

11. We are committed to the principle of multiplication of ourselves by evangelizing, discipling, training, and delegating ministry to others who are faithful.

12. We will multiply ourselves and train others using the method of apprenticeship.

13. The primary method of making disciples is the decentralized small group. We see one-on-one approaches as valid, sometimes necessary, but only a secondary method for most in our church.

14. Reasonable accountability is an indispensable method in making disciples.

15. We will offer nurturing/equipping ministries at multiple commitment levels to develop sequential growth for disciples.

16. Our evangelism will focus on multiple, specific groups rather than using a generic approach.

17. Our organizational structure and leadership styles will flex and change as we move through our life cycle as a church.

18. We will promote the belief that the church's most important identity and ministry takes place while it is decentralized.

                                                   —Bob Gilliam

Appendix 5

Analogies for Staff Ministry

Interview Questions: "Which analogy or combination of analogies as stated best describes your current or most recent staff ministry relationships?"

1st   2nd

____ ____ 1. One analogy is that of a **star**

All full-time paid ministers are serving toward a total ministry, with each minister a distinct and equal point of the star in significance and identity. All points represent professional specialists in an area of competency more so than any other pastor.

____ ____ 2. The analogy of a **ship**

The senior pastor is a captain, determining priorities and essentials for emphasis, time, and other resources. As helmsman, he must steer and coordinate.

____ ____ 3. The analogy of a **sports team**

The senior pastor is a coach and quarterback calling the plays, requiring loyalty and fidelity of all staff members, who are trained and disciplined toward a common goal and plan determined by staff and lay leadership (point guard).

____ ____ 4. The analogy of a **van**

All staff may participate in giving advice, planning and working together to formulate strategies and programs, but only one person can drive (the senior pastor). He or she has the responsibility of guiding, pacing, and arriving safely at the destination.

___ ___ 5. The analogy of a **proper hybrid**

All staff have a unity with diversity, with vigor and productivity not possessed by individual original strains. Staff uniqueness is encouraged as strengths in competencies, styles, and personalities so they mesh with each other.

___ ___ 6. Other analogy:

Adapted from *Review and Expositor*, Winter Issue, 1961, pp. 46–47, 55.

Appendix 6

A Look at the Six Views of Culture

After looking at 2 Corinthians 6:16–18 and Ephesians 5:8–10, answer the following questions in reference to the cultural position assigned to your group from chapter 3 in Gibbs.

1. How would this group define culture?

2. How would they define Christian separation? Give illustrations of what that would look like in their lifestyles?

3. How would this group view the schooling issues?

4. How would this group view the moral and ethical issues of society? (In their preaching/teaching, the political arena, in opposing these issues)

5. How would this group practice their evangelism?

6. What graduate schools and other Christian organizations would they be identified with?

7. What groups of society in Tex Sample's *Lifestyles and Mainline Churches* would most often be identified with this group?

Appendix 7

Evangelism Leadership Bibliography

Abraham, William. *The Logic of Evangelism.* Grand Rapids: William B. Eerdmans Publishing Co., 1989.

Aldrich, Joseph C. *Life-style Evangelism: Crossing Traditional Boundaries to Reach the Unbelieving World.* Portland: Multnomah Press, 1981.

Dayton, Edward R. and Fraser, David A. *Planning Strategies for World Evangelization.* Grand Rapids: William B. Eerdmans Publishing Co., 1978.

DeWitt, David A. *Answering the Tough Ones: Common Questions About Christianity.* Chicago: Moody Press, 1980.

Greenway, Roger S., ed. *The Pastor-Evangelist: Preacher, Model, and Mobilizer for Church Growth.* Grand Rapids: Baker Book House, 1987.

Johnston, Arthur. *The Battle for World Evangelism.* Wheaton: Tyndale House Publishers, Inc., 1978.

Little, Paul E. *How to Give Away Your Faith.* Chicago: InterVarsity Press, 1966.

McCloskey, Mark. *Tell It Often, Tell It Well: Making the Most of Witnessing Opportunities.* San Bernardino: Here's Life Publishers, 1988.

McGavran, Donald A. *Effective Evangelism: A Theological Mandate.* Phillipsburg: Presbyterian and Reformed Publishing Company, 1988.

Packer, J. I. *Evangelism and the Sovereignty of God.* Chicago: InterVarsity Press, 1961.

Petersen, Jim. *Evangelism for Our Generation: The Practical Way to Make Evangelism Your Lifestyle.* Colorado Springs: Navpress, 1987.

Posterski, Don. *Reinventing Evangelism: New Strategies for Presenting Christ in Today's World.* Downers Grove: InterVarsity Press, 1989.

Rainer, Thom S. *Evangelism in the Twenty-first Century: The Critical Issues.* Wheaton: Harold Shaw Publishers, 1989.

Sisson, Dick. *Evangelism Encounter: Bringing the Excitement of Evangelism Back into the Body.* Wheaton: Victor Books, 1988.

Veerman, David R. *Youth Evangelism: When They're in Your Neighborhood but Not in the Fold.* Wheaton: Victor Books, 1988.

Appendix 8

Church Attendance Survey Items

(date)

Dear Friends,

Would you do me a small favor that should take only a few minutes of your time?

I am working as a church consultant for _____ to help them enrich their ministry. Their records show that you were a part of this congregation for a short period of time. Your answers to the attached questions could serve as a helpful means to strengthen the church. All answers will remain anonymous, so please be honest and straightforward.

Thank you for your cooperation. The questionnaires will come to my office where I will study them and share only the tabulated results with the church.

Yours in Christ,

Dr. Harold J. Westing
Center for Leadership Development
Denver, Colorado

Church Attendance Evaluation

A. I (we) attended your church:
   _____   1-4 weeks
   _____   2-5 months
   _____   6-12 months
   _____   a year or more

B. My (our) age bracket is:
   _____   1-21 years
   _____   22-29 years
   _____   30-45 years
   _____   46-65 years
   _____   over 65

C. I (we) consider myself (ourselves):
   _____   born-again Christian(s)
   _____   non-believer(s)

D. I (we) currently:
   _____   attend another church
   _____   am (are) looking for another church

E. I (we) discontinued attending because:
   (check one or more)
   1. ____   moved away
   2. ____   were not welcomed adequately
   3. ____   the services did not meet spiritual needs
   4. ____   did not appreciate the style of worship
          _____   too informal
          _____   too formal
   5. ____   did not appreciate the use of the school building
   6. ____   the preaching did not meet needs
   7. ____   the educational program did not meet needs
   8. ____   there were not sufficient programs for the family
   9. ____   there was a lack of opportunities for service
   10. ____ there were inadequate parking facilities
   11. ____ theological difference (please specify) _____

   _____
   _____
   _____
   _____

12. _____ other _____
_____
_____
_____
_____

F. Did you attempt to communicate the concerns which you checked under section "E" to the staff or elders?

_____ yes _____ no

If you did try to communicate with the staff or elders, did you find them responsive to your concerns?

_____ yes _____ no

G. Even though I (we) no longer attend, I (we) appreciated the following strengths:
(check one or more)
1. _____ worship content
2. _____ educational programs
3. _____ warmth of the staff and congregation
4. _____ the style of the church worship services
5. _____ the weekly small groups
6. _____ the preaching
7. _____ ministry of music
8. _____ other factors (please specify) _____
_____
_____

H. What other important factors should the church leadership be aware of that would help them more adequately carry out their ministry? _____
_____
_____
_____
_____
_____

I. What or who helped you attend the church for the first time?
1. _____ a friend brought me
2. _____ family member
3. _____ advertisement

4. _____ knew of services by word of mouth
5. _____ came out of curiosity
6. _____ a stranger invited me

J. Other comments: _____
_____
_____
_____
_____

Appendix 9

Unleashing the Church

1. **Strategy/Goal Oriented vs. Event/Activity Oriented**
   This emphasizes the fact of the plan. Build a ministry on a thought-out strategy, not on a series of events. Parachurch groups are strategy oriented—they know why they are doing what they are doing. Churches tend to be event oriented—it is easy for programs to become ends in themselves and not a part of an overall plan. Activities should be a means to an end that has been thought through.

2. **Vision Oriented vs. Maintenance Oriented**
   This emphasizes the scope or thrust of the plan. There tends to be a maintenance mentality in churches instead of an aggressive thrust. Churches tend to have a "come to us" versus a "we'll go to you" mentality.

3. **Organism Based on Headship of Christ vs. Organization Based on Human Plans**
   The Lord Jesus Christ is the Head of His church, not the pastor, or elders or anyone else. He is the One who guides, directs, leads, provides resources, etc. There must be a conscious dependence upon Him so that His purposes for the church might be accomplished.

4. **Every Member a Minister vs. Every Member a Spectator**
   Each member in the body of Christ has the responsibility to be responsive to the Head. He has a place for them to function in His body and has given them spiritual gifts that they might minister. The ministry is in the hands of the laity.

5. **Freedom to Initiate Ministries vs. Stifling of Initiative**
   The people must know that along with the responsibility to be responsive to the Head is the responsibility to be obedient to what the Lord Jesus would want them to do. The people must be given the freedom to initiate ministries.

6. **Spirit-led, Intrinsic Motivation vs. Human-led, Extrinsic Motivation**
   Jesus is the Head of the church and what people do they do because God has given them the desire to do it, not because someone has talked them into doing it. This emphasizes the "want-to" motivation versus the "have-to" motivation.

7. **Structure Follows Ministry vs. Ministry Follows Structure**
   Never produce ministry out of structure, but structure out of ministry. Build the structure around the initiative of Spirit-led people. Committees should be formed from people who are ministering.

8. **Leadership Position Based on Influence vs. Credentials**
   A person doesn't become a leader based on his/her credentials. A person becomes a leader because he/she is having an influence in the lives of people.

9. **Flexibility of Structure vs. Sacredness of Structure**
   If structure flows from ministry, then it follows that the structure must be flexible. The Head of the church is directing us in a certain way today. Therefore, our structure is based on His leading. However, He may lead us differently one year from now. If so, we must be willing to change that which is necessary to follow His leading.

10. **Trust in People vs. Control Over People**
    People who have a desire for a ministry must be trusted by the leadership of the church to follow the Lord in the development of that ministry.

11. **Freedom to Fail vs. Pressure to Succeed**
    People who are responsible to the Head, who take the initiative to begin a ministry and who are trusted by the leadership, must be given the freedom to fail.

12. **Responsibility with Authority vs. Responsibility Without Authority**
    We must not separate responsibility and authority. Responsibility for a ministry means authority to do the ministry.

13. **Ministry Oriented vs. Superstar/Superstructure Oriented**
    The focus must be on ministry rather than on the egos of people or the organizational framework.

    —Bear Valley Church
    Denver, Colorado

Appendix 10

Philosophy of Ministry: Grace Evangelical Free Church, Mason City, Iowa

Statement of Vision: "A Heart for People"

Statement of Mission: It is our mission to make disciples of Jesus Christ in North Iowa and beyond, attracting and leading unbelievers to Jesus, and developing them toward Christlikeness.

Out of our statement of vision and mission grow the priorities that enable us to accomplish our mission.

I. It is our mission to make disciples of Jesus Christ in North Iowa and beyond.

   A. Priority #1: focusing people's vision to make disciples (Matt. 28:18–20)

      1. North Iowa Orientation
      2. Enhancing Image in Community
      3. Global Christians
      4. Sense of Urgency
      5. Action Plans

   B. Priority #2: finding lost people through intentional evangelism (Acts 1:8)

      6. Church Growth
      7. Evangelism
      8. Membership
      9. Networking

II. . . . developing those who believe toward Christlikeness.

   A. Priority #3: folding believers into the life of the church (Acts 2:42–47)

      10. Care and Counseling
      11. Proportionate Sacrificial Giving
      12. Unified Diversity
      13. Role of Staff

B. Priority #4: feeding believers through corporate, congregational, and cell ministries (2 Tim. 4:1–5; 3:16)

14. Relevant Bible Teaching
15. Growing by Discipling
16. Celebration
17. Congregation and Cell Group Structures

C. Priority #5: framing ministry structures that release believers to co-labor with Christ, utilizing their God-given abilities and talents (1 Peter 4:10–11; Eph. 4:11–12)

18. Elder-guided Ministry
19. Leadership Development
20. Planning and Organization
21. Facilities
22. God-given Abilities and Talents
23. Lifestyle
24. Multiple Ministries
25. Political Practices
26. Teachable

Appendix 11

Philosophy of Ministry: Sun River Church: Sacramento, California

I love visionaries. Joe (the imaginary Joe is found in every church or group) was a visionary. In fact, Joe's enthusiasm and love for the Lord were contagious, and he was a great impetus to the vision of the church. But Joe produced a different idea each week. One week he would walk into my office with an idea of how we could reach all the Vietnamese refugees in our city. Two weeks later he wanted to sponsor a "World Vision" hunger campaign with our young people. The next week he was ready to take a group of young people to Haiti to help construct a hospital. Joe wanted the church to do it all, and in fact, many of these programs would be effective. But they weren't the church's ideas. They were Joe's. He would burn out many people in the process and roll over anyone who did not agree with him—me included.

It is refreshing to work with someone who wants to move out. But with two or three visionaries like Joe, the church can become spastic, jerking and groping this way and that without any real direction.

How do you work with a visionary? How do you know what God wants the church to do? Who's vision is God's plan for the church? Just how much freedom does the church leadership give to the membership to have dreams and visions?

A picture has helped me live in this tension at Sun River. I see a road—a wide road that allows freedom. But the road has guardrails that keep the visionary moving in the right direction and protects him from disastrous hazards. In order for us to know what God wants us to do we have established the following guidelines which act as guardrails to guide our church. Within them we have freedom, but they keep us moving the same direction. These guidelines outline our philosophy of ministry.

I. We Are a Bible Church—Not a Tradition Church

The seven words that killed the church were, "We have always done it that way!" Even though we are a young church, it is possible to establish traditions that become more important than the leading of the Holy Spirit. The Bible, not tradition (even Baptist tradition), is our authority in all matters of faith and practice.

II.   We Are a Lay Ministry Church—Not a Staff-centered Church

At Sun River we are committed to a biblical principle that the ultimate work of the church in the world is to be done by the saints—plain, ordinary Christians—and not by the professional clergy or a few selected laymen. We must never lose the impact of the apostle Paul's statement that apostles, prophets, evangelists, and pastor-teachers exist for the equipping of the saints for the work of ministry, for the building up of the body of Christ (Eph. 4:12).

The word "equip" (*katartismon*) is a Greek word from which we get our English word, "artisan"—an artist or craftsman, someone who works with his hands to make or build things. The work of the hired staff is to "equip" the people (ministers) in the church for ministry. We on the staff are to first model effective ministry in our own lives and then essentially get the people of the church ready for action.

Our philosophy is to bring on our staff only those who can equip the broader scope of ministers of our church. Pam's responsibility is to recruit, motivate, and equip all of those ministers who would work with children. Bob's role is to recruit, motivate, and equip all of those ministers who would work with junior high through college students. And Paul's responsibility is to recruit, motivate, and equip all of those who would work with adults. My role is to use the Word of God to cleanse and feed the flock. The Word of God is the instrument of growth in the lives of Christians. I am also to seek out, train, and motivate those who would lead the church (staff and elders).

III.   We Are *a* Church—Not *the* Church

We are not the only church in town. God has planted many branches of His church in the Sacramento area and each church is a part of His body. In some towns the Gospel is preached in over 50 languages. But no one church preaches the Gospel in all 50 languages.

We cannot be the whole body of Christ. We are only part of that body. Therefore we do not feel guilty for not having certain ministries. We cannot meet every need. How do we determine our ministries?

We believe that God will send to us the gifted people we need to effectively minister in the programs that God wants us to have. There are three results of this philosophy.

First, we don't have to beat our heads against the wall trying to recruit people to fill a certain need. If a certain ministry begins to die, it could be that we no longer have the leadership for that ministry. We need to let it die until God brings along the right people to administer and lead. And if the Lord brings someone with a new vision and gifts for Sun River Church, we want to be open to that special ministry. The specialized ministries depend on the gifted people that God sends to our church.

Second, we want to be aware of the parachurch ministries represented in our body. Sun River ministry is not limited to what happens within our walls. Some of our people will be called on to serve the Lord in Campus Life, Young Life, InterVarsity, Navigators, Nurses Christian Fellowship, Bible Study Fellowship, and other effective ministries. We should not fight these ministries, but rather encourage them as they also build up the body.

Third, we encourage members to use their gifts creatively in the church. Sun River Church is not limited to its existing programs. We do not want to spread guilt, however, if a member feels it is time to move elsewhere. Although it is unhealthy to hop from one church to another every year, a person does not have to be in one church his whole life. Individuals and churches change, and sometimes a move is necessary.

I would hope that each person would find an effective ministry for at least three to five years—preferably more—in the same church. But if after a certain time he or she is led to change, we should not accuse one of being a church-hopper.

IV.   We Are a Reproducing Church—Not a Super Church

I am convinced that God has given Sun River the gifts to build a super church. People are hungry for Bible teaching and fellowship. We offer both. If we had the room, our church would continue to grow and grow. When we build our new worship center, the maximum number of members we can have on this property is about 1,500 members. So what do we do after we reach that number? We cannot close the doors and say, "No more!" We have two options. We could sell our property, buy more property and build church facilities to hold 5000 members. And nothing would be wrong with that. Super churches can meet the needs of a community and have a tremendous world outreach. But this is not our philosophy of ministry.

The second option is what I believe that God wants us to do: to reproduce locally and worldwide. I believe that we are to build new churches. Each new branch of Sun River Church would reach to its own community. We want to time each campus carefully, much like Arcade did in planting Sun River. We want to purchase property, start a first building and call a pastor for the new church. This takes time, but when done correctly the church will grow. I dream that by the year 2000 Sun River will be the mother of three other churches and each of these churches can have a membership of about 1500 people. Maybe even one of them will be a super church!

From a worldwide perspective this philosophy addresses our missions program. Our goal is to pay off our indebtedness within ten years (by 1990). We want to pay off our $6,000 per month interest payments as fast as we can. During that time we want to teach and challenge the church about missions. But in the next phase of our church life (1990-2000), we want to become a center for world missions. I am hoping that half of our total budget will be used for missions. This missions fund would be used to start new churches, relieve famine, send teams from our church to help missionaries (i.e., a construction team to build a hospital) and missionary support. I have a dream that when our own people (whose missionary gifts have been recognized by the church) desire to go to the mission field, we as a church will fully support them. We will be able to say to the prospective missionary, "You need not take the time to raise your support—GO!"

V.   The Church Is People—Not a Building

Sun River Church is not located at the corner of Trinity River and Sunrise. Our buildings and offices are located there, but our church is scattered all over Sacramento. We are to go out into the world and be salt and light in our jobs, communities, school, homes and businesses.

There are several applications of this philosophy. First of all that makes us a soul-winning church, but not an evangelistic meeting church. We do not bring the world into the church buildings to be saved, but we send the saved into the world to evangelize. God has given each one of us gifts, and we are to use these gifts to bring people to Christ. For example, some win their right to witness with the gift of helps, others with the gift of mercy, and others with the gift of administration. It is our ministry as members of Sun River Church to move out into the community and use our gifts to witness. We do not bring people to our meetings so that our professional staff can lead them to Christ.

Second, we do not build elaborate facilities. Our buildings are a testimony to our community in that they are functional and appear nice. But they are not ostentatious. We believe that the majority of our money should be put into ministry rather than buildings.

VI. We Are a Worshiping/Teaching Church—Not a Lobbying Church

Baptists hold to the principle of the separation of church and state. The role of the church is to lead people to Jesus Christ and teach biblical morality. We are not to become an organizational political caucus to lobby for the changing of the civil laws.

Individual members of Sun River are very involved in many political issues, acting as salt and light in the community. That is the way we sense God directed the apostle Paul to organize the New Testament churches. Paul never led the church as an organization to demonstrate against slavery in the first century. He merely taught the principles of how to be moral in an immoral world. That is our calling.

We meet to worship and study the principles of God's Word. We are called to lead people into a personal relationship with a Holy God through the Lord and Savior Jesus Christ and to teach the principles of morality. We are not to usher in the millennium—a time of perfect peace. We do not feel that the United States is God's special blessed country or that we are to keep it pure through legislation. We believe that we only keep our country pure by humbling ourselves, praying and seeking God's face (2 Chron. 6:14).

Closing

In closing I want to make two observations about these guidelines. First, although we believe that this is the direction in which God has led us for this time. That does not mean that God will not redirect us at some point. I am a firm believer in setting goals. We have five-year goals, ten-year goals and twenty-year goals. We are planning on completing our physical plant and being debt free by 1990. By 1990 we want to have planted a new church in Elk Grove. However, even with goals we must be aware that the Holy Spirit may change those plans. We must never forget James 4:13–17 which talks about the person who brags about his plans. We always place our goals under the direction of God's will.

Last, these guidelines are merely principles to help us fulfill our purpose as a New Testament church, based on the teaching of God's Word. We state this purpose:

We exist for the glory of God as a worshiping community.
We exist for believers as a nurturing community.
We exist for the world as a redeeming community.

(November 1988)

Appendix 12

10 Rules for Growth

What can we learn from these new Christians recently inducted into the church? Three faculty members—Paul Borden, Tim Weber and Harold Westing—work with the Institute for Church Development, the Denver Seminary program that evaluates churches. They offered some observations based on our interviews and their experience with scores of congregations.

1. **Focused churches work from a clear statement of purpose.** This statement reflects a vision large enough to stir the blood, yet specific enough to be achieved in a generation. A clear vision should be succinct enough to be stated on a bumper sticker.

2. **The best church boards do not serve their church—they serve their communities through the church.** They possess a vision driven by ministry. They do not view themselves as competitors with other evangelical congregations in their area, but as workers together with God. A board lives with the reality that new members will be attracted to people like themselves, but they also figure out how they can serve those individuals who don't fit into the profile of their congregations.

3. **Growing churches minister to people's needs.** Their leaders develop strategies to satisfy those needs rather than merely perpetuating activities of the organization. Most new people enter a church as consumers, asking what a church can do to serve them rather than what they can do to serve others. They expect a church to provide basic services (preaching, worship, youth programs, small groups, music). The church that provides the best services for that family or individual will probably be the one they will attend.

4. **Biblical churches wrestle with the tension of motivating members to do what they ought to do in contrast to what people want to do about their responsibilities to God and others.** Leaders must devise strategies that move Christians from where they are to where they need to go.

5. **Friendly churches extend friendship to everyone.** Many congregations are warm and inviting to those on the inside. Outsiders, however, sometimes have to storm their way into the ranks. Strong churches cultivate a band of women and men who give up socializing with friends on Sunday to network visitors into their fellowship. This networking makes visitors feel comfortable not only in the worship services but also in the Sunday school classes and small groups. While outsiders first appear at worship services, they usually become active members only when they become involved with other activities in the church.

6. **Effective churches treat their members as adults.** They trust them. The leaders understand that the line of penetration is from the pulpit to the pew to the pavement. They recognize that every Christian's gifts and call to serve Christ are as valid as the pastor's. Most believers desire to serve God. Their biggest problem is knowing how or where. Many need permission to represent their Lord in the marketplace. These churches realize that wholeness is not found in the individual but in the congregation. Balance resides in the body, not in its individual members. Kenneth Boulding, in *The Meaning of the Twentieth Century*, observed that "there are many things that one man can do because other people are not doing them. If everyone at the same time decided to go downtown, draw money out of the bank or even pay their debts, the whole system would collapse." That principle applies to the church. What mayhem, if everyone decided to sing in the choir or signed up to usher. We release others for ministry by tending our own. Strong leaders do not insist that members choose between service in the church and ministry in the community. Christians in a church work together to minister not only when the church is gathered, but when it is dispersed in the society.

7. **Powerful churches persuade people who want to minister that they can do it.** A weak church convinces its members that they can't. They imply that ordinary Christians don't have the proper credentials, education or training, or they limit ministry to six or seven activities that take place at the church building. Church bureaucracies that serve themselves stifle service. Wise church leaders expand people's view of

ministry. They not only prepare people for ministry—they place them in ministry and train them as they serve.

8. **Strong churches also provide a variety of ways to do evangelism.** People who might hesitate to go door to door to canvas the neighborhood may cultivate friends for Christ. Other Christians who don't make friends easily may open their homes to an unwed mother for several months while she is having her baby.

9. **Godly churches know their greatest asset in doing God's work isn't programs but people.** According to church growth expert Win Arn, seventy to eighty percent of those attracted to a church come because they have been invited by relatives and friends. Only ten percent come because of the pastor. All of the other efforts of the church account for the rest of the visitors.

10. **Vital churches not only take people in—they include people in.** They respond to visitors as prospects. Some may need a personal relationship to Jesus Christ. Then they look at those prospects as men and women who need a relationship with Christ's people. Church members need at least four experiences as part of a congregation: celebration (worship), social interaction (fellowship), intimacy (small support groups), and ministry (service). Different gatherings will be designed to accomplish different purposes.

To sum up, growing churches always have growing pains. They constantly struggle with the tension between form and freedom. Organization is essential, but too much stifles ministry, inhibits creativity, leads to low morale and places too many people in second-line ministries. This depresses a congregation and creates an environment for gossip and dissatisfaction. On the other hand, while freedom is necessary for creativity, excitement and dynamism in ministry, too much leads to chaos, frustration, and eventually anarchy. The proper balance between form and freedom is never completely settled in the life of a church. Leaders live with it as part of their calling.

—Reprinted with permission of Denver Seminary

Appendix 13

FOUNDATIONS

What we want to become · · · OUR VISION:

Every attender a devoted follower of God.
Every follower a sacrificial servant.
Every servant a loving messenger.

Why we exist · · · OUR PURPOSE:

Based on the Bible as the standard of truth, the purpose of Mission Hills Baptist Church is to honor God by bringing lives into harmony with Him and one another through balanced emphasis on worship, fellowship, discipleship, and evangelism.

How we do our work · · · OUR PHILOSOPHY OF MINISTRY:

We believe that every member of God's family has been given the ministry of Jesus, which is to bring people to God and each other. We also believe that each member of God's family has God—given abilities to fulfill this ministry.

Therefore, in all areas of our church's life, we will seek to motivate, train, equip, and organize people to do Jesus' ministry. We will do this intentionally through informal lifestyle modeling and through formal training programs.

In order to empower God's people and increase effectiveness we will develop ministry teams to work together in the specific avenues of ministry to which God calls us.

Who is responsible · · · OUR STRUCTURE:

	Senior	Special
Worship	Mid	SCA
Missions	Young	ELC
Stewardship	Single	Training/
Shepherding	Youth	Equipping
	Children	

OUR ENVIRONMENT FOR RESULTS:

Where people fit in · · ·

Prayer
Operate by faith
Purpose
Simple organization
Communications
Willingness to change
Unity of Leadership
Leadership trained in ministry
Functional goals and objectives

OUR INVOLVEMENT:

Where people fit in · · ·

Community & Congregation
Celebration
Cell
&
1 to 1

OUR PROCESS: why people stay and catch the vision · · ·

Attraction

Involvement

Reproduction

Multiplication

Implementations . . .

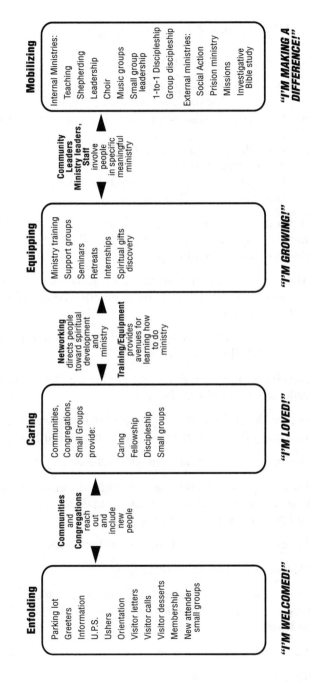

Enfolding

Parking lot
Greeters
Information
U.P.S.
Ushers
Orientation
Visitor letters
Visitor calls
Visitor desserts
Membership
New attender
small groups

Communities
and
Congregations
reach
out
and
include
new
people

Caring

Communities,
Congregations,
Small Groups
provide:

Caring
Fellowship
Discipleship
Small groups

Networking
directs people
toward spiritual
development
and
ministry

Training/Equipment
provides
avenues for
learning how
to do
ministry

Equipping

Ministry training
Support groups
Seminars
Retreats
Internships
Spiritual gifts
discovery

**Community
Leaders
Ministry leaders,
Staff**
involve
people
in specific
meaningful
ministry

Mobilizing

Internal Ministries:
Teaching
Shepherding
Leadership
Choir
Music groups
Small group
leadership
1-to-1 Discipleship
Group discipleship
External ministries:
Social Action
Prision ministry
Missions
Investigative
Bible study

"I'M WELCOMED!"

"I'M LOVED!"

"I'M GROWING!"

*"I'M MAKING A
DIFFERENCE!"*

Increasing levels of involvement, commitment, growth, and obedience

Mission Hills Baptist Church Strategies

1. Meaningfully involve its people in:

   a. Worship—knowing God's worthiness and celebrating His person so that our lives are transformed.
   b. Fellowship—sharing our total lives with one another in Jesus Christ.
   c. Discipleship—building a life-style into each person that honors Jesus Christ.
   d. Evangelism—bringing the unsaved to faith in Jesus Christ and active in the Body of Christ.

2. Encourage commitment in each believer and train them to use their spiritual gifts so that they effectively minister in the church and community.

3. Make excellence the standard of programs so they are continued or added only in terms of effectively fulfilling the church's purpose.

4. Employ competent, godly pastoral staff to equip the church body to fulfill its purpose.

5. Develop long-range goals and implement yearly objectives endorsed by the church body.

6. Follow the godly leadership elected within the church whom God has gifted to enable the church body to fulfill its purpose.

7. Assimilate members and attenders into small groups.

8. Provide dynamic corporate worship experiences that are characterized by God's presence, uplifting music, prayer, and practical biblical teaching.

9. Encourage the unity and strength of family life.

10. Minister to the needs of singles.

11. Determine the felt needs of people outside the church and reach out to meet those needs as a step toward bringing them to Jesus Christ.

12. Seek to grow both spiritually (depth) and numerically (breadth).

13. Teach and encourage stewardship of time, talent, and treasure.

14. Encourage commitment to membership in the church body.

15. Encourage local and foreign missions as a vision and practice of the individual Christian as well as the church body.

16. Support an internship program designed to train competent, godly Christian leaders for the church of Jesus Christ.

17. Develop plans for and implement action to plant daughter churches of like mind and ministry.

18. Encourage youth and adults to consider local and foreign missions as viable options for life service.

Appendix 14

Elizabethtown Evangelical Free Church Strategies

MISSION: To glorify God in corporate worship and personal devotion; to evangelize our community and equip the believer to use God's Word for personal ministry and growth.

VISION: Arising out of a felt need in the community, it is our desire for a church: with a strong evangelical emphasis; sensitive to the needs and perspective of the unchurched in the community; able to provide an atmosphere of challenge and worship and sound biblical teaching; emphasizing discipleship and personal outreach; stimulating active personal and spiritual growth; drawing individuals into a closer walk with God.

MODEL: A "seeker sensitive" model of ministry targets pre-Christians through 1) sermons which are biblical, relevant, thought-provoking, and practical; 2) quality contemporary music; 3) compelling drama and media presentation; 4) creative programming for children, teens, and adults; and 5) a welcoming, caring approach where we accept people for who they are and help them build friendships in the context of small groups.

CORE VALUES:

1. **Church Reproduction:** Commitment to the principle of church planting. Understanding that reproduction is an essential component of the fuller life cycle of the church and a core ingredient of a healthy church.
2. **Missions:** Active participation in the support of missions, both at home and abroad.
3. **Evangelism Outreach:** Commitment to bring people to Christ through love and forgiveness, not guilt and shame.
4. **Disciplemaking:** Commitment to Christ as Lord and to personal holiness. Recognition of the need for specific, intentional training to disciple others.
5. **Practical Daily Living:** Commitment to training in stewardship of time, money, and talents. Belief that the church "happens" in our daily lives, not just within the four walls

of the church building, as the believer is motivated by the experience of Christ's love and forgiveness.

6. **Mobilization of Believers:** Empowerment of lay people to discern and fulfill their God-given passion and calling with each member using his or her own unique spiritual gifts. Promotion of church involvement so that each believer feels and acts as though he or she has ownership in the church.

7. **Celebrative & Reflective Worship:** Contemporary, meaningful style of worship using creative and culturally relevant approaches to reach pre-Christians. Effective communication of God's Word to change lives and apply to us today.

8. **Flexibility:** Willingness to set aside comfort levels formed from our traditional upbringing in order to bring people to Christ, without compromising standards and values taught by the Bible.

9. **Excellence in Programming:** Commitment to quality in programming (e.g., worship services, children's ministries, nursery, Christian education), while at the same time understanding that ministry to people is more important than programs themselves. Recognition that we have only one chance to make a positive first impression.

10. **Small Groups:** Development of care groups to meet the spiritual, emotional, and physical needs of people in a relevant and effective way.

11. **Exercising Faith and Prayer:** Acknowledgment of spiritual warfare and claiming of God's power in our lives.

Appendix 15

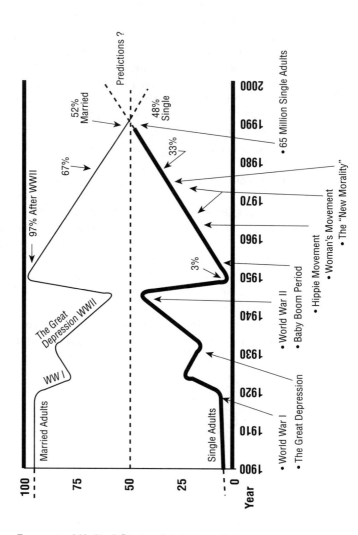

Single/Married Demographics in Twentieth-century America

Percent of United States Adult Population

Endnotes

[1] James Carter, *The Mission of the Church* (Broadman Press: 1974), p. 7.

[2] Ibid., p. 5.

[3] George Barna, *The Power of Vision* (Regal Books: 1991), p. 28.

[4] Aubrey Malphurs, *Developing a Vision for Ministry in the 21st Century* (Baker Book House: 1992), p. 31.

[5] David Moore, pastor of Community Creek Church of Desert Psalms, CA., comment from interview.

[6] Alan Wilkins, *Developing Corporate Character* (Jossey and Bass: 1989), p. 85.

[7] George Barna, *The Power of Vision* (Regal Books: 1991), p. 38-39.

[8] Chuck Colson, "A New Awakening," *Newsweek*, August 9, 1976.

[9] Langdon Gilkey, *Shanton Compound* (1976), p. 76.

10 *Webster's New World Dictionary of the American Language* (World Publishing Co.: 1960), p. 1609.

[11] Bill Hull, *The Disciple-Making Church*, (Revell: 1990), p. 64.

[12] Hunter Lewis, *A Question of Values*, (Harper and Row Publishers: 1990), pp. 9-12.

[13] Alan L. Wilkins, p. 89.

[14] Randy Kinnison, pastor of Bethany Baptist Church in Portland, Oregon, comment from interview.

[15] Bear Valley Church newspaper, "Leadership and Authority," *Heart Beats*, Nov. 88. Disequilibrium in Leadership.

[16] Kinnison, comment from interview.

[17] Joe Ellis, *Church on Purpose* (Standard Publications: 1978), p. 106.

[18] Kent R. Hunter, *Your Church Has Personality* (Abingdon Press: 1985), p. 18.

[19] Bruce Larson and Ralph Osborne, *Emerging Church* (Word Books: 1970) p. 92.

[20] Hunter, p. 63.

[21] Robert Dale, *Search Magazine* (Summer, 1978), p. 38.

[22] Bill Hybels, sermon about his philosophy of ministry.

[23] Lyle Schaller, *Vision.*

[24] Peter Wagner, "Developing a Philosophy of Ministry," *Pastor's Update.*

[25] George Barna, *The Power of Vision* (Regal Books: 1992), p. 112.

[26] Dale, p. 35.

[27] James Humes, *Churchill; Speaker of the Century* (Stein and Day: 1980), p. 269.

[28] Donald Gerig and Gary Litwiller, "When Problem-solving Is Now Practice," *Leadership Journal* (Summer 1992), p. 77.

[29] Tom McKee, Pastor of Sun River Church, Sacramento, California, comment from interview.

[30] Harold Westing, *Multiple Church-staff Handbook* (Kregel Publications: 1985).

[31] Roy Oswald and Speed Leas, *The Inviting Church* (Alban Institute: 1988), p. 65.

[32] Doug Murren, *The Baby Boomerang* (Regal: 1990).

[33] Cheryl Forbes, *Imagination—Embracing a Theology of Wonder* (Multnomah Press: 1986), p. 53.

[34] Steven Arcovey, *The Seven Habits of Highly Effective People*, (Fireside Book: 1989), p. 106.

[35] Warren Bennis and Burt Nanus, *Leaders, the Strategy for Taking Charge* (Harper and Row: 1987), p. 33.

[36] Ibid., p. 39.

[37] Chemistry Match is available from the Institute for Church Development, 43 Inverness Drive East, Englewood, CO 80112.

[38] Forbes, p. 15.

[39] Forbes, p. 157.

[40] From interview with Tommy Barnett.

[41] Interview with Tom McKee.

[42] Bruce Larson and Ralph Osborne, *Emerging Church* (Word Books: 1970), p. 92.

[43] William Easum, *The Church Growth Handbook* (Abingdon Press: 1990), p. 93.

[44] From *Pastor's Update* tape by Peter Wagner.

[45] Kent R. Hunter, *Your Church Has Personality* (Abingdon Press: 1985), p. 41.

[46] Leith Anderson, *Dying for Change* (Bethany House: 1990), p. 150.

[47] Aubrey Malphurs, *Developing a Vision for Ministry in the 21st Century* (Baker Book House: 1992), p. 96.

[48] Perry and Shawchuck, *Revitalizing the 20th Century Church* (Moody Bible Institute: 1982), p. 21.

[49] Ibid.

[50] Robert Clark, Lin Johnson, and Allyn Sloat, eds., *Christian Education Foundations for the Future* (Moody Press: 1991), p. 456.

[51] William Banowsky, *Is the Past Relevant?* (publisher and page unknown).

[52] Lyle Schaller, *The Middle-Size Church* (Abingdon Press: 1985), p. 7.

[53] Ibid., p. 94.

[54] Alan Wilkins, *Developing Corporate Character* (Jossey and Bass: 1989), p. 5.

[55] Ibid., p. 88.

[56] Jim Detmer, "Moving in the Right Circles," *Leadership Journal* (Fall 1992), p. 86. See full description of the three "C's" in this article.

[57] Jim Petersen, "Eclipse of the Gospel," *Discipleship Journal* 55 (1990), p. 11.

[58] Gene Getz, *The Church I Never Intended to Start* (Biblical Renewal, November/December 1987).

[59] Leith Anderson, *Church of the 21st Century* lecture on the growth of a seven-day-a-week church.

[60] Jim Petersen, "Eclipse of the Gospel," *Discipleship Journal*, 55, (1990), p. 14.

[61] Gene Getz, "The Church I Never Intended to Start" *Renewal*, November/December (1987), p. 7.

[62] Ralph Neighbor, *The Seven Last Words of the Church* (Zondervan: 1979), p. 107.

[63] Wallace Hensley, *Form or Frenzy* (Encounter Media: Houston, Texas).

[64] Ibid., p. 1.

[65] Arnold Mitchell, *Nine American Life Styles* (Warner Books: 1984).

[66] Joel Garreau, *Edge City: Life on the New Frontier* (Doubleday), page unknown.

[67] Lyle Schaller, in a speech at the Church of the 21st Century Conference in Dallas, Texas, in July, 1992.

[68] Teck Sample, *U.S. Lifestyles and Mainline Churches* (Westminster/John Knox Press: 1990).

[69] Raymond Ortlund, "Sharing God's Concern for the World," *Bibliotheca Sacra* (Jan. 1981), p. 291.

[70] Bob Gilliam's research from the Institute for Church Development data bank.

[71] C. S. Lewis, *Letters to Malcolm: Chiefly on Prayer* (Harcourt, Brace: London, UK, 1964), p. 4.

[72] A reflection of a study done in James F. White's *Protestant Worship: Traditions and Transition* and spiritual protestant in the *Dictionary of Christianity in America*.

[73] This graph is designed by Professor Paul Borden, Dick Bunger, and Harold Westing of Denver Seminary.

[74] Craig Erickson, *Participation in Worship* (Westminster/John Knox Press: 1989), p. 25.

[75] Donald Hustad, "Music Speaks, But What Language?" *Christianity Today* (May 6, 1977), p. 16.

[76] Findings from the data base from the Institute for Church Development.

[77] Craig Erickson, *Participating in Worship, History, Theory, and Practice* (Westminster/John Knox Press: 1989), p. 1.

[78] Donald Hustad, "Let's Not Just Praise the Lord," *Christianity Today* (Nov. 6, 1987), p. 28.

[79] Margaret Clarkson, "What Makes a Hymn 'Good,'" *Christianity Today* (June 27, 1980), p. 22.

[80] Donald Hustad, "Music Speaks, But What Language?" *Christianity Today* (May 6, 1977), p. 16.

[81] Ann Gascon, "For Many Hispanics, Worship Is a Fiesta," *Worship Leader*, June/July 1992, p. 26.

[82] Hustad, p. 28.

[83] "Talking to God" (*Newsweek*: January 6, 1992), p. 39.

[84] Larry Crabb at the Foundations Conference in San Francisco, 1992.

[85] *The McIntosh Church Growth Network*, September, 1991.

[86] William Easum, *Church Growth Handbook* (Abingdon: 1990), p. 45.

[87] Ibid.

[88] Leith Anderson, *A Church for the 21st Century* (Bethany House: 1992), pp. 21-22.

[89] Kennon L. Callahan, *Effective Church Leadership* (Harper and Row: 1990), p. 1.

[90] Jim Abrahamson, "In Search of the Effective Church," *Leadership Journal* (1990), p. 52.

[91] Roger Greenway, *The Pastor Evangelist* (Presbyterian Reformed Publishing House: 1987), p. 59.

[92] Kirk Hadaway, "Growing off the Plateau: A Summary of the 1988 Church on the Plateau Survey," *Church Growth Today,* vol. 4, no. 3 (1989). The 33-page report is available from Research Service Department, 127 Ninth Avenue North, Nashville, TN 37234.

[93] Douglas Webster of the staff at Cherry Creek Presbyterian Church, "De-Marketing the American Church." A talk given in Denver Seminary chapel in 1990.

[94] Greenway, p. 53.

[95] Eugene Peterson, source unknown.

[96] Greenway, p. 60.

[97] Leith Anderson, *A Church for the 21st Century* (Bethany House: 1992), p. 20.

[98] John Wimber, "Signs and Wonders Today," *Christian Life Magazine* (Special Journal prepared by the editors of Christian Life Magazine), p. 10.

[99] Ibid, p. 10.

[100] Hubbard lists an extensive set of cautions and guidelines to be considered when exploring the initiation of signs and wonders in the congregation.

[101] Ibid., p. 5.

[102] Peter DeWitt, "Signs and Wonders Today," *Christian Life Magazine*, p. 5.

[103] Ibid., p. 27.

[104] Peter Wagner, *Understanding Church Growth* (Eerdmans: 1990) pp. 145–147.

[105] Ibid.

[106] George Barna, *What Americans Believe* (Regal: 1992), p. 193.

[107] Douglas Webster of the staff at Cherry Creek Presbyterian Church, "De-marketing the American Church." A talk given in Denver Seminary chapel in 1990.

[108] Kennon L. Callahan, *Effective Church Leadership* (Harper and Row: 1990).

[109] Peter Wagner, "Developing a Philosophy of Ministry," *Pastor's Update*.

[110] Os Guinness and John Seel, *No God But God* (Moody Press: 1992), p. 178.

[111] Ibid., p. 183.

[112] Warren Bennis and Burt Nanus, *Leaders, the Strategies for Taking Charge* (1985), p. 21.

[113] George Barna, *User Friendly Churches* (Regal Books: 1991) p. 143.

[114] The address for IDAK is 7931 Northeast Halsey, Banfield Plaza Building, Portland, OR 97213. The address for Chem Match is at the Institute for Church Development, 43 Inverness Drive East, Englewood, CO 80112.

[115] Bear Valley Church newspaper, "Leadership and Authority," *Heart Beats* (November 1988).

[116] J. Gary Inrig, "Call to Serve; Toward a Philosophy of Ministry," *Bibliotheca Sacra* (Oct.-Dec. 1983), p. 336.

[117] Bruce Larson and Ralph Osborne, *The Emerging Church* (Word Books: 1970), p. 129.

[118] Barna, p. 168.

[119] Paul Hersey and Kenneth H. Blanchard, *Management of Organizational Behavior* 5th edition (Prentice Hall: 1988), p. 137.

[120] Barna, p. 162.

[121] Kennon Callahan, *Twelve Keys to an Effective Church* (Abingdon Press: 1979), p. 45.

[122] J. Robertson McQuilkin, "Whatever Happened to Church Discipline," *Christianity Today* (March 29, 1974), p. 8.

[123] Barna, *What Americans Believe* (Regal Books: 1992), p. 252.

[124] Leith Anderson, *A Church for the 21st Century* (Bethany House: 1992), p. 174.

[125] Guiness and Seel, p. 87.

[126] Lyle Schaller, *Getting Things Done* (Abingdon Press: 1986), p. 216.

[127] Osborn, Ronald, *Creative Disarray: Models of Ministry in a Changing America* (Chalice Press: 1991) from the index.

[128] William Willimon, *What's Right with the Church* (Harper and Row: 1985), p. 130.

[129] Carl Laney, *Church Discipline: Rebuilding the Family Fellowship*, Punch Line of Western Seminary.

[130] Oliver Price, "How to Begin Church Discipline," *Moody Monthly* (May 1979), p. 37.

[131] J. Robertson McQuilkin, "Whatever Happened to Church Discipline?" *Christianity Today* (March 29, 1974), p. 8.

[132] Suburban Bible Church, "Our Position on Church Discipline," Highland, Indiana.

[133] McQuilkin, p. 9.

[134] See also Michael Griffith, *God's Forgetful Pilgrims* (Eerdmans: 1978).

[135] Anderson, p. 48.

[136] Kent R. Hunter, *Your Church Has Personality* (Abingdon Press: 1985), p. 116.

[137] John S. Thompson, "Look What They've Done to My Song," *Reader's Digest*, December 1990, p. 106.

[138] A publication of the Conservative Baptist Association of America, Wheaton, IL.

[139] *Challenge of the '80s Update* Vol. 18, no. 2 (CBA of America).

[140] Lyle Schaller, Church of the 21st Century Conference in Dallas, Texas, 1992.

[141] George Peters, *A Theology of Church Growth* (Zondervan: 1981), p. 166.

[142] Ken McGarvey, "The Independent Church Myth," *Christianity Today* (July 29, 1991), p. 8.

[143] Raymond Ortlund, "A Biblical Philosophy of Ministry," *Bibliotheca Sacra* (Apr.-June 1981), p. 9.

[144] Discipleship defined by Peter Wagner.

[145] Bill Hull, *The Disciple-Making Church* (Revell: 1989), p. 18.

[146] Ibid., p. 32.

[147] Don Bubna, *Leadership Journal*, Fall 1988, p. 69.

[148] Frank Tillapaugh, *Unleashing Your Potential* (Regal Books: 1988).

[149] Robert Bellah, *Habits of the Heart* (Harper and Row: 1985), p. 121.

[150] Ibid., p. 122.

[151] Knute Larson, *Growing Adults on Sunday Morning* (Victor: 1992), p. 23.

[152] Callahan, p. 67.

[153] Ibid., p. 31.

[154] E. Mansell Pattison, *Pastor and Parish/A System Approach* (Fortress Press: 1977), p. 25.

[155] Knute Larson, *Growing Adults on Sunday Morning* (Victor Press: 1992), p. 41.

[156] Institute for Church Development data base is the resource for this information.

[157] Larson, p. 27.

[158] Ibid.

[159] Dick Murry, *Strengthening the Adult Sunday School Class* (Abingdon Press: 1984), p. 30.

[160] Roy Oswald and Speed Leas, *The Inviting Church* (Alban Institute: 1989), appendixes

[161] Ronald Sider, "Cautions Against Ecclesiastical Elegance," *Christianity Today* (August 17, 1979), p. 15.

[162] Howard A. Snyder, IV, *The Problem of Wineskins* (NavPress: 1975), p. 70.

[163] Kent R. Hunter, *Your Church Has Personality* (Abingdon Press: 1985), p. 31.

[164] Robert E. Webber, "Church Buildings," *Christianity Today* (August 7, 1981), p. 16.

[165] "Seekers or Saints: The Church's Conflict of Interest," a leadership forum, *Leadership Journal* (Fall 1991).

[166] Loren Mead, *The Once and Future Church* (Alban Institute: 1991).

[167] Paul Johnson, "The Passion-Driven Church," *Leadership* (Spring 1992), p. 64.

[168] Bruce Shelley, *The Consumer Church* (IVP: 1992), p. 49.

[169] Joe Ellis, *The Church on Purpose: Keys to Effective Church Leadership* (Broadman: 1982), p. 33.

[170] Alan R. Tippett, *Church Growth and the Word of God* (Eerdmans: 1970), p. 9.

[171] Eddie Gibbs, *I Believe in Church Growth* (Eerdmans: 1981), p. 48.

[172] Peter Wagner, *Understanding Church Growth* 3rd edition (Eerdmans: 1990), p. 24.

[173] Ibid., p. 27-28.

[174] Robert McQuilkin, *How Biblical Is the Church Growth Movement?* (Moody Press: 1973), p. 60.

[175] Gibbs, p. 88.

[176] Leith Anderson, *A Church for the 21st Century* (Bethany House: 1992), p. 21.

[177] Elton Trueblood, *Incendiary Fellowship* (Harper and Row: 1967), p. 28.

[178] Orlando E. Costas, *The Church and Its Mission: a Shattering Critique from the Third World* (Tyndale: 1974), p. 116.

[179] Personal interview with Rick Warren in July, 1992.

[180] Anderson, p. 54.

[181] *Win Arn Church Growth Report*, no. 13.

[182] Roger Greenway, *The Pastor-Evangelist* (Baker Book House: 1987), p. 98.

[183] Jay Carty in a lecture at Denver Seminary.

[184] Ratz, Tillapaugh, and Augsburger, *Mastering Outreach and Evangelism* (Multnomah Press: 1990), p. 63.

[185] James H. Rutz, *The Open Church* (The Seed Sowers:1992), p. 112.

[186] McQuilkin, p. 60.

[187] Costas, p. 98.

[188] McQuilkin, chapter 1.

[189] The Lausanne Committee for World Evangelization, *The Pasadena Consultation*, p. 6.

[190] Gibbs, pp. 52–53.

[191] Finding from the Institute for Church Development data base.

[192] A thorough study of the article by Perry Downs entitled, "Child Evangelism," *Christian Ed Journal* III-2, p. 11, is helpful in understanding the age of accountability question in childhood conversion.

[193] Data from the Institute for Church Development.

[194] Bob Gilliam, and Sharon Johnson, *A State of the Church Report on Evangelism in the EFCA* (1991) p. 12.

[195] Ratz, Tillapaugh, and Augsburger, p. 70.

[196] Fuller School of Church Growth, Workers Analysis.

[197] Bob Gilliam and Sharon Johnson, pp. 12.

[198] Ibid.

[199] "Basic Bible Truths," Bethel Baptist Church, 325 Baker Creek Road, McMinnville OR 97128.

[200] Ratz, Tillapaugh, and Augsburger, pp. 22–24.

[201] Peter Wagner, *Our Kind of People* (John Knox Press: 1979). This book is the most complete treatise on the homogeneous unit principle.

[202] Lyle Schaller, *The Parish Paper-Yokefellow Institute*, Vol. 12, no. 2.

[203] Figures come from the Institute for Church Development.

[204] Lyle Schaller, *Getting Things Done* (Abingdon: 1986), p. 115.

[205] Ralph Winter, "Existing Churches: Ends or Means" *(Christianity Today* (Nov. 19, 1973), p. 11.

[206] See Peter Wagner, *Our Kind of People* (John Knox Press: 1979); Lyle Schaller, *Getting Things Done* (Abingdon Press: 1986), p. 110–125; and Shanks, *Exploring Church Growth* (Eerdmans: 1983).

[207] Bruce Shelley, *Consumer Church* (IVP: 1992), p. 158.

[208] Edwin M. Yamaguchi, "How the Early Church Responded to Social Problems," *Christianity Today* (Nov. 24, 1972), p. 186.

[209] Shelley, p. 158

[210] Wagner, *Church Growth and the Whole Gospel* (Harper and Row: 1981), p. 13.

[211] Wagner, *The Strategies for Church Growth.*

[212] Ray S. Anderson, *Theological Foundations for Ministry* (Eerdmans: 1979), p. 534.

213 Webster's Universal Dictionary Harvard Edition Series (1970).

[214] F. H. Henry Karlys, *Christian Personal Ethics* (Eerdmans: 1957,) p. 145.

[215] John R. W. Stott, *Christian Mission in the Modern World* (IVP: 1975), p. 96.

[216] Stott, *Christian Mission in the Modern World* (IVP: 1975) p. 96.

[217] William Willimon, *What's Right with the Church* (Harper and Row: 1985), p. 56.

[218] Ibid., p. 88.

[219] Ibid., p. 42.

[220] Ibid., p. 64.

[221] Ibid., p. 57.

[222] Ibid.

[223] Stott, *Christian Mission in the Modern World* (IVP: 1975), p. 25.

[224] Peter Wagner, *Church Growth and the Whole Gospel* (Harper and Row: 1981), paragraph five from the Lausanne Covenant.

[225] Raymond Ortlund, "A Biblical Philosophy of Ministry," *Bibliotheca Sacra* (April-June 1981), p. 5.

[226] Loren Mead, *The Once and Future Church* (Alban Institute: 1991), p. 25.

227 Forum Files Vol. 2, no. 3 (Leadership Network, Tyler, Texas), p. 1.

[228] Research done by Bob Gilliam of the Evangelical Free Church of America with data from the Institute for Church Development.

[229] Kennon Callahan, *Twelve Keys to an Effective Church* (Harper and Row: 1983), p. 112.

[230] William Easum, *The Church Growth Handbook* (Abingdon: 1990), p. 97.

[231] Easum, p. 101.

[232] Callahan, p. 111.

[233] George Barna, *What Americans Believe* (Regal: 1991), p. 224.

[234] Share Inc., *Church Finances.*

[235] Easum, p. 101.

[236] John LaRue, "The Typical Church Budget," *Your Church Magazine* (November–December 1991).

[237] John 8:43 NIV.

[238] Henry Drummond, *Natural Law in the Spiritual World* (John Lovell Co., n.d.).

[239] Ibid., p. 99.

[240] Pierre Berton, *The Comfortable Pew* (Lippincot: 1965).

[241] Col. 1:28–29 NIV.

[242] 1 Cor. 3:9 NIV.

[243] Eph. 3:16 NIV.

[244] Eph. 4:15–16 NIV.

[245] Os Guinness and John Seel, *No God But God* (Moody Press: 1992), p. 142.

246 The Business of Paradigms, video by Joel Barker, Chart House.

247 The Win Arn Growth Report, No. 34, published by Church Growth, 1921 South Myrtle Avenue, Monrovia, CA 91016. See Growth Report #32 for a full story.

[248] Martin F. Saarinen, *The Life Cycle of a Congregation* (Alban Institute: 1986), p. 5.

[249] 2 Tim. 4:7–8 NIV.

[250] Carl Wilson, *With Christ in the School of Disciple Building* (Zondervan: 1976).

[251] 2 Peter 3:18 NIV.

[252] Eph. 4:15 NIV.

[253] James 1:2 NIV.

[254] James Stockdale, article or book unknown.

[255] Dr. Paul Brand, "Why One Doctor Prays for Pain," *Eternity Magazine*, Oct. 75, p. 78.

[256] Ibid.

[257] Hans Selye, "On the Real Benefits of Eustress," *Psychology Today*, March 1978, p. 63.

[258] Matt. 10:34-37 NIV.

[259] Bill Hull, *The Disciple-making Church* (Revell)

[260] Cheryl Forbes, *Imagination* (Multnomah: 1986), p. 18.

[261] Ibid., p. 18.

[262] There are 32 squares in the puzzle.

[263] Forbes, p. 19.

[264] Source unknown.

[265] Raymond Ortlund, "A Biblical Philosophy of Ministry," part 4, *Bibliotheca Sacra* (October-December 1981), p. 295.

[266] Ibid., p. 19.

[267] Jay Cocks, "Let's Get Crazy" *Time Magazine* (June 11, 1990), p. 40.

[268] Daniel J. Boorstin, "The Creators, " *U.S. News and World Report* (August 31, 1992), p. 99.

[269] Don Toshach, "The Creative Church," *Inside Story* (CBA of Southern California, August 1990).

[270] Charles Garfield, *Peak Performers* (Morrow Publishers: 1986) p. 276.

[271] Tosbach, p. 2.

[272] Book review entitled, "Will Change Undo the Church?" *Christianity Today* (October 26, 1992), p. 81. It deals with Leith Anderson, *A Church for the 21st Century* (Bethany House: 1992); Jim Petersen, *Church Without Walls* (Nav Press: 1992); and Bruce Shelley and Marshall Shelley, *The Consumer Church* (Intervarsity Press: 1992).

[273] Orlando E. Costas, *The Church and Its Mission; A Shattering Critique from the Third World* (Tyndale: 1974), p. 149.

[274] Loren Mead, *The Once and Future Church; Reinventing the Congregation for a New Mission Frontier* (Alban Institute: 1992), p. 55.

[275] Leith Anderson, *Dying for Change* (Bethany House: 1990); Lyle Schaller, *Change Agent* (Abingdon: 1980); Mike Tucker, *The Church That Dared to Change* (Tyndale House: 1975).

[276] Paul Hersey, and Kenneth H. Blanchard, *Management of Organization Behavior*, 5th Edition (Prentice Hall: 1988), p. 342.

[277] Kenneth Blanchard at the "Church for the 21st Century" conference in Dallas, July 1992.

[278] Interview with Randy Kinnison, 1992.

[279] Alan Wilkins, *Developing Corporate Character* (Jossey and Bass: 1989), p. 5.

[280] Hersey and Blanchard, p. 164.

[281] Peter Drucker, "Don't Change Corporate Culture—Use it," *The Wall Street Journal* (Thursday, March 26, 199.

[282] Alan Wilkins, *Developing Corporate Character* (Jossey and Bass: 1989), p. 65.

[283] 1 Corinthians 3:9.